2008

Recommended

Country Hotels

of Britain

Including supplements of Town and Country Hotels with Conference, Leisure and Wedding Facilities

NEW! Haunted Hotels Supplement

Foreword

Why not sample the delights of a British country holiday by visiting one of the charming properties listed in this edition of RECOMMENDED COUNTRY HOTELS? Here you will find a wide variety of hotels and houses including historic manor houses, impressive castles and country cottages, as well as larger hotels with leisure facilities such as spas, gymnasiums, swimming pools and tennis courts.

For those who prefer something that little bit different we have included a guide to some of the HAUNTED HOTELS to be found throughout Britain. You can read about the history and ghostly inhabitants of each property, as well as the facilities on offer, and there is usually a brief description of the location and the area.

No matter which you choose, you will find that all of our proprietors offer a warm welcome and the highest standards of accommodation and service.

Anne Cuthbertson
Editor

ISBN 978-1-85055-397-7

Maps: ©MAPS IN MINUTES™ / Collins Bartholmew 2007

Typeset by FHG Guides Ltd, Paisley.
Printed and bound in Malaysia by Imago.

Distribution. Book Trade: ORCA Book Services, Stanley House,
3 Fleets Lane, Poole, Dorset BH15 3AJ
(Tel: 01202 665432; Fax: 01202 666219)
e-mail: mail@orcabookservices.co.uk
Published by FHG Guides Ltd., Abbey Mill Business Centre,
Seedhill, Paisley PA1 ITJ (Tel: 0141-887 0428 Fax: 0141-889 7204).
e-mail: admin@fhguides.co.uk

Recommended Country Hotels of Britain is published by FHG Guides Ltd,
part of Kuperard Group.

Cover design: FHG Guides
Cover Picture: courtesy of hauntedhotelguide.com

Contents

England and Wales • Counties

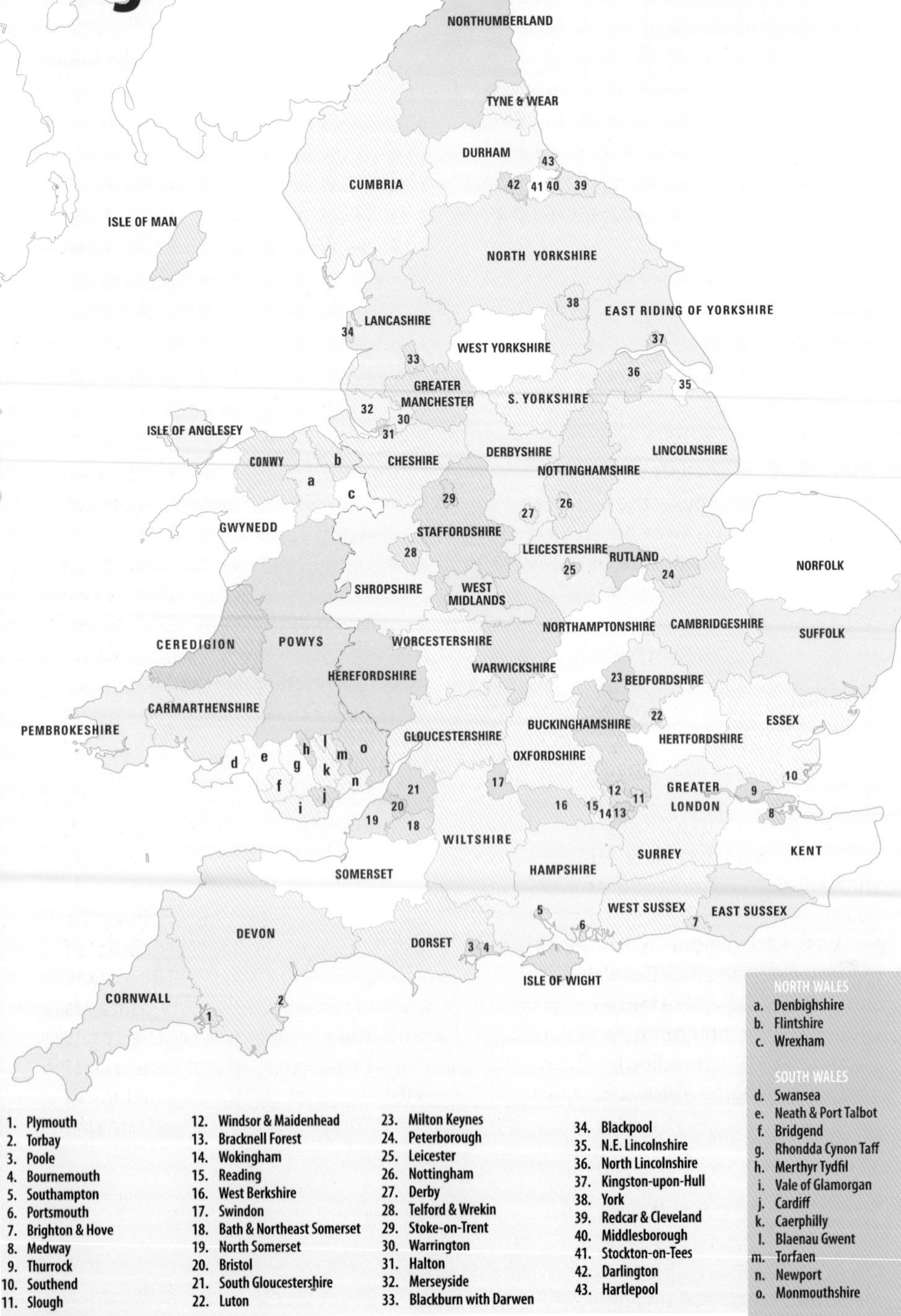
NORTHUMBERLAND
TYNE & WEAR
DURHAM
43
42
41
40
39
CUMBRIA
ISLE OF MAN
NORTH YORKSHIRE
38
EAST RIDING OF YORKSHIRE
34
LANCASHIRE
WEST YORKSHIRE
37
33
36
35
GREATER MANCHESTER
S. YORKSHIRE
32
30
31
ISLE OF ANGLESEY
CONWY
b
a
c
CHESHIRE
DERBYSHIRE
LINCOLNSHIRE
NOTTINGHAMSHIRE
29
26
27
GWYNEDD
STAFFORDSHIRE
28
LEICESTERSHIRE
RUTLAND
25
24
NORFOLK
SHROPSHIRE
WEST MIDLANDS
NORTHAMPTONSHIRE
CAMBRIDGESHIRE
SUFFOLK
CEREDIGION
POWYS
WORCESTERSHIRE
WARWICKSHIRE
HEREFORDSHIRE
23
BEDFORDSHIRE
CARMARTHENSHIRE
22
BUCKINGHAMSHIRE
ESSEX
PEMBROKESHIRE
GLOUCESTERSHIRE
HERTFORDSHIRE
l
h
m
o
d
e
g
k
OXFORDSHIRE
n
f
17
10
21
12
11
GREATER LONDON
9
i
j
20
16
15
14
13
8
19
18
WILTSHIRE
SURREY
KENT
SOMERSET
HAMPSHIRE
WEST SUSSEX
EAST SUSSEX
5
6
7
DEVON
DORSET
3
4
ISLE OF WIGHT
CORNWALL
2
1
NORTH WALES
a. Denbighshire
b. Flintshire
c. Wrexham
SOUTH WALES
d. Swansea
e. Neath & Port Talbot
f. Bridgend
g. Rhondda Cynon Taff
h. Merthyr Tydfil
i. Vale of Glamorgan
j. Cardiff
k. Caerphilly
l. Blaenau Gwent
m. Torfaen
n. Newport
o. Monmouthshire
1. Plymouth
2. Torbay
3. Poole
4. Bournemouth
5. Southampton
6. Portsmouth
7. Brighton & Hove
8. Medway
9. Thurrock
10. Southend
11. Slough
12. Windsor & Maidenhead
13. Bracknell Forest
14. Wokingham
15. Reading
16. West Berkshire
17. Swindon
18. Bath & Northeast Somerset
19. North Somerset
20. Bristol
21. South Gloucestershire
22. Luton
23. Milton Keynes
24. Peterborough
25. Leicester
26. Nottingham
27. Derby
28. Telford & Wrekin
29. Stoke-on-Trent
30. Warrington
31. Halton
32. Merseyside
33. Blackburn with Darwen
34. Blackpool
35. N.E. Lincolnshire
36. North Lincolnshire
37. Kingston-upon-Hull
38. York
39. Redcar & Cleveland
40. Middlesborough
41. Stockton-on-Tees
42. Darlington
43. Hartlepool

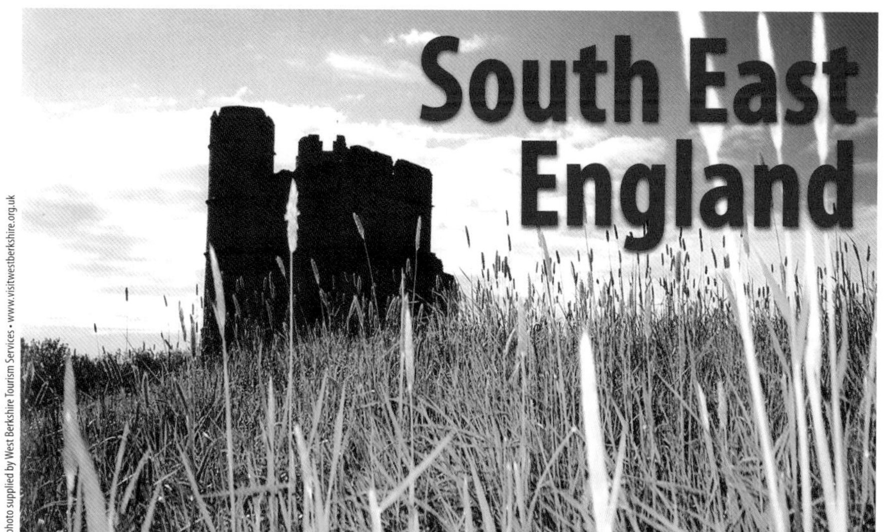

South East England

photo supplied by West Berkshire Tourism Services • www.visitwestberkshire.org.uk

WITH A POPULATION of almost seven million, London is by far the largest city in Europe, sprawling over an area of 620 square miles. For first-time visitors a city sight-seeing tour by double-decker bus or by boat along the River Thames is a 'must'. Even for those already familiar with the main attractions, there's always something new in London. Buckingham Palace is now open to the public and proving a very popular attraction. Visitors are welcome from the end of July to the end of September and will see 19 out of the 660 rooms in the Palace, including the Throne Room and most of the other State apartments.

A visit to London is not complete without seeing the new Docklands – an 8½ square mile area with a fantastic range of old and new architecture (including Britain's tallest building), pubs and restaurants, shops, visitor attractions and parks – all just a short journey from the City Centre.

With its orchards, hopfields, bluebell woods and vineyards it's not surprising that Kent is known as 'The Garden of England'. Historic Kent towns like Canterbury, Rochester and Broadstairs are a contrast with Dover, still the busiest passenger seaport in Europe and gateway to the Channel Tunnel.

The South East has many and varied resorts, including Brighton, with its two piers, prom, graceful Georgian houses, antique shops, and the famous Royal Pavilion, built at the request of the Prince of Wales, later Prince Regent and George IV. Eastbourne is another fine family resort, while in the quieter nearby town of Bexhill, low tides reveal the remains of a forest – part of the land bridge by which Britain was joined to Europe 10,000 years ago.

Seaside towns also cluster along the Hampshire coast around the port of Southampton, itself a picturesque town. And in the extreme east of the county is Portsmouth, a town irrevocably tied to its seafaring heritage. There are naval museums and ships to see, including Nelson's famous flagship from Trafalgar, *The Victory*.

www.visitbritain.com
www.uk.visitlondon.com
www.visitsoutheastengland.com

South West England

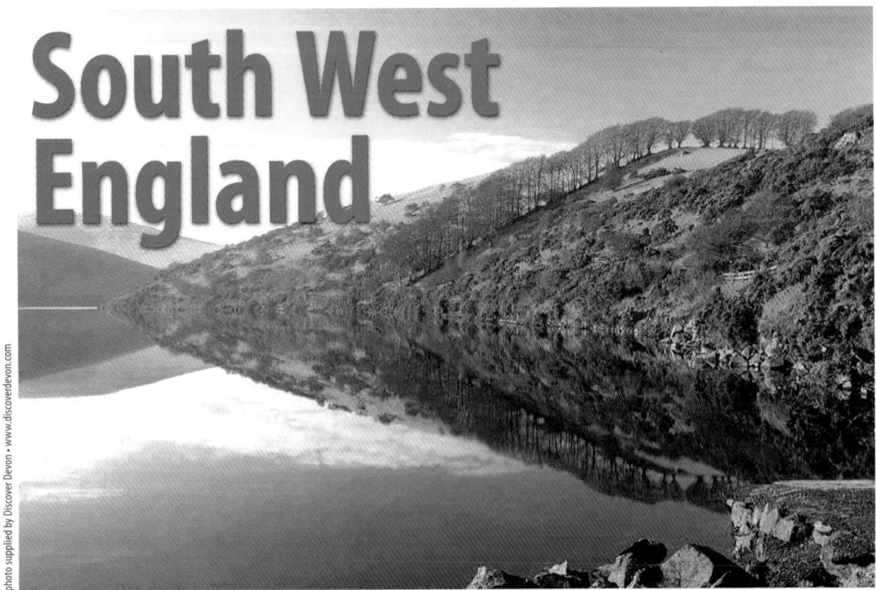

photo supplied by Discover Devon • www.discoverdevon.com

WHATEVER SORT of holiday destination you're looking for, you'll find it in South-West England. As well as the elegant shops and Georgian crescents of Bath, other south-west towns have the very latest in big shopping centres, speciality shops and nightlife. There are stretches of wild moorland, chalk hills, limestone gorges and thatched-house villages and there are miles of golden sand washed by Atlantic breakers. From Orcombe Rocks, Exmouth to Studland Bay in Dorset, the Jurassic Coast Natural World Heritage Site gives a unique insight into life in the past through the rocks exposed along the 95 miles of beautiful coastline.

Devon has both coast and countryside. Plymouth on the south coast has been a naval base of the greatest importance to the defence of the realm since the days of Sir Francis Drake. The city was hastily rebuilt after destruction in the Second World War, but nothing can spoil the glorious vista of the Sound viewed from Plymouth Hoe where Drake finished his game of bowls.

Cornwall reaches into the Atlantic Ocean for almost 100 miles.Take a walk along any part of this strikingly beautiful coast, enjoy a cream tea in one of the charming villages sheltering in a cove and you will understand why Cornwall has been the inspiration for so many artists, novelists and poets. Often free from frost in winter, the soft spring climate favours Cornwall as an ideal destination for holiday breaks.

Say Somerset and most people would automatically think of cider, Cheddar cheese and county cricket matches. But there's a lot more to Somerset – there's Exmoor which is Lorna Doone territory and home to the wild Exmoor ponies and herds of red deer. The National Park of Exmoor has a coastline with some marvellous clifftop walks. Further along this coast are Somerset's main seaside resorts, Minehead and Burnham-on-Sea.

www.visitsouthwest.co.uk

East of England

photo supplied by Essex Development & Regeneration Agency • www.realessex.co.uk

EAST ANGLIA, once a Saxon kingdom cut off from the rest of England by marshland and forest, remains to this day a relatively unexplored part of Britain. It is an area of low, chalky hills, pleasant market towns, working windmills adding charm to the fields, wide sweeping views over the flattest land and glorious sunsets. Along East Anglia's North Sea coast, the visitor can choose between bustling seaside resorts or long stretches of deserted sandy beaches. Boating enthusiasts come from all over the world for holidays afloat on the Norfolk Broads, an ancient man-made network of shallow tree-fringed lakes, rivers and canals. East Anglia's inland towns are full of history and proud to tell their stories at visitor centres and museums. Specialist museums abound. The Imperial War Museum at Duxford Airfield has the largest collection of military and civil aircraft in Britain. Duxford was a Battle of Britain station and the flatness of East Anglia gave it the wartime distinction of having the largest number of airfields in the country. Steam, vintage and miniature railway museums, classic car collections, bicycle museums: East Anglia has them all, as well as the famous Lace Museum (with magnifying glasses provided) in Norfolk and a Working Silk Museum at the restored silk mills in Braintree and a Motorboat Museum tracing the history of motor boats, racing hydroplanes and leisure boats. At Lowestoft harbour you can step aboard the last survivor of more than 3000 drifters that came every autumn to Yarmouth and Lowestoft, following the plentiful shoals of herring. Visual displays portray the hardships of the herring workers, male and female, who brought prosperity to the two ports for more than a century but only poverty to themselves. It was a different way of life – above stairs at least – for the inhabitants of the great mansion houses of East Anglia in their heyday. The Queen's favourite country seat in England, Sandringham House, is open to the public from the end of July to the end of October.

www.visiteastofengland.com

The Midlands

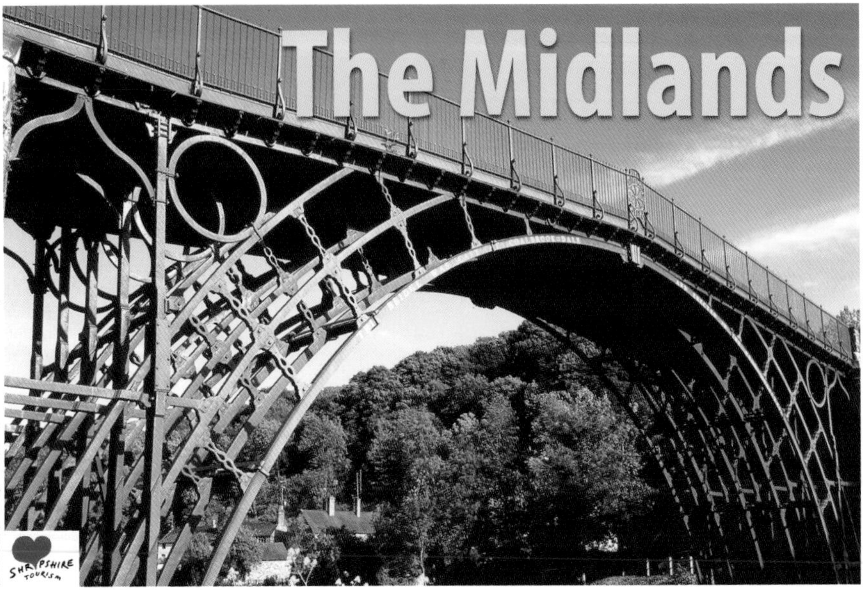

photo supplied by Shropshire Tourism • www.shropshiretourism.info

FOLLOWING The Romantic Road is not what immediately comes to mind when the English Midlands are being considered as a holiday destination. Nevertheless, the Romantic Road is a very suitable title for a guide to the picture-postcard villages of the Cotswolds which is available from Cheltenham Tourism. The gentle hills and honey-coloured houses of the Cotswolds are deservedly popular with tourists in summer. Quieter, but just as beautiful in their way, are other scenic areas of the Midlands: the Wye Valley, the Vale of Evesham, Sherwood Forest, once the haunt of the legendary Robin Hood and, near the Welsh border, the wooded valleys known as the Marches around the towns of Hereford and Shrewsbury

In a secluded valley in this area a discovery was made that changed the face of the world when Abraham Darby perfected his revolutionary techniques for the mass production of cast iron. Today there are no fewer than seven museums in the Gorge, which has been designated a World Heritage Site.

To keep the children happy there is also a Teddy Bear Museum and the Ironbridge Toy Museum. Children are welcome at the Heritage Motor Centre at Gaydon, the largest collection of British cars in the world; quad biking over rough terrain track is available for children.

Staffordshire is the home of the Potteries and some of the best china and porcelain in the world is made there. Visit Stoke-on-Trent for the complete China Experience, factory tours, ceramic museums and, to take home as a souvenir of the Midlands, world famous names like Wedgwood, Royal Doulton and Spode china at amazing discounts.

www.visitheartofengland.com

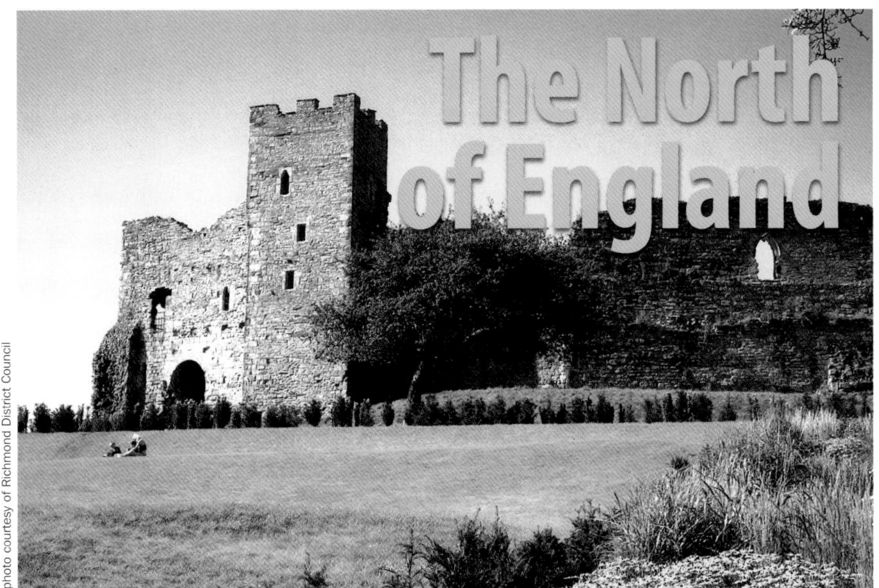

photo courtesy of Richmond District Council

THERE ARE SOME PEOPLE who prefer a holiday where every day is packed with action and every evening filled with fun. Others see a holiday as the exact opposite, a chance to get some peace and quiet in the wide open spaces. Whatever sort of holidaymaker you are, the North of England has plenty to offer you. The North has some of the best living museums and 'hands-on' visitor centres in Britain, where the latest presentation techniques are equally fascinating to adults and children. How does the world look to a fish, a dog, a bee? Find out – and learn to make rainbows too – at the Colour Museum in the once-grimy city of Bradford. Also in Bradford is the National Museum of Photography, Film and Television which has Britain's biggest cinema screen, a thousand times bigger than your TV screen at home – and not content with that, it also has the world's only Cinerama cinema, the world's biggest lens, smallest camera and first-ever photographic likeness! Just as interesting are the smaller heritage museums to be found in practically every town and village in the North. Britain's National Railway Museum is in York, the birthplace of the steam railway. If a day trip behind a steam engine is more your style, ask for the Yorkshire Tourist Board's leaflet 'Steaming Along' with details of seven steam railways and the dates of the kiddies' specials – the Thomas the Tank Engine week-ends.

The seaside resorts of the North have provided happiness for children and relaxation for Mums and Dads for generations. In Lancashire, on the west coast, Southport, St Annes, Blackpool, Morecambe – often it's the same resort families choose year after satisfied year. The twin resorts of Whitley Bay and Tynemouth are on the North Tyneside coast. From bright lights to walking on the fells, from heritage visits to Sunday shopping, you'll find them all in the North of England!

www.golakes.co.uk
www.visitnorthumbria.com
www.visitenglandsnorthwest.com
www.yorkshirevisitor.com

Scotland

photo supplied by Visit Scotland / Perthshire

THE HIGHLANDS AND ISLANDS include much of what is often thought of as the 'real' Scotland. Stretching north from Fort William and Ben Nevis in the west to Inverness and the Moray Firth in the east, this unspoiled area contains some of Britain's most remote, least populated and most beautiful districts. The North West Highlands is the first area of Scotland to be awarded UNESCO-endorsed European Geopark status. The area which encompasses parts of Wester Ross and the whole of North West Sutherland has been designated as a Geopark on the basis of its outstanding geology and landscape, the strength of its partnership approach to sustainable economic development and its existing geological interpretation.

On the eastern borders of the Highlands lie Aberdeenshire and Moray, with their rugged peaks and rolling farmlands. Rich in fish, whisky, oil and castles, these counties boast 'Royal' Deeside, with Braemar and Balmoral as a tourist 'honeypot' and share with their neighbouring counties some of the most impressive scenery in Britain. Perth & Kinross and Angus offer a wealth of leisure activities: ski-ing in the glens, fishing on Loch Leven or Loch Earn, golf at Gleneagles or Carnoustie, climbing Lochnagar, pony trekking round Loch Tay, or sea-bathing at Arbroath or Montrose. The many attractive towns like Pitlochry, Aberfeldy, Crieff, Forfar etc and the busy cities of Perth and Dundee offer civilised shopping, eating and accommodation facilities.

Convenient road, rail and air links make Central and South-West Scotland a popular tourist destination. Argyll has a long, much indented coastline, looking out onto a scatter of islands such as Mull, Jura, Gigha and Islay. This is a popular outdoor resort area and has excellent hotels and a wide choice of self catering accommodation. Oban is the principal centre and a busy port for the Inner and Outer Hebrides. The lively city of Glasgow is well worth a visit and has a growing reputation for its superb cultural, entertainment, shopping and sporting facilities. Ayrshire naturally means Rabbie Bums and Alloway, and also means golf – Prestwick, Troon and Turnberry are courses of international renown. Make time for a trip across to the lovely Isle of Arran – 'Scotland in miniature'.

Central Scotland is surprisingly rich in scenery and historic interest. The 'bonnie banks' of Loch Lomond, the Trossachs, Stirling Castle and Bannockburn are just some of the treasure stored here in the heart of Scotland. Excellent holiday centres with plenty of accommodation include Stirling itself, Killin, Aberfoyle, Callander, Lochearnhead and Dunblane. The rolling hills and fields of the Lothians, with Edinburgh at the heart, sweep down to the Forth as it enters the North Sea.

Edinburgh is the country's capital and a year-round tourist destination. It is always full of interest – the castle, the Palace of Holyrood, museums, galleries, pubs and entertainment. North Berwick and Dunbar are popular coastal resorts and this area, like Fife and Ayrshire, is a golfers' paradise. Opening onto the sea between the Lothians and Berwick-on-Tweed (which is technically in England), are the very attractive Scottish Borders. The ruined abbeys of Dryburgh, Jedburgh, Kelso and Melrose are a main attraction, as are the mills and mill-shops for the woollens which have made towns like Hawick and Galashiels famous.

photo supplied by Visit Scotland / Perthshire

A short break in St Andrews and the Kingdom of Fife is the ideal escape from the pressures of everyday life. Curl up in a comfy chair by a roaring fire in an ancient castle hotel. Sample superb cuisine in gracious surroundings in a stately home. Or treat the family to a self-catering break in a house with a view. And no matter what time of year you choose to come, you can be sure that there will be plenty of things to see and do. With its dry climate, most sports, including golf, can be played throughout the year. And as the scenery changes character with each season, you will notice something new no matter how many times you return. It is, of course, golf that has placed Fife on the world stage. St Andrews is the "Home of Golf", and the town, and Fife in general, boasts many fine courses which can be played all year round.

For walkers, the Southern Upland Way runs from Cockburnpath on the east coast, through the Borders to Portpatrick, near Stranraer from where ferry services leave for Northern Ireland. We are now in Dumfries & Galloway whose hills and valleys run down to the Solway Firth within sight of the English Lake District. This is a popular touring and holiday region, with its green and fertile countryside, pleasant small towns and villages, and many attractions to visit.

www.visitscotland.com

photo courtesy of Cottrell Park Golf Club, Cardiff

SCENERY, history and the quality of life are the main ingredients of a holiday in Wales, which makes this a perfect destination for a holiday.

You can't go far in Wales without a view of mountains or the sea. And you can't go far in Wales without being in a National Park! Wales has three of these, each with its own special character. In the north, the Snowdonia National Park has mountains, moors, lakes and wooded valleys, dominated of course by Snowdon, the highest peak in England and Wales. At its northern edge is Anglesey and the North Wales Coast resorts, all popular tourist areas. But the atmosphere of the National Park is best experienced in the small towns and villages at its heart, such as Llanberis, Beddgelert, Betws-y-Coed and Capel Curig.

Approximately 100 km to the south and east is the Brecon Beacons National Park. From Llandeilo by the Black Mountain in the west, through the Brecon Beacons themselves to the Black Mountains and Hay-on-Wye on the border with England, here are grassy, smooth hills, open spaces, bare moors, lakes and forests. All that is lacking is the sea – and it's the sea which has made the Pembroke Coast National Park possible. From Tenby in the south to Cardigan in the north, the park offers every kind of coastal scenery: steep cliffs, sheltered bays and harbours, huge expanses of sand and shingle, rocky coves and quiet wooded inlets.

But 'scenery' doesn't end with the national parks. Wales also has five areas nominated officially as being of 'Outstanding Natural Beauty'. The Gower Peninsula, west of Swansea, is a scenic jewel – small but sparkling! The Wye Valley from Chepstow to Monmouth includes the ruined Tintern Abbey and many historic sites including Chepstow itself, Raglan and Caerleon.

The Isle of Anglesey, apart from its quiet beauty, claims the world's longest placename, Llanfairpwllgwyngyllgogerychwyrndrobwllllantysiliogogogoch – usually: shortened to Llanfair PG! The Llyn Peninsula, west of Snowdon is perhaps the most traditionally Welsh part of Wales and finally, the Clwydian Range behind Rhyl and Prestatyn, where St Asaph has the smallest cathedral in Britain.

www.visitwales.com

hauntedhotelguide.com

For True Believers or Open-minded Sceptics, this supplement gives you the opportunity to visit som of the Most Haunted Hotels in the Country.

Experience the Unexplained!

hauntedhotelguide.com was developed in late 2005 in response to the overwhelming demand for a definitive directory of haunted accommodation throughout the UK. With the public's interest in all things paranormal constantly growing, and with increasingly popular TV shows like "*Most Haunted*", "*Dead Famous*" and "*Derek Acorah's Ghost Towns*" every hotel seems to have a ghost or two to boast about.

Whether you are a hardcore ghost fan or open-minded sceptic, **hauntedhotelguide.com** will provide you with invaluable haunted history about the ghostly goings-on at each hotel, along with the usual information you would expect to find from a regular hotel guide. With around 500 haunted hotels throughout the country, it should be easy to find the perfect location for your stay.

Whilst many other hotel guides concentrate on facilities provided, often the really interesting things, such as where to find the ghost of a servant girl in the Station Hotel or where the bones of the 'Blue Boy' of Chillingham Castle were discovered, are overlooked... Not by us... As you'd expect, we positively encourage reports such as these as we believe that the haunted history of a hotel is just as important as its facilities and we feel that the possibility of seeing a ghost tends to remain etched in your mind much longer than the amount of sherry you received on the welcome tray!

With detailed descriptions and images of the Haunted Hotels and Haunted Inns in this supplement and on our site, **hauntedhotelguide.com** is totally unique: Discover the Green Lady of Comlongon Castle; investigate the presence of a spectral monk in the Tansy Room at Hazlewood Castle, or try and spot the Ghostly Lady Jane in Dalston Hall.

Many of our hotels have been investigated by our Mediums, psychics and paranormal investigators. James Griffiths *(Derek Acorah's Ghost Towns)*, one of our mediums, has certainly had a few 'interesting' experiences to say the least:

'Having had the opportunity to visit some of the most haunted hotels throughout the UK, I can honestly say that they do live up to expectations! Being rather rudely pulled out of bed at the dead of night by the poisoned spectre of a lady does leave you wondering whether you will be charged extra for it in the morning as you were sure it wasn't mentioned in the brochure... Finding yourself confronted by a sword-wielding soldier within a castle gate house with only a torch and your mobile phone to defend yourself makes you question your decision to venture out on Halloween! And investigating a hotel in a village renowned for at least 12 ghosts, wondering which one they are all staying at and praying it's not yours, make's you realise there truly is another world waiting to be discovered...'

James Griffiths

This first edition of the **hauntedhotelguide.com** supplement is only a taster as next year, along with FHG guides, we are producing a full 100 page haunted supplement showcasing the most haunted hotels throughout the UK. If you want to find out to find out more about the hotels in this supplement or if you want to discover a haunted hotel near you, take a look at **hauntedhotelguide.com.**

We hope you enjoy the guide and may all your experiences be unexplainable...

The luxurious **Flitwick Manor** is a Georgian gem. If you are fortunate enough, you may witness the ghost of an ex-housekeeper who is said to haunt the corridors...

Nestling in the tranquillity of acres of rolling gardens and wooded parkland, Flitwick Manor is a luxury hotel in the South East of England. This country house hotel, located near Woburn, is a classical Georgian house that continues its ancestral traditions of hospitality.

The cosy lounge of Flitwick Manor is elegantly furnished, providing the perfect retreat for those seeking peace and relaxation.

For private functions or business meetings, this country house hotel offers the ultimate in luxury in the South East, all just one hour from the centre of London.

With two AA rosettes, the restaurant at this luxury hotel is rated as one of the finest in the country and offers the ideal combination of fine dining in a delightful setting.

The 17 individually designed guestrooms and suites, furnished with fine antiques and period pieces, blend effortlessly together to offer guests a comfortable and endearing stay. If you're looking for a luxury hotel in the South East, look no further than Flitwick Manor.

Flitwick Manor

Church Road , Flitwick
Bedfordshire MK45 1AE
Tel: 01525 712242
Email : flitwick@menzieshotels.co.uk
www.menzies-hotels.co.uk

HOTEL FEATURES

• 24 hour room service
• Award-winning restaurant
• Drawing room
• Gardens and woodlands
• Tennis Court • Croquet Lawn
• Helicopter landing pad

Haunted History

hauntedhotelguide.com

Flitwick Manor is reputedly haunted by an ex-housekeeper who, over 100 years ago, was dismissed for allegedly poisoning one of the Lyall family, the former owners of the Manor. After the Old Housekeeper (whose proper name no-one knows) died, it seems her spirit decided to take up residence again at Flitwick.

She keeps herself to herself and doesn't stray much from the bedroom she has made her own. Staff at Flitwick Manor know the housekeeper's favourite chair - she even leaves an impression in the seat after sitting down!

Whilst building work was being carried out on Flitwick Manor, a concealed room was discovered behind some panelling. It has been suggested that this could have been the housekeeper's quarters. Ever since then the spirit has been making herself known to guests throughout the hotel. One guest was woken to find her sitting on the end of his bed, and a duty manager witnessed the ghost in one of the corridors...

he stunning 16th Century **Lion and Swan Inn** in Congleton is steeped in istory... A dark haired female spirit said to have lived during the Middle Ages ften makes an appearance...

ituated at the heart of the attractive market town of Congleton, the strikingly mbered Lion and Swan Hotel is a traditional coaching inn which boasts 21 ttractive bedrooms with every modern amenity, a first class restaurant which rides itself on a high standard of cuisine, and a friendly bar which is open to esidents and non residents alike featuring a wide selection of real ales, lagers, vines & spirits..

Our restaurant, open for Breakfast, Lunch and Dinner seven days a week, erves an eclectic selection of dishes freshly prepared in house using locally ourced fresh ingredients. The fireplace in the restaurant is a particular delight nd source of mystery with its complex and intriguing carvings...

Lion & Swan Hotel

Swan Bank, Congleton,
Cheshire
Tel: 01260 273 115
Email: info@lionandswan.co.uk
www.lionandswan.co.uk

he carvings on the fireplace are often interpreted as demonic symbolism. his may have something to do with the **Lion and Swan's** ghost - a young, rown haired woman, who often appears around a new moon, wearing othing but a pair of clogs and a smile!

his young spirit reputedly dates back to the Middle Ages. It is alleged that she vas unable to conceive and drank a potion to aid conception. However, nstead of creating new life, the potion took hers. She has been seen on many ccasions tending the fire beneath the carved fireplace...

he Tudor Suite is also renowned for its mysterious goings on. It sometimes has cold atmosphere, and most of the unexplained noises emanate from here t night.

HOTEL FEATURES

- Remote Control Colour Television
- AM/FM radio alarm clock
- Hairdryer • Ironing Facilities
- Full tea and coffee making facilities.

he **George and Dragon Hotel** in Chester is an imposing building situated just utside the city walls. As Chester is one of the most haunted cities in the UK, it no surprise that this hotel has its own ghosts as guests...

short walk from Chester City centre, the George and Dragon is a traditional ostelry that blends well with a modern lively bar. Our open plan lounge, with hree fireplaces, creates a warm and cosy atmosphere to enjoy our well tocked cellar and traditional food. The character building which now stands n the site is around 100 years old, but there has been a public house or oaching inn, of some kind, on the site for a lot longer.

here is also believed to be a burial ground of Roman origin on the site, which possible given that Chester, or Dewa was an important Roman town.

George & Dragon

1 Liverpool Road
Chester, Cheshire CH2 1AA
Tel: 01244 380714
Email : 7783@greeneking.co.uk
www.oldenglishinns.co.uk

Haunted History hauntedhotelguide.com

Chester boasts over 2000 years of documented history. Its crypts, narrow treets and alley ways play host to many infamous ghosts and spirits and the **George and Dragon Hotel** is no exception. This hotel is reputedly haunted by legion of Roman soldiers.

he George and Dragon is situated on the site of the old Roman road leading ut from Chester. Roman military law forbade the burial of soldiers within the ity walls of Dewa and so many were buried immediately outside and some ould quite feasibly be buried beneath the hotel.

Over the centuries the sound of marching feet beneath the floors has been eard by staff and guests alike. Strangely, the sound seems loudest in the ellars, which would have been closer to the original Roman ground level...

HOTEL FEATURES

- Hairdryer
- Iron & Ironing Board
- Tea/Coffee • TV
- All en suite with shower room

Dalston Hall

Carlisle
Cumbria CA5 7JX
Tel: +44 (0)1228 710271
Email: enquiries@dalstonhall.com
www.dalston-hall-hotel.co.uk

HOTEL FEATURES

- En suite bathroom
- Tea & Coffee making facilities
- TV • Award Winning Restaurant
- Wedding Licence
- Conference Facilities

Dalston Hall is a luxurious 15th Century Mansion with a fascinating history. Lady Jane is said to appear in Tudor dress in the gallery above the manorial hall. Other ghosts include a Handyman, 'Sad Emily' and a Young Girl...
Guests can expect a venue with a difference, and as witnessed by the GMTV 'Haunted' team, a few ghosts! The hotel offers a peaceful and tranquil setting to guests, and the perfect retreat in the beautiful countryside on the northern edge of the Lake District, ideally placed for the national treasure Hadrian's Wall.
The hotel has recently undergone considerable refurbishment involving the ground floor public areas being restyled but still keeping the original character of this 15th Century family Mansion. The bedrooms have also been restyled to an elegant character but each has their own unique luxurious style.

Haunted History hauntedhotelguide.com

Dalston Hall plays host to many ghosts, the first of which, the spirit of a Victorian handyman, has been seen wandering the grounds. In the Baronial Hall you may find Dalston Hall's oldest ghost – known to the staff as Lady Jane. She appears in Tudor dress and may well be a member of one of the Dalston families who owned the Hall for such a long time.
The cellars of the hotel are haunted by the sinister Mr Fingernails and many of the bedrooms are reputed to have spectral guests: Room 4 is said to be haunted by a poor maid who threw herself from the Pele tower and in Room 12 guests have complained of being woken by girls' voices whispering...

Walworth Castle

Walworth, Darlington
Durham DL2 2LY
Tel: +44 (0)1325 485470
Email:
enquiries@walworthcastle.co.uk
www.walworthcastle.co.uk

HOTEL FEATURES

- Four-Poster Beds
- Sumptuous Furnishings
- Castle Gardens
- Fabulous Views
- TV

Set in 18 acres, **Walworth Castle** is one of the country 's finest historic hotels, parts of which date back to the 12th century
Walworth Castle Hotel just outside Darlington in County Durham, was built in 1189 and is one of the few castle hotels in England. Recently refurbished to an extremely high standard by owners Rachel and Chris Swain, Walworth Castle Hotel really is the ideal venue to sample England's Living History
Each of the 34 bedrooms and numerous reception rooms has its own particular character many with individually designed upholstery. The feature rooms have been recently refurbished to an extremely high standard
Walworth Castle boasts two fabulous restaurants (one award-winning) and a traditional 'pub'. The choice of hospitality at Walworth Castle Hotel really is second to none.

Haunted History hauntedhotelguide.com

According to legend, the Lord of the Manor was having an affair with one of the servant girls. Unfortunately, for both parties, the maid fell pregnant. Realising that it would be a great disgrace to his family to father a child with a servant he decided to take drastic action. At the time of the affair, the castle was being renovated so the Lord of the Manor decided to seize the opportunity and had the maid walled up inside a spiral staircase.
It is alleged that she can still be heard climbing the staircase behind the library leading to the turrets of **Walworth Castle**
Other ghostly apparitions at the castle include the spectral replay of a brother's feud resulting in one killing the other, the horse buried in the gardens and the running boy in the corridors...

he stunningly beautiful Redworth Hall dates back to 744. Redworth was the site of many battles during the Civil War and it appears that some of the soldiers killed battle are still lingering…

edworth Hall Hotel is a breathtaking Jacobean ountry house in County Durham. You'll feel as if you're the middle of nowhere here as you survey the aptivating, landscaped gardens and enchanting oodland. From the moment you sweep up the long riveway to the hotel, you know you're in for a treat. ou can enjoy the escapism of this picture postcard etting and within 5 minutes be heading towards ewcastle, historic Durham or York.

his original building still retains many of its original eatures including an ornate staircase, the Great Hall nd several four-poster bedrooms. The Hall also boasts vo award winning restaurants and a leisure club.

side from the hotel itself, you'll find it's the charm and ospitality of north-east folk at Redworth Hall that will ake your stay an incredible one.

Redworth Hall

Redworth,
Durham DL5 6NL
Tel: +44 (0)1388 770 600
Email:
redworthhall@paramount-hotels.co.uk
www.paramount-redworthhall.co.uk

HOTEL FEATURES

- Concierge
- Currency exchange
- Safety Deposit Boxes
- Restaurant
- Lounge / Bar
- Barber / Beauty Services

Haunted History

hauntedhotelguide.com

Redworth Hall has a fantastic haunted history and boasts at least two ghosts…

The first is that of a woman who, it appears, felt the urge to throw herself from the top of the Jacobean Tower after her lover left her. She is said to walk the corridors and rooms at the front of the Hall, particularly the bedrooms.

The second ghost relates to one of the former owners of the Hall, Lord Surtee. One of the Lord's many children was 'ill of mind' and his unique way of coping with this was to chain the child up to one of the Great Hall's Fireplaces… day & night . The laughter and crying of young children is sometimes heard in this area of the Great Hall.

Enjoy your stay!

Elvey Farm

Elvey Lane , Pluckley
KENT TN27 0SU
Tel: 01233 840 442
Email:
bookings@elveyfarm.co.uk
www.elveyfarm.co.uk

Beautiful **Elvey Farm** dates back to the early 15th Century. This small country hotel is situated in Pluckley, the Most Haunted Village in England, and is renowned for its Ghostly Guests... Elvey Farm is a medieval farmstead in the village of Pluckley, Kent. The Hall House was built in 1430 and little has changed since then. Once used as a 75 acre farm for cereals and sheep, Elvey is now run as a small country hotel. Guests stay in the converted stable block and barn, and enjoy brand new contemporary bathrooms and excellent personal service, with glorious views over the Kent countryside.

Whether you're sipping champagne on the veranda outside your suite, or you're riding your own horse through our excellent bridleways, you'll be surrounded by the quietest, the prettiest and the most idyllic countryside in Kent.

At breakfast you have fresh eggs from our own chickens, sausages from local farms, tomatoes and fried potatoes from our own gardens. In the evenings, you can sample wine or cider from Kent's vineyards, and admire crafts from local artists. Elvey has been run by local people for centuries. That's why we say Elvey is Kentish to the core.

HOTEL FEATURES

- Double rooms in the converted stables
- Brand new contemporary en-suite bathrooms
- Stunning views across the fields.
- A beautiful Dining Room with low beams
- Roaring log fire
- Fabulous Full English Breakfast

Haunted History

hauntedhotelguide.com

According to the Guinness Book of Records, Pluckley is the most haunted village in England. There have been numerous sightings – and at last count, there are 42 Ghosts in the village alone.

Elvey Farm has long been known as the only haunted hotel in the area. Edward Brett, a farmer at Elvey, is reputed to have shot himself here. He may have died over a hundred years ago, but many say Edward is still here. The previous owners of the farm saw Mr Brett on many occasions walking the corridors at night. Many guests have seen him too... Some say he is so vivid, it's as though he's alive today. Guests have reported a strange smell, resembling burning hay. There have been reports of a poltergeist – and paranormal investigators have confirmed the farm is bristling with activity. The present owners have already experienced Edward Brett – his voice has twice been heard whispering in the old dairy where he shot himself.

Many people come to Pluckley to find the ghosts – many people descend on Elvey Farm. At Hallowe'en, the whole village is packed. But there's far more than a ghost here. It's an idyllic location, surrounded by fields, orchards and hop gardens. It's Kent at its best – ghosts and all...

ne **Ffolkes Arms** at Hillington is a friendly family run hotel which offers first class ccommodation and a wide range of services and facilities. It holds a dark ecret however, as it is reputedly haunted by a young nanny who committed uicide...

ne hotel, which bears the name of the Ffolkes family, was constructed over nree hundred years ago and became well known as a very popular Coaching Inn, being located on the main mailing route from the Midlands in Norwich. For a period of time the attic rooms of the hotel were used as an vernight gaol for the prison carriages on their way to the prison in Norwich. nis now provides the hotel with 20 bedrooms, all tastefully furnished, and omplete with en-suite facilities. The rooms also ensure added comfort; each aving twin or double beds, remote control colour television, direct dial elephone, tea making facilities, hair dryer and trouser press.

Ffolkes Arms Hotel

Lynn Road, Hillington,
King's Lynn,
Norfolk, PE31 6BJ
www.ffolkes-arms-hotel.co.uk

ne **Ffolkes Arms** is reputedly haunted by a young nanny, who apparently nrew herself out of one of the attic bedrooms during the latter part of the 9th century and was, quite gruesomely, embedded on the iron railings hich then ran along the front of the inn.

er benign spirit is known to wander the bedrooms and corridors of this eautiful hotel.

HOTEL FEATURES

- En suite facilities
- Television
- Direct Dial Telephone
- Tea and Coffee Making Facilities
- Hair Dryer

ne **Schooner Hotel,** situated in Alnmouth, Northumberland has been twice warded the title of The Most Haunted Hotel in Great Britain and is reputed to ave over 60 individual ghosts...

ne Famous Schooner Hotel and Restaurant, a Listed 17th century coaching n only 100 yards from the beach, river and golf course, has been the hub of lnmouth village since its first customer back in the 1600's, and remains one of ne most well known and respected hotels in the North East of England. otable persons said to have stayed at The Schooner include Charles ickens, John Wesley, Basil Rathbone, Douglas Bader and even King George and there is always the chance of meeting our Resident Ghost - "Parson myth"! There is little doubting that our motto "Comfort with Character" is stly deserved, and this can be seen by the number of guests who return to ne Famous Schooner time and time again.

Schooner Hotel

Alnmouth, Alnwick
Northumberland NE66 2RS
Tel: +44 (0)1665 830216
Email: info@theschoonerhotel.co.uk
www.theschoonerhotel.co.uk

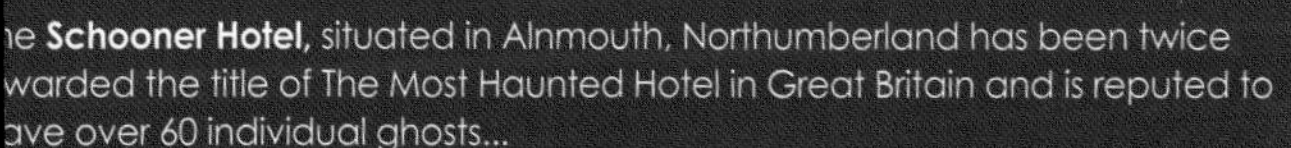

ne **Schooner Hotel** has been twice awarded the title of The Most Haunted otel in Great Britain by The Poltergeist Society and is reputed to have over) individual ghosts. The hotel has a somewhat unclear history, but there are ports of suicides, murders and even of babies being thrown into the fire. It is very 'active' hotel with over 3000 recent sightings, ranging from ghosts essed in military uniform to apparitions of a little boy. The sound of reaming, whispers and knocking are also a very common occurrence and e regularly experienced by staff and guests alike.

HOTEL FEATURES

- En suite facilities
- Television
- Tea and coffee making facilities
- Licensed Bar & Restaurant
- Conference Facilities

Chillingham Castle

Chillingham, Alnwick
Northumberland NE66 5NJ
Tel: +44 (0)1668 215359
Email:
enquiries@chillingham-castle.com
www.chillingham-castle.com

HOTEL FEATURES

- Colour television, microwave, fridge and electric cooker
- Stunning Grounds
- Log burning stoves
- Logs and kindling for fires

Stunning **Chillingham Castle** with its alarming dungeons and torture chamber has, since the twelve-hundreds, been continuously owned by the family of the Earls Grey and their relations. The Castle is also home to a number a ghosts, the most famous being the 'Blue Boy'...
In a glorious and secluded setting in Northumberland's famously beautiful countryside, Chillingham Castle offers holidaymakers the unbelievable experience of staying in a medieval fortress.
Parts of the Castle and the coach house have been converted into comfortable holiday apartments, offering the opportunity for a memorable holiday.
The extensive grounds are accessible to holiday makers. Within a few miles of the coast and being in close proximity to several golf courses, Chillingham is ideally situated for a unique holiday, with fishing, golf and stately home visits.

Haunted History hauntedhotelguide.com

We have a number of ghosts at **Chillingham Castle**. The most famous is the "Blue Boy" whose moans are often heard around midnight. These noises hav been traced to a spot near a passage cut through a ten foot wall, behind which the bones of a young boy and fragments of blue clothing were discovered! People sleeping in that room even today, have been known to see the figure of a young boy dressed in blue, and surrounded by light.
Another ghost, Lady Mary Berkeley, searches for her husband who ran off wi her sister. Lady Mary, desolate and broken hearted, lived in the castle by herself with only her baby daughter as a companion. The rustle of her dress can be heard as she passes people by...

The George Hotel

High Street, Dorchester-on-Thames
Oxfordshire OX10 7HH
Tel: 01865 340404
E-mail: info@thegeorgedorch-ester.co.uk
www.thegeorgedorchester.co.uk

HOTEL FEATURES

- En suite bathroom
- Colour TV • Alarm clock Radio
- Direct Dial Telephone
- Cathedral or garden views
- Tea & coffee making facilities

The **George Hotel** is a fifteenth century coaching inn set in the heart of Oxfordshire. In the days of the stagecoach it provided a welcome haven for many an aristocrat including the first Duchess of Marlborough, Sarah Church However, in more recent times we have seen famous guests of a different hu such as author DH Lawrence.
The Buildings of The George Hotel have changed little since their heyday as coaching inn. It retains all the beauty and charm of those days whilst offering every modern amenity.
The Hotel provides 17 en-suite bedrooms set in peaceful surroundings; all individually decorated and furnished with fine antiques. Our owners have created a décor which suits the requirements of modern times and facilities whilst maintaining the spirit of the past.

Haunted History hauntedhotelguide.com

This beautiful hotel is directly opposite Dorchester Abbey and is well renowned for its spectral visitors. Being so close to the Abbey it is little surprise that a mischievous monk often frequents Room 6. The spirit of an old lady ha also been 'picked up' by a number of mediums. She is present in Room 3 of the hotel and on occasion, her reflection has been seen through the windows.
Another visitor to the **George Hotel** frequents one of the bedrooms in particular – The Vicar's Room. This room is reputed to be haunted by a ghost of a sad-looking girl dressed in a white gown.

e beautiful **Bull Hotel** at Long Melford dates back to the Fifteenth Century. e Ghost of Richard Evered, murdered there in 1648, still roams the Hotel... original timber work, both outside and inside is unusually well preserved. at of the exterior was discovered in 1935 when a hundred year old brick nt was removed. On a beam in the lounge is carved a 'Wildman' or Voodwose', a mysterious being frequently depicted in the decoration of the iddle ages, reputedly to ward off evil spirits.

e Bull Hotel, boasting 25 en-suite bedrooms, was tastefully refurbished in 03 and is renowned for its excellent cuisine and chef's specialities...

Bull Hotel

Hall Street, Long Melford
Sudbury, Suffolk CO10 9JG
Tel: 01787 378494
Email:
bull.longmelford@greeneking.co.uk
www.thebull-hotel.com

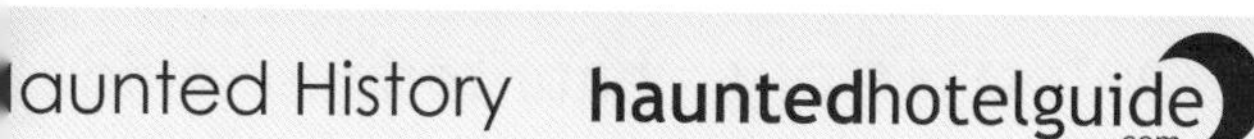

e **Bull Hotel** is quite famous for its ghosts. Indeed it is mentioned in a number books on the subject. According to the legend, a man named "Richard ered" was murdered there in 1648. The crime had a strange twist however, the victim's body disappeared overnight! It is said that the spirit of Richard ered roams the Bull Hotel now.

ong with a number of apparitions, the Bull is also known for its poltergeist tivity: a large oak door opens and closes by itself; chairs move around the ning room of their own accord and the sound of breaking crockery has en heard by several guests. One person even had a copper jug thrown at em.

definitely a place we would recommend!

HOTEL FEATURES

- Colour Television
- Mini Stereo
- Direct Dial Telephones
- Ironing Boards • Irons • Hairdryers
- Tea & coffee making facilities

eeped in history **Brownsover Hall** is now a fabulous hotel. It is said to be unted by One Handed Boughton - a former inhabitant of the hall who lost arm during Elizabethan times...

e Hall Hotel is a Grade 11 Listed Victorian Gothic mansion nestling in 7 acres woodland and garden. This magnificent building has a dramatic interior h sweeping staircase and crackling log fires. With rich colours and plenty of aracter and charm the Brownsover Hall Hotel has a distinct unique charm. e Hall borders three counties, making it the ideal base for visiting Warwick, atford-upon-Avon and the North Cotswolds.

Brownsover Hall

Brownsover Lane, Old Brownsover
Rugby, Warwickshire CV21 1HU
Tel: +44 (0)1788 546100
Email:
gm.brownsoverhall@foliohotels.com
www.foliohotels.com/brownsoverhall

aunted History hauntedhotelguide.com

nember of the Boughton-Leigh family, who had his hand severed at the e of Queen Elizabeth I, is reputed to haunt **Brownsover Hall** despite many empts to exorcise the ghost. The spirit was finally imprisoned in a glass ttle and thrown into a nearby lake. Everything was fine at the Hall until the ttle was discovered by a group of fishermen and returned to the Hall und 100 years ago...

spirit of One-handed Boughton, as he was known, is reputed to haunt the unds, and many unexplained noises, footsteps and voices can often be ard emanating from the tower...

HOTEL FEATURES

- Gilbert Scott Restaurant
- Warwick Bar
- WiFi internet access
- Nearest Rail Link: Rugby 1mile
- Nearest Airport: Birmingham

The Old Bell Hotel

Abbey Row, Malmesbury
Wiltshire SN16 0AG
Tel: 01666 822344
Email:
www.oldbellhotel.com

HOTEL FEATURES

- En Suite Facilities
- Televisions with integral
- DVD players, Sky TV
- Wired broadband internet access.

Built in 1220 and reputed to be the oldest purpose built hotel in England, The **Old Bell Hotel** is still offering quintessentially English warmth, comfort and hospitality nearly eight hundred years later.

Standing alongside Malmesbury's medieval Abbey, in England's first capita the hotel provides outstanding levels of service and retains the ambience o a bygone age.

There are 31 en suite bedrooms, 15 in the main house , each furnished in an individual style, some with antique furniture, and a further 16 in the Coach House

Haunted History hauntedhotelguide.com

The **Old Bell Hotel** is renowned for its mysterious goings on - which is not surprising a the east wing of the hotel is built directly on part of the former abbey.

The hotel's most famous ghost is said to be the spirit of a lady who was unhappily married in the abbey. Her ghost, known as the Grey Lady, has reputedly been see wandering about the bedrooms, in particular the James Ody Room.

Many more strange happenings have occurred at the Old Bell including glasses rising into the air and smashing by themselves in the Danvers Room; wardrobes mysteriously jamming themselves against doors in the Foe Room and night porters reporting a cold atmosphere when walking down the corridor towards the Salon. Could these experiences all be attributed to the Grey Lady... or are there more mischievous spirits at the Old Bell?

Station Hotel

Castle Hill, Dudley
West Midlands DY1 4RA
Tel: +44 (0)1384 253418
Email:
sales@stationhoteldudley.co.uk
www.stationhoteldudley.co.uk

HOTEL FEATURES

- En suite bathroom
- Colour TV
- Radio
- Tea & Coffee Making Facilities
- Wedding Facilities

The **Station Hotel,** originally built in the early 20th Century has played host to many famous guests, including Bob Hope and Laurel and Hardy. The spirit o a girl murdered in the hotel is said to roam the corridors...

The Station Hotel offers a warm and friendly atmosphere. Set in the heart of the Midlands, the hotel is easily accessible from Junction 2 of the M5 which only five minutes drive away.

Originally built in 1910, The Station was demolished in 1936 in order to build a larger hotel. This became particularly popular with theatrical artists playing the Hippodrome Theatre, once situated opposite. Laurel & Hardy, Bob Hope Bing Crosby and George Formby are amongst the famous names that have stayed at this historic Hotel.

Haunted History hauntedhotelguide.com

Going back to the beginning, researching the building was almost impossib due to the misplacement of many archive records. However, it is up to you decide whether the folklore stories told about the hotel over the years are true or not.....

The story tells of a hotel manager who enticed a servant girl into the cellar. Spurning his advances and threatening to tell his wife, the girl was murdered by the hotel manager. He strangled and stabbed her then hid her body in a barrel. 'Most Haunted's Derek Acorah 'picked up' the ghost of the murdere girl as well as the spirit of writer George Lawley and the spirits of two young children. The other, as yet unnamed spirit Acorah picked up on, is rumoured to be sitting waiting for someone in the infamous ROOM 214.

unning **Hazlewood Castle** is steeped in history and was t mentioned in the Doomsday Book carried out for King lliam. Ghostly apparitions and sounds are regularly perienced...

t in seventy-seven acres of tranquil parkland Hazlewood astle, a former monastery and retreat has been oughtfully and tastefully designed to offer a distinctly ferent lifestyle experience. Hazlewood combines the egance of the Castle with the excellence of the food d service offered to all our guests. Whether visiting zlewood for the first time with friends or as a delegate at e of our major conferences you will always be greeted h a warm welcome.We have twenty-one bedrooms d suites at Hazlewood. Nine of them are situated in the ain castle and twelve are in our annex area "St argaret's" which is located in our picturesque Courtyard. bedrooms are beautifully decorated to the highest ndards, with great care taken to enhance their natural auty. All bedrooms are individual and vary in shape and es, designed to provide a relaxing haven full of ckknacks (and little rubber ducks!).

Hazlewood Castle

Paradise Lane, Hazlewood
Tadcaster
North Yorkshire LS24 9NJ
Tel: 01937 535353
Email: info@hazlewood-castle.co.uk
www.hazlewood-castle.co.uk

HOTEL FEATURES

- Beautiful Restaurant
- Weddings
- Satellite television
- Tea and Coffee making Facilities
- Modem Links for E-mail and Internet Access
- En suite Bathrooms

Haunted History

hauntedhotelguide.com

Hazlewood Castle is steeped in history and it is no surprise that it has its fair share of ghosts.

Many of the bedrooms throughout the hotel are haunted. Tansy bedroom, for example, is mentioned in a ghost book as having a monk dressed in black 'making his presence felt' in the room.

Staff and guests alike have seen and felt strange presences in Lavender bedroom, Rose Bedroom and the Jasmine Suite.

Downstairs in the hotel, a priest has been seen walking from the direction of the Great Hall into the Library and then disappear. As the castle was a former monastery, the monks and priests would walk from the Great Hall to the Tower to go down into the cloisters, which is where the fireplace is now positioned in the Library

Voices have also been heard at Hazlewood Castle... A voice saying "goodnight" was heard by a chef as she was leaving the Restaurant Anise to enter Reception but no-one was there, and over the Christmas period of 2003 one guest complained repeatedly overnight of a baby crying keeping her awake. However, no babies were in the adjoining rooms.

Beautiful **Mosborough Hall** dates back hundreds of years and is steeped in history. It is now a luxurious ho and is also home to a number of ghosts, including th White Lady and a Spectral Dog...

A wealth of quality, service and history wait for you a Mosborough Hall Hotel. The Hotel was lovingly restore in 1974 from a magnificent 750 year old Manor Hous No expense has been spared, with each room havin been carefully restored and decorated to retain the historic ambience that is rarely enjoyed today. An ancient doorway leads from the friendly reception t the oak bar, with minstrel gallery and old stone mullioned windows, inviting you to relax in comfort a you take a drink, perhaps before enjoying the super cuisine for which the restaurant has been long celebrated. The Restaurant consistently maintains its Rosettes award-winning standard with fresh home made breads, chocolates and patisseries.

Mosborough Hall has a selection of 47 rooms to cove all tastes; from Four Poster Feature Rooms with authentic wall panelling for that special occasion, t recently renovated Contemporary Rooms.

Mosborough Hall

High Street, Mosborough
Sheffield
South Yorkshire S20 5EA
Tel: 0114 248 4353
Email: hotel@mosboroughhall.co.uk
www.mosboroughhall.co.uk

HOTEL FEATURES

- Beautiful Award-winning Restaurant
- Weddings
- Conference Facilities
- Satellite Television
- Tea and Coffee making Facilities
- Telephone Modem Links for E-mail and Internet Access

Haunted History

hauntedhotelguide .com

Mosborough Hall was an ancient Manor House, the earliest parts of which date back to medieval times. It survives today as Mosborough Hall Hotel and still retains its stately charm behind a somewhat foreboding exterior appearance. Partly hidden by tall, stark trees, an air of mystery is enhanced by a high stone wall which hides the intimacies of the Hall from passers-by using the quiet Hallow Lane. There was a doorway through the wall, which was used by servants when they collected milk or eggs from the farm opposite. Many tales were told of strange noises and voices heard around this doorway, sufficient enough to raise a prickle on the back of the neck when walking past in the dim light of a fading evening.

Stories of a doctor waking up in his bed dripping with blood, a spectral dog and The White Lady of Mosborough Hall are enough to make the blood run cold. The White Lady, thought to have been a governess at the hotel killed by the squire with whom she was in love, is regularly seen throughout the hotel.

eautiful **Comlongon Castle** dates back to the 1300s. his truly breathtaking building is now a luxurious hotel. he hotel also boasts a ghost - that of the 'Green ady', thought to be the spirit of Marion Carruthers... omlongon Castle, near Gretna in Scotland, is a estored 14th Century Medieval Scottish Castle Vedding Venue and luxurious Baronial Hotel with 14 dividually themed luxury en-suite 4-poster bedrooms. he wedding castle hotel has two Oak panelled estaurants for receptions and a private residents' bar. ur chefs specialise in local produce, changing their enus daily.

his Romantic Medieval Castle is the perfect wedding enue for your wedding castle reception or elebration in Scotland. Steeped in Scottish Border story, Comlongon Castle is more than just fantastic otel – it has fantastic displays of armour, weapons and anners, whilst the opulent bedrooms boast 4-poster eds and jacuzzis providing a stunning blend of edieval and modern luxury.

Comlongon Castle

Clarencefield , Dumfries
Dumfries and Galloway DG1 4NA
Tel: 01387 870283
Email:
reception@comlongon.co.uk
www.comlongon.com

HOTEL FEATURES

- Four-Poster Suites
- En suite Facilities
- Breathtaking Surroundings
- Jacuzzi Baths

Haunted History

hauntedhotelguide.com

Marion Carruthers is a presence that has been felt within **Comlongon Castle** for over four centuries. Since her death in 1570 there have been numerous sightings of a "Green Lady" wandering the grounds of the estate. The smell of apples often precedes these apparitions.

Over the last decade sightings have been concentrated upon one room in particular. Guests have reported numerous sightings of a figure in a long dress either sitting on the four-poster bed or drifting between the bed and door. Most stories from guests mention the moving of jewellery, particularly watches and bracelets, from one location to another.

Sightings at one period numbered almost once a month, so much so that staff began to talk of the suite as "Marion's room". Upon the introduction of new jacuzzis in several rooms, including Marion's, it seemed the obvious choice to name this as the Carruthers suite.

If you wish to book this room please inform reception. We are always interested in information you gather...

Ardoe House Hotel

South Deeside Road, Blairs
Aberdeen AB12 5YP
Tel: 01224 860 600
Email: H6626@accor.com
www.mercure.com

HOTEL FEATURES

- 24 hour room service
- Satellite Television
- Tea and Coffee making Facilities
- Swimming Pool
- State of the Art Beauty Salon

Ardoe House dates back to 1878. The hotel's traditional decor including wood panelled walls, enormous fireplaces and a grand staircase are not the only reminders of its past - some of the hotel's previous inhabitants still remain Ardoe House is a luxurious modern hotel, beautifully crafted from an imposing 19th century mansion house and inspired by the royal residence of Balmoral Castle, a few miles upstream.

Throwing open your window to capture the morning light as it spills over the River Dee is one of the pure delights of a stay at the Ardoe House. We've created over one hundred bedrooms in this historic setting, each one capturing the distinctly romantic mood of the surrounding countryside.

Depending on your mood you can choose to dine in our elegant AA rosette winning restaurant or enjoy a meal in the relaxed surroundings of the Laird's Bar, where you can enjoy a dram in front of a crackling fire in Winter.

It is, quite simply, beautiful.

Haunted History hauntedhotelguide.com

Ardoe House is no stranger to mysterious noises and ghostly apparitions. The hotel is said to be haunted by the white lady, thought to be Katherine Ogston, the wife of soap merchant Alexander Milne Ogston. Her spirit has been seen throughout the hotel but most of the 'activity' seems to centre round a portrait of Katherine on the main stairs.

There are conflicting reports as to who this ghost is. Whilst some maintain that the White Lady is the spirit of Katherine Ogston, others believe that the ghost is the spirit of the daughter of a former owner who committed suicide...

Maesmawr Hall Hotel

Caersws, Powys, SY17 5SF.
Tel: 01686 688255
Fax: 01686 688410
Email:
information@maesmawr.co.uk
www.maesmawr.co.uk

HOTEL FEATURES

- En suite rooms
- Stunning Views
- Welsh Coastline and attractions nearby

Maesmawr Hall Hotel, Caersws is situated in the beautiful valley of the Severn This stunning period house is privately owned and personally supervised by the resident proprietors, Tim and Matthew Lewis.

The hotel is one of the most complete and picturesque of the old half-timbered houses of Montgomeryshire and a fine example of the central chimney timber-framed houses which are characteristic of Mid Wales.

The general appearance of the house suggests a mid 17th Century dwelling but it has been established that the house was in existence before 1600.

The hotel has 17 en-suite bedrooms with modern facilities, many of which have been recently refurbished to a high standard and offer stunning views over the grounds and the breathtaking countryside beyond

Whether it's simply an overnight stay with bed and breakfast, or a longer holiday, Maesmawr Hall combines the quiet tranquillity of a country house with the atmosphere of a popular venue.

Haunted History hauntedhotelguide.com

All old houses with the slightest self respect claim to possess a ghost and **Maesmawr Hall** is no exception! The Grey Lady, an unknown spectre and Robin Drwg (Wicked Robin), assuming the form of a bull, are said to roam the Hall.

Robin Drwg was a renowned rapscallion in his day and it appears that he caused much mischief and alarm to those who encountered him. He was eventually overcome by the efforts of seven parsons of undoubted ability and laid in Llyn Tarw (the Bull's Pool)....

Whether the endeavours of the worthy gentlemen were successful or not is a matter of conjecture, but it is claimed that his half man/half beastly form still lurks!

hin Castle (the "Red Fort") originally dates from fore 1277 and dominates the historic Welsh rural arket town of Ruthin. The infamous Grey Lady is a gular visitor to this beautiful hotel...

thin Castle's wood panelled entrance hall is warmly and several of the inner rooms have the added rmth of beautifully carved stone and wood eplaces with open fires that make them cosy despite eir scale. Original oil paintings line the Inner Hallway d are to be found in several of the public rooms.

e castle has a proud, centuries-old tradition of oviding hospitality and comfort, including hosting merous Royal guests. It is difficult not just to feel elcome here but also to feel part of the great history the castle and those that have come before.

e Castle boasts 62 individually designed bedrooms. ost of the rooms enjoy views over the 30 acres of rdens, parkland and woods of the estate and wards the surrounding Welsh countryside. Many oms have four-poster beds and original fireplaces urrently not in use) and most have original antique eces of furniture.

Ruthin Castle

Ruthin
Denbighshire LL15 2NU
Tel: 01824 702664
Email:
reception@ruthincastle.co.uk
www.ruthincastle.co.uk

HOTEL FEATURES

- Fully equipped Gym
- Award-winning Restaurant
- Hairdryer, bath and/or shower
- Remote control colour television
- Beautiful Grounds
- Hospitality Beverages

Haunted History

hauntedhotelguide.com

here are endless tales of hauntings in and around the castle. However there is a lot of historic evidence which gives the rumours credence and many believe them to be true.

he castle ghost is known as the 'Grey Lady' as she is dressed from head to foot in grey. One of the nost popular explanations as to who this spirit may be is that she was the wife of the second in command at the castle when it was 'the Red Fort' and was first inhabited by the armies of Edward I. he story goes that the 'Grey Lady' discovered that her husband, a powerful man, was having an affair and took it upon herself to murder his lover with an axe! Once this heinous crime was discovered, he 'Grey Lady' was arrested and sentenced to death. However, she was buried outside the walls of he Castle so as not to bury her on consecrated ground. Her grave can still be seen today, as can her pirit wandering around the battlements of the Castle.

Craig-y-Nos Castle nestles in the lovely Upper Swanse[a] Valley next to the River Tawe. The castle was the forme[r] home of opera diva, Adelina Patti and is now a beautiful hotel with a very haunted history...
Craig-y-nos Castle is situated in an area of outstandin[g] natural beauty. With its wonderful location and the authentic ambience of a Welsh Castle, Craig-y-Nos has plenty to offer. Whether you want a relaxing brea[k], an over night stay, or if you are joining us as part of a function, you can be sure of a totally unique experience.
The Castle benefits from a number of bars and restaurants and is fully equipped to cater for conferences and wedding parties.
Craig-y-nos Castle has a wide variety of accommodation ranging from budget rooms to en-suite and luxury guest rooms overlooking the gardens. Each room is unique in design and is furnished in a traditional fashion in keeping with the Castle's history. The castle also benefits from Spa facilities, gymnasium and spa that enjoy unsurpassed panoramic views of the Brecon Beacons.

Craig-y-Nos Castle

Powys SA9 1GL
Email:
bookings_craigynos@hotmail.com
www.craigynoscastle.com

HOTEL FEATURES

- Fantastic Location
- Character Bedrooms
- Ghost Tours
- Beacons Spa Facilities
- Wonderful Public Rooms
- En suite Facilities

Haunted History

hauntedhotelguide.com

Old castles, with their colourful and often turbulent histories, often conjure up pictures of ghosts and paranormal goings-on. **Craig-y-Nos Castle** is no exception and has established a reputation amongst "ghost watchers" who have experienced apparitions, poltergeist activity and strange noises first hand. As the former home of Opera Diva Adelina Patti, who was embalmed in its cellars, and later as a Tuberculosis Hospital, where many succumbed to their illness, the Castle has a rich history of both dramatic and tragic events...
As well as being haunted by the Opera Diva herself, the Castle is home to many more spirits including a small boy accompanied by a soldier, often seen at the bottom of the staircase. The Nicolini Bar, formerly the Library of Patti's second husband Ernesto Nicolini, is haunted by a male spirit who is often heard shouting orders. There is also a well documented malevolent spirit who resides in the cellar.
A number of television programmes have been produced illustrating the paranormal activities at Craig-y-Nos Castle and due to the overwhelming interest from the general public wanting to experience them for themselves the castle now organises "Ghost Watch Tours".

e **Skirrid** Mountain Inn is situated in Llanvihangel Crucorney; a small village t off the A465; approximately 5 miles north from the centre of Abergavenny d 18 miles from Hereford.

reputed to be the oldest Inn in Wales and it's history can be traced back far as the Norman Conquest.

e inn has an ancient wood-panelled restaurant where you can sit and joy delicious home cooked food from the menu. There are fireplaces with al fires, two bars, one with a pool table, an old ship's bell for calling last ders, and three comfortable luxury visitor's bedrooms, two with four poster ds.

The Skirrid Inn

Llanvihangel Crucorney,
Abergavenny,
Monmouthshire, NP7 8DH
Tel: 01873 890258
www.skirridmountaininn.co.uk/

HOTEL FEATURES

- En suite facilities
- Four-poster beds
- Colour Television
- Tea and Coffee making
- Wonderful views

aunted History hauntedhotelguide.com

e **Skirrid Inn,** the oldest in Wales, is well known for its haunting happenings d there's good reason to take these "sightings" seriously due to the inn's uesome history. The Skirrid has been an inn since 1110 but is most famous for use as Judge Jeffrey's courtroom in the wake of the Monmouth rebellion. e brutal judge famously hanged 180 rebels in 1685 from a beam beneath e Skirrid's staircase. The beam stands today and bears chaffing marks from e hangman's rope.

o-one can be entirely sure who actually haunts the bedrooms and stairways the Inn but many people believe that 'hanging' Judge Jeffreys could not t, or that some of the 180 people he sent to the gallows have come back revenge.

unning **Ross Castle**, situated on the shores of Lough Sheelin, dates back to 36 and, not surprisingly, is steeped in history. The ghosts of two star-crossed ers are often witnessed...

uated amidst majestic trees in the tranquil countryside on the County eath and Cavan border, Ross Castle commands magnificent views of ugh Sheelin, a 4500 acre lake famous for its brown trout and liberally cked perch and large pike.

e secluded setting and spacious, comfortable accommodation offer the itor an exclusive retreat. The Castle is the perfect place to relax and wind, away from the stresses and strains of modern city life, or as a venue a private party or function.

Ross Castle

Mountnugent
County Meath
Ireland
Tel: +353 (0) 43 81286
Email : book@ross-castle.com
www.ross-castle.com

HOTEL FEATURES

- Tea and Coffee making facilities.
- En suite Bedrooms
- Four-Poster Room
- Use of Leisure Facilities at Ross House

aunted History hauntedhotelguide.com

all started back in 1536, when **Ross Castle** was first built. Legend has it that e Lord of Delvin, who built the castle, had a beautiful daughter, Sabina, no happened to fall in love with Orwin, the son of an Irish Lord. Fearing that eir love would not be accepted by their families, they decided to elope. ey set off in a sail boat but were unfortunately caught in a terrible storm. win was tipped overboard and was killed instantly. Sabina was thrown out the boat and was rescued by onlookers. They brought her back to the astle where she slept for three days. When she finally awoke, she found win, who was laid out in the chapel on the grounds of Ross Castle. She died ortly after that.

Kinnitty Castle

Kinnitty, Birr
County Offaly
Ireland
Tel: +353 (0)509 37318
Email: info@kinnittycastle.com
www.kinnittycastle.com

Stunning **Kinnitty Castle** has everything you would expect from an historic castle hotel and much more. We have our own resident ghost – The Monk!
Kinnitty Castle is located in the heart of Ireland, close to the picturesque village of Kinnitty in County Offaly. Approximately one hour 30 minutes from both Dublin and Shannon airports, it nestles in the foothills of the beautiful Slieve Bloom Mountains and is in Ireland's or designated Environment Park.
The whole area is steeped in Irish history and there is c wide range of things to see and do.
The hotel has 37 en suite bedrooms, all decorated in keeping with the castle's romantic old-world style. Wit two restaurants offering a selection of delicious dishe and two bars, the hotel is the ideal venue for holidays and special occasions alike. Our private panelled banqueting hall provides a secluded setting for weddings, conferences and themed functions. Excellent cuisine, fine wines, open turf fires, candleligh and excellent service create a very warm and welcoming atmosphere that is special to Kinnitty Castle.

HOTEL FEATURES

- Luxury en suite accommodation
- Bars and Restaurants
- Gate Lodge Spa
- Activities such as shooting, fishing, tennis & equestrian sports

Haunted History

hauntedhotelguide.com

The Castle has a long and colourful history which dates back to ancient times. Located on an ancient druidic ceremonial ground, where leylines cross and mystical forces are prevalent, the area around Kinnitty is considered by many to be a very mystical and magical place. The castle is also known for its infamous ghostly guest... the monk.
The monk has often been seen wandering through the glorious Banqueting Hall, stunning both staff and visitors alike. He has been known to communicate with staff members on occasion, sometimes even prophesying about future events which have unbelievably come true! Other rooms throughout the castle are haunted, in particular the Geraldine Room and the Elizabeth room where eerie presences have been felt.

Cornwall

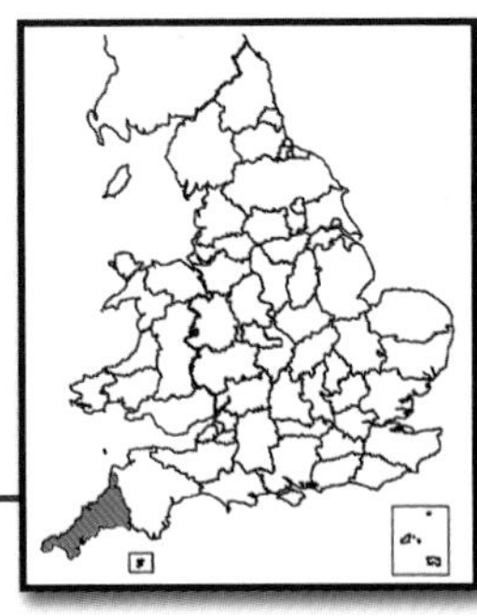

THE BOTTREAUX – restaurant, bar, rooms

Boscastle, Cornwall PL35 0BG • Tel: 01840 250231

This 200-year-old building is located in the heart of the old village, 10 minutes' walk from the harbour and shops. Guest bedrooms, lounge and bar have been refurbished to a high standard of comfort. The six double rooms (and one twin room) are en suite, with colour TV, tea/coffee making facilities and telephone; most have super king-size beds and high quality mattresses. This is a stylish and comfortable place to stay. Open to guests and non-residents, the AA Two Rosette Restaurant offers an atmospheric setting for romantic candlelit dinners. The select fixed-price menu changes on a daily basis, specialising in seafood dishes, using locally sourced ingredients of the finest quality.

Closed during November and open for weekends only in January and February.

e-mail: info@boscastlecornwall.co.uk • www.boscastlecornwall.co.uk

FULLY LICENSED. 7 BEDROOMS, ALL WITH PRIVATE BATHROOM. CAMELFORD 5 MILES. S£££, D££.

STRATTON GARDENS HOUSE

Cot Hill, Stratton, Bude, Cornwall EX23 9DN

Tel: 01288 352500 • Fax: 01288 359153

e-mail: moira@stratton-gardens.co.uk

www.stratton-gardens.co.uk

This charming 16th century Listed house in historic Stratton offers quality accommodation, fine food and friendly, traditional hospitality. Enjoy the comforts of the spacious en suite bedrooms, all of which are individually furnished and have colour television, tea/coffee making facilities and hairdryers. Relax and feel at home in our comfortable lounge and sample the delights of the licensed restaurant and attractive terraced gardens. Stratton Gardens House is a peaceful hideaway, only one-and-a-half miles from Bude's wonderful beaches and dramatic coastline, an ideal base for bird-watching, walking, exploring the coast or moors, or simply unwinding.

OPEN ALL YEAR. RESIDENTIAL & RESTAURANT LICENCE. 6 BEDROOMS, ALL WITH PRIVATE BATHROOMS. NON-SMOKING HOTEL. CHILDREN WELCOME. LAUNCESTON 15 MILES. S£, D£.

A useful index of towns/counties appears on pages 173-174

Penmorvah Manor Hotel and Courtyard Cottages

Falmouth, Cornwall TR11 5ED

- 3 Star Country House Hotel and 4 Star Self Catering Courtyard Cottages.
- Situated in 6 acres of mature gardens and woodland.
- Exceptional fine dining at Restaurant 1872.
- Ideally located for exploring Cornwall's many gardens and attractions.
- Close to the harbour town of Falmouth and Coastal Paths.
- Ground floor bedrooms available and ample parking.

Tel: 01326 250277 • Fax: 01326 250509

e-mail: reception@penmorvah.co.uk

www.penmorvah.co.uk

AA ★★★

FULLY LICENSED. 27 BEDROOMS, ALL WITH PRIVATE BATHROOMS. CHILDREN AND PETS WELCOME. CONFERENCE FACILITIES. CIVIL WEDDING CEREMONIES. FALMOUTH 2 MILES. S£££, D£££.

Trelawne Hotel

Nestling on the coastline between the Helford and Fal rivers in a beautiful and tranquil corner of Cornwall, this fine country house hotel enjoys a magnificent outlook across Falmouth Bay to the Roseland Peninsula. Maenporth beach is a short distance away and there are numerous idyllic coves nearby. The tastefully furnished and centrally heated bedrooms have en suite facilities, as well as colour television, radio, telephone and tea and coffee makers. There is a charming cocktail bar where new friends are easily made, and there is an indoor pool and games room. The cuisine comes high on the list of attractions at this well-run hotel, dishes being prepared by award-winning chefs and backed by an extensive wine list.

Mawnan Smith, Falmouth, Cornwall TR11 5HS

Tel: 01326 250226 • Fax: 01326 250909

LICENSED. 16 BEDROOMS, 14 WITH PRIVATE BATHROOMS. CHILDREN AND PETS WELCOME. LEISURE FACILITIES. FALMOUTH 5 MILES. S££, D££.

Beautifully situated in prize-winning gardens with views across Falmouth Bay, Green Lawns Hotel is an old established hotel which still retains and prides itself on the traditional standards associated with first class cuisine, comfort and service. Offering elegant, luxury accommodation, classic cuisine and leisure.
A superb base for exploring and touring enigmatic West Cornwall.

Western Terrace, Falmouth, Cornwall TR11 4QJ

Tel: 01326 312734 • Fax: 01326 211427

e-mail: info@greenlawnshotel.com • www.greenlawnshotel.com

AA ★★★ Silver

OPEN ALL YEAR EXCEPT CHRISTMAS. FULLY LICENSED. 39 BEDROOMS, ALL WITH PRIVATE BATHROOMS. NON-SMOKING ACCOMMODATION AVAILABLE. CHILDREN AND PETS WELCOME. LEISURE FACILITIES. CONFERENCE FACILITIES. CIVIL WEDDING CEREMONIES. TRURO 8 MILES. S££, D££.

Meudon Hotel

Mawnan Smith, Falmouth, Cornwall TR11 5HT
Tel: 01326 250541
Fax: 01326 250543
wecare@meudon.co.uk
www.meudon.co.uk

The most picturesque part of the Cornish coast between the Fal and Helford rivers is the enviable setting of this luxury hotel where the cuisine is something of a legend, with locally caught seafood especially worthy of mention. Eight acres of beautiful sub-tropical gardens lead down to the hotel's own private beach. Here one may relax in utter peace with rare flowering plants and shrubs providing a blaze of colour.

Appointments throughout the hotel are of the highest standard; comfortable lounges and a modern en suite bedroom wing all enjoy fine garden views. A wide range of leisure amenities are available in the area, as well as the hotel's own yacht and free golf. Walk the cliff path where delightful unspoilt villages and peaceful coves wait to be explored.

AA 85% ★★★

FULLY LICENSED. 29 BEDROOMS, ALL WITH PRIVATE BATHROOMS. NON-SMOKING ACCOMMODATION. CHILDREN AND PETS WELCOME. LEISURE FACILITIES. FALMOUTH 4 MILES. S££££, D££££.

The Majestic Old Lady of Fowey....

comfortably sits on the bank of the River Fowey estuary, and offers unrivalled views overlooking the water to the quaint fishing village of Polruan. Built in 1882, she commands the best location in the area, nestled next to the water's edge. Open for morning coffee, bar snack lunches, afternoon Cornish cream teas, and both 3 and 5-course evening meals at AA 2 Rosette standard.

Non-residents very welcome.

The Fowey Hotel

The Fowey Hotel
The Esplanade, Fowey PL23 1HX
FREEPHONE: 0800 243708
www.richardsonhotels.co.uk
info@thefoweyhotel.co.uk

LICENSED. 37 BEDROOMS, ALL WITH PRIVATE BATHROOMS. CHILDREN AND PETS WELCOME. EDEN PROJECT 8 MILES. S££££, D£££.

Readers are requested to mention this FHG guidebook when seeking accommodation

*Dogs stay for **FREE** during Low Season at Mullion Cove Hotel*

MULLION COVE HOTEL

... located on the Cornwall Coast Path in a spectacular position on the Lizard Peninsula. Stunning country and coastal walks. Hotel facilities include a doggy friendly lounge, dog welcome pack, comfortable bedrooms and excellent food. **Tel: 01326 240328**

Email: enquiries@mullion-cove.co.uk
www.mullion-cove.co.uk

OPEN ALL YEAR. FULLY LICENSED. 32 BEDROOMS, ALL WITH PRIVATE BATHROOMS.
CHILDREN AND PETS WELCOME. LEISURE FACILITIES. CONFERENCE FACILITIES. S£££, D£££.

The Best Western Restormel Lodge Hotel is situated in the beautiful Fowey Valley. The restaurant is noted for high quality traditional cooking, using the very best of Cornish farm and sea produce, with an excellent choice of reasonably priced wines. The en suite bedrooms are elegantly furnished and fully equipped for your comfort. From April to October there is a heated outdoor swimming pool. Many Cornish beauty spots are within a short drive, and the Eden Project is six miles away.

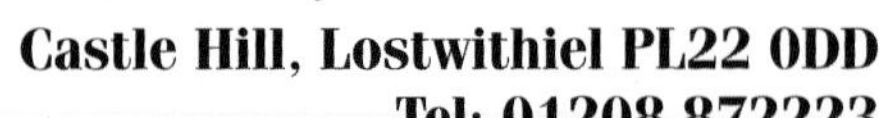

LICENSED. ALL BEDROOMS WITH PRIVATE BATHROOMS. CHILDREN WELCOME, PETS BY ARRANGEMENT. LEISURE FACILITIES. BODMIN 5 MILES. S£££, D£££.

Trevalsa Court Country House Hotel

School Hill, Mevagissey, Cornwall PL26 6TH
Tel: 01726 842468 • Fax: 01726 844482
stay@trevalsa-hotel.co.uk • www.trevalsa-hotel.co.uk

High above one of the Duchy's favourite fishing villages and with direct access to sheltered Polstreath Beach with its gently sloping sands and safe bathing, this sprucely decorated hotel takes in panoramic views along the coast. This superb example of the English country hotel, with its oak-panelled hall and dining room, sumptuously furnished lounge and mullioned windows, recalls the ambience of a bygone age. The cuisine places great emphasis on the presentation of fresh, superbly cooked food backed by courteous and efficient service. All rooms have first-class en suite facilities, colour television and tea/coffee making facilities. A haven of quiet contentment by the sea.

OPEN ALL YEAR. FULLY LICENSED. 12 BEDROOMS, ALL WITH PRIVATE BATHROOMS.
CHILDREN OVER 12 YEARS WELCOME. ST AUSTELL 5 MILES. S££££, D£££/££££.

e-mail: relax@polurrianhotel.com • www.polurrianhotel.com

Set in 12 acres with stunning views across Mount's Bay. The hotel has two pools, gym, snooker room, tennis court, sun terraces and secluded gardens. Most of the recently refurbished bedrooms have sea views. Our restaurants offer excellent food in stylish surroundings. Whether it is a more casual atmosphere in the High Point Restaurant or a formal dinner in the main Dining Room, we have something for everyone.

Mullion, Lizard Peninsula, Cornwall TR12 7EN • Tel: 01326 240421 • Fax: 01326 240083

OPEN ALL YEAR. FULLY LICENSED. 39 BEDROOMS, ALL WITH PRIVATE BATHROOMS.
CHILDREN AND PETS WELCOME. LEISURE FACILITIES. CONFERENCE FACILITIES. CIVIL WEDDING CEREMONIES.
HELSTON 5 MILES. S£££, D£££.

Whipsiderry Hotel

Trevelgue Road, Porth, Newquay TR7 3LY
Tel: 01637 874777 • info@whipsiderry.co.uk
www.whipsiderry.co.uk

Newquay has many fine beaches and many fine hotels and this warm and friendly hotel is among the very best. Standing in spacious grounds, in which there is a superb heated swimming pool and children's play area, the hotel overlooks Porth Bay with beautiful Whipsiderry Beach, backed by honeycomb cliffs, nearby. The cuisine is high on the list of attributes, the excellent six-course menus complemented by an extensive wine list. Public and private rooms are delightfully decorated and appointed and leisure opportunities include specially arranged fishing trips and perhaps a chance to watch the friendly local badgers at play in the garden. ***Family-run for 36 years.***

RESIDENTIAL AND RESTAURANT LICENCE. 20 BEDROOMS, ALL WITH PRIVATE BATHROOMS.
CHILDREN AND PETS WELCOME. LEISURE FACILITIES. NEWQUAY 1 MILE. S££, D££.

Penventon Hotel

Cornwall's Premier Independent Hotel, The Penventon offers superb facilities at "affordable" prices for every social or business occasion Central for touring Cornwall, our inspirational breaks can be arranged for 2 to 7 days.

Bedrooms

• All appointed to a high standard, with bath or shower en suite.
• Colour TV, direct dial telephone, controllable central heating and tea/coffee making facilities.
• Suites offer one or two bedrooms with lounge areas, some with patios. • Special weekend and weekly rates available.

Dining

• AA Rosetted menus • Choose from over 100 classic French, Italian and English dishes in the Dining Galleries.
• Local fish, shellfish and meat traditionally served.
• Favourite melodies played on piano grande each evening.

Leisure

• Centrally heated Aphrodite's Health and Leisure Complex.
• Large sauna, steam bath, spa hydrobath, fitness suite.
• Luxury robes and towels always provided
• STATZ "VERTICLE" sun room, allowing the fastest tan available.
• Poolside bar and menu.
• Open 7 days a week, normally adults only.
• Resident beautician and masseuse for health and beauty treatments.

ROSETTED

★★★ HOTEL

The Penventon Hotel
Redruth, West Cornwall TR15 1TE
Telephone: 01209 20 3000 • Fax: 01209 20 3001
e-mail: manager@penventon.com
www.penventon.com

A perfect setting for a perfect holiday

Set in over four acres of secluded gardens and woodlands, this elegant Queen Anne residence is a wonderful place to relax and unwind.

- 47 en suite bedrooms with colour TV and tea/coffee facilities, hairdryers and radios.
- Standard, Superior and De Luxe rooms
- Table d'hôte restaurant • Large wine selection
- 3 comfortable lounges
- Croquet, putting
- 45ft heated swimming pool (May to September)
- ¾ mile from beach • ¾ hour drive to Heligan and the Eden Project.

Rosemundy House Hotel, St Agnes, Cornwall TR5 0UF
Tel: 01872 552101 • Fax: 01872 554000
e-mail: info@rosemundy.co.uk • www.rosemundy.co.uk

OPEN ALL YEAR. RESIDENTIAL/RESTAURANT LICENCE. 47 BEDROOMS, ALL WITH PRIVATE BATHROOMS. NON-SMOKING ACCOMMODATION AVAILABLE. LEISURE FACILITIES. S£££, D££££.

THE GARRACK
HOTEL & RESTAURANT
ST IVES, CORNWALL TR26 3AA
Tel: 01736 796199 • Fax: 01736 798955
reception@garrack.com • www.garrack.com

THE GARRACK HOTEL stands in two secluded acres, with breathtaking views over Porthmeor beach, just 15 minutes' walk from picturesque St Ives. Owned and run by the same family for over 40 years, it is a place of comfort and traditional hospitality, for you to eat well, sleep soundly and leave relaxed.

- *A la carte and fixed price menus including seafood, meat and vegetarian dishes using fresh Cornish and West Country ingredients*
- *Wine list offering exceptional value for money*
- *18 individually styled en suite bedrooms, most with ocean view; ground floor rooms available.*
- *Indoor pool, sauna, exercise equipment, all-day licensed coffee shop*

LICENSED. 18 BEDROOMS, ALL WITH PRIVATE BATHROOM. CHILDREN WELCOME. LEISURE FACILITIES. PENZANCE 7 MILES.

PENVENTON HOTEL *(on facing page)*

OPEN ALL YEAR. LICENSED. ALL BEDROOMS WITH PRIVATE BATHROOM. LEISURE FACILITIES. CONFERENCE FACILITIES. CIVIL WEDDING CEREMONIES. TRURO 8 MILES.

Comprising an amalgam of four houses built into the hillside and with stunning views out to sea, this skilfully converted hotel is an eclectic blend of ancient and modern; its outstanding facilities match its beautiful position. Each of the bedrooms has a different character and these include two family suites which can accommodate up to three children. A delightfully designed dining room with a mosaic floor and a cool Mediterranean atmosphere is the ideal setting for appreciation of a varied cuisine and, in the natural way of things, fish dishes figure prominently amongst the fresh local produce, whilst special mention must be made of the delicious home-made ice cream and West Country cheeses.

HOTEL TRESANTON St Mawes, Cornwall TR2 5DR

Tel: 01326 270055 • Fax: 01326 270053
e-mail: info@tresanton.com • www.tresanton.com

OPEN ALL YEAR. FULLY LICENSED. 29 BEDROOMS, ALL WITH PRIVATE BATHROOMS. CHILDREN WELCOME, PETS ALLOWED IN 2 ROOMS. CIVIL WEDDING CEREMONIES. TREGONY 10 MILES. S££££, D££££.

Country House

Luxury country house set amidst the beautiful Camel Valley.
Ideally situated for enjoying all that Cornwall has to offer.

Tel: 01208 841262
www.tredethyhouse.co.uk • enquiries@tredethyhouse.co.uk
Helland Bridge, Wadebridge, Cornwall PL30 4QS

OPEN ALL YEAR. 11 BEDROOMS, ALL WITH PRIVATE BATHROOMS. CONFERENCE FACILITIES. BODMIN 3 MILES.

Please mention **Recommended Country Hotels**
when making enquiries about accommodation featured in these pages

Visit the FHG website
www.holidayguides.com
for details of the wide choice of accommodation
featured in the full range of FHG titles

Devon

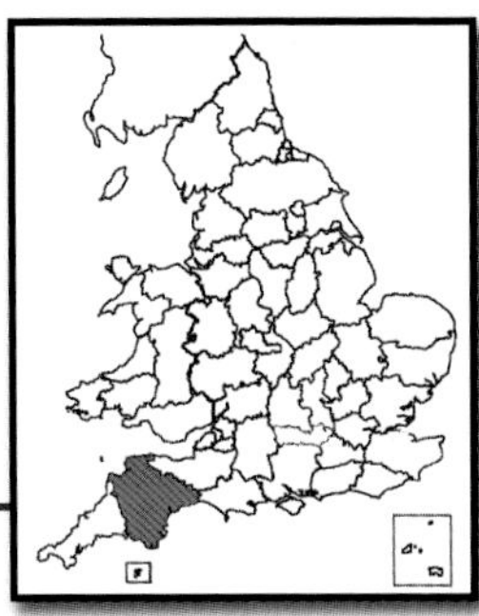

The hotel stands in 20 acres of cliff, coast and garden, and the Hotel Restaurant overlooks the sea and cliffs with spectacular views of the bay. Mini-breaks are available as well as special weekly rates, all of which offer a five-course meal including seafood platters with lobster, smoked salmon and steak. Every Saturday there is a Swedish Smorgasbord and Carvery followed by dancing till late. All bedrooms have colour TV, telephone, teamaking and are en suite. There is an unique indoor swimming pool with rolling back sides to enjoy the sun, as well as a whirlpool, sauna, steam-room and fitness area with gym equipment.

Children have free accommodation sharing parents' room.
Children under 5 years completely free, including meals.

You'll love the special atmosphere of Sandy Cove, why not find us on our website at www.sandycove-hotel.co.uk *or ring to request a brochure*

Combe Martin Bay,
Devon EX34 9SR
Tel: 01271 882243
01271 882888

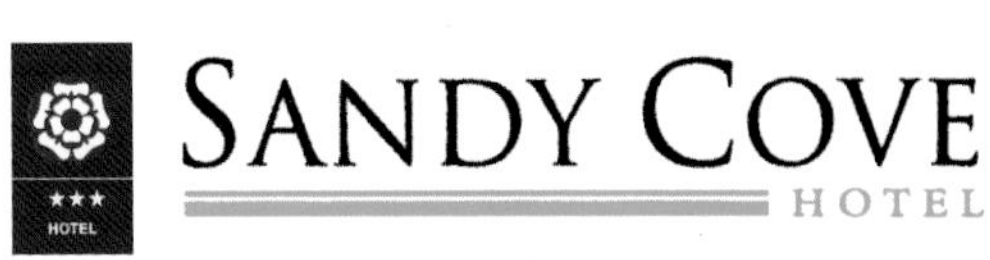

OPEN ALL YEAR. FULLY LICENSED. 39 BEDROOMS, ALL WITH PRIVATE BATHROOMS. CHILDREN AND PETS WELCOME. LEISURE FACILITIES. CIVIL WEDDING CEREMONIES. ILFRACOMBE 3 MILES. S£££, D£££.

Please note

All the information in this book is given in good faith in the belief that it is correct. However, the publishers cannot guarantee the facts given in these pages, neither are they responsible for changes in policy, ownership or terms that may take place after the date of going to press. Readers should always satisfy themselves that the facilities they require are available and that the terms, if quoted, still apply.

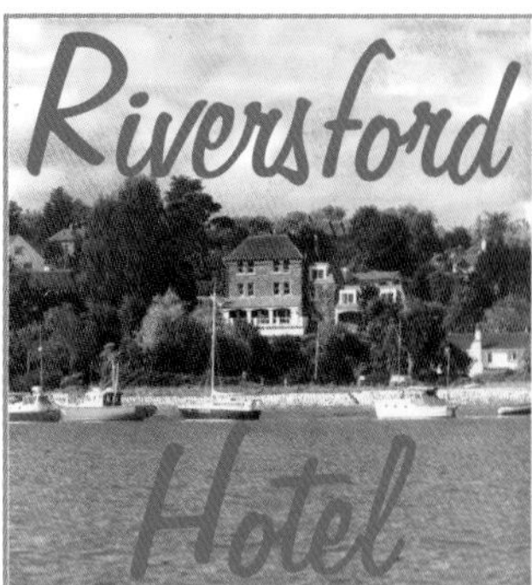

Limers Lane, Bideford, Devon EX39 2RG

- Riversford is a beautifully situated hotel overlooking the River Torridge.
- Bideford lies only a 10-minute walk away, while a gentle stroll along a leafy woodland path will lead you to the fishing village of Appledore.
- Our restaurant has earned a fine reputation for some superb dishes, seafood being our speciality.
- Most of our en suite rooms overlook the river; four-poster rooms and suites available.

Tel: 01237 474239 • Fax: 01237 421661
e-mail: Riversford@aol.com
www.Riversford.co.uk

ALL ROOMS WITH PRIVATE BATHROOM. CHILDREN WELCOME. EXETER 36 MILES. S££, D££££.

FOSFELLE COUNTRY HOUSE HOTEL

Hartland, Bideford, Devon EX39 6EF

This 17th century manor house is set in six acres of grounds in peaceful surroundings with large ornamental gardens and lawns. Fosfelle offers a friendly atmosphere with excellent food, a licensed bar, and a television lounge with log fires on chilly evenings; central heating throughout. There is a games room for children. The comfortable bedrooms, some en suite, all have washbasins and tea making facilities; family rooms and cots are available. Within easy reach of local beaches and ideal for touring Devon and Cornwall. Trout and coarse fishing, clay shooting available at the hotel; riding and golf nearby. Open all year. Reductions for children. **AA Listed.**

Telephone: 01237 441273

OPEN ALL YEAR. FULLY LICENSED. 7 BEDROOMS, 4 WITH PRIVATE BATHROOMS.
CHILDREN AND PETS WELCOME. CLOVELLY 4 MILES. S£, D£.

Yeoldon House Hotel

Durrant Lane, Northam, Near Bideford, Devon EX39 2RL

With its lawns sloping down to the River Torridge, this expansive, stone-clad country house exudes comfort and well-being and for a real taste of the delights of North Devon makes a recommended holiday base. A land of majestic scenery on Exmoor and in Lorna Doone country awaits and there are countless uncrowded coves and sandy beaches leading off miles of coastal footpath. Accommodation is splendidly appointed, whether it be grand four-poster room or cosy, country-style bedroom; all have en suite facilities, colour television, direct-dial telephone and tea and coffee-makers. Under the kind attention of the Steele family, the imaginative fare on offer in Soyer's Restaurant is of the highest calibre and is beautifully presented.

Tel: 01237 474400 • Fax: 01237 476618 • e-mail: yeoldonhouse@aol.com • www.yeoldonhousehotel.co.uk

FULLY LICENSED. 10 BEDROOMS, ALL WITH PRIVATE BATHROOMS. CHILDREN AND PETS WELCOME. CIVIL WEDDING CEREMONIES. BIDEFORD 2 MILES. S££££, D£££.

HIGHBULLEN HOTEL *(on facing page)*

LICENSED. 42 BEDROOMS, ALL WITH PRIVATE BATHROOMS. CHILDREN WELCOME. LEISURE FACILITIES. CONFERENCE FACILITIES. SOUTH MOLTON 5 MILES. S££££. D££££.

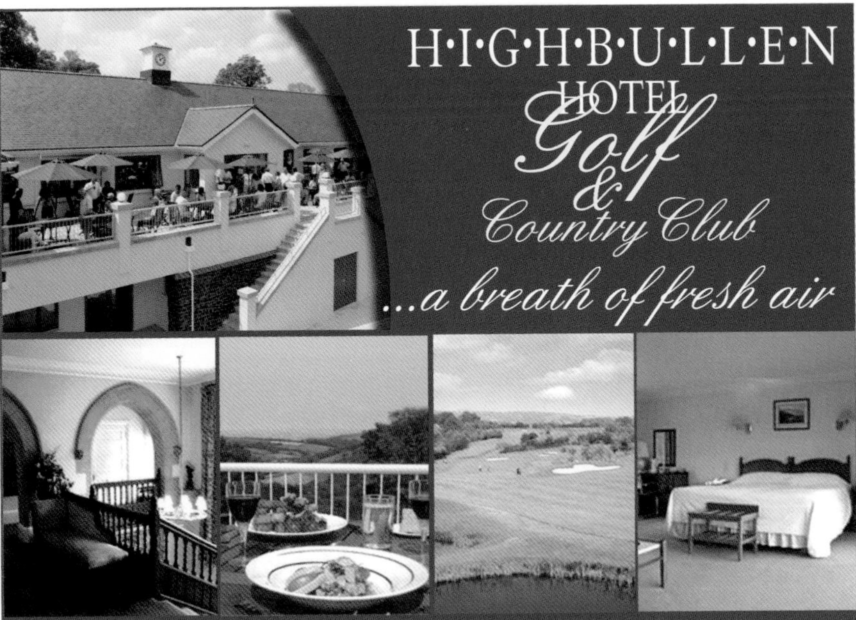

Highbullen Hotel, Golf & Country Club is beautifully set in a richly wooded 200 acre parkland estate. Boasting breathtaking views towards the romantic Devon landscapes of Exmoor and Dartmoor, the 42 bedroom hotel is truly a hidden treasure, nestling between the Mole and Taw valleys in mature wooded seclusion. Few establishments in the South of England can match the wealth of sporting and leisure facilities available on site at Highbullen.

- Double or twin-bedded room with private bath, central heating, TV and direct dial telephone. Seasonal Breaks available from November to March.
- Elegant Restaurant... Terraced Brasserie, offering a wealth of dining options, Highbullen is synonymous with fine food.
- Superb award-winning 18 hole par 68 golf course, salmon and trout-fishing, indoor and outdoor tennis courts, including four new grass courts to Wimbledon specifications. Fitness suite, aerobics studio, indoor and outdoor swimming pools, health and beauty spa, squash, indoor bowls, croquet, indoor putting green, golf simulator, boules, snooker, sauna, steam room, jacuzzi – the list goes on... our sporting and leisure professionals are there to cater for your every need.
- The whole ethos at Highbullen is to let you decide exactly what you want from your stay, whether it's lazing in the quiet spot on the river with a cold bottle of Chablis, or playing three hard sets of tennis before a light Brasserie lunch.

Highbullen Hotel, Chittlehamholt, Umberleigh, North Devon EX37 9HD

Tel: 01769 540 561 Fax: 01769 540 492 • E-mail: info@highbullen.co.uk

www.highbullen.co.uk

Mill End feels more like a comfortable country house than a hotel. You'll find framed maps and watercolours, fresh flowers and burning logs, nooks and crannies where you can curl up with a good book. Stroll by the river or enjoy a cream tea on the lawn. Comfortable bedrooms, some on the ground floor, enjoy delightful views of the gardens or the rolling Devon countryside. The award-winning restaurant offers the finest local produce in season, cooked to order, with mouth-watering desserts and a tempting cheese board featuring local specialities.

Dartmoor National Park, Chagford TQ13 8JN
Tel: 01647 432282 • Fax: 01647 433106
e-mail: info@millendhotel.com
www.millendhotel.com

LICENSED. 15 BEDROOMS, ALL WITH PRIVATE BATHROOMS. CHILDREN WELCOME. MORETONHAMPSTEAD 4 MILES. S££££, D££££/£££.

Fox & Hounds

Country Hotel

Eggesford, Chulmleigh
Devon EX18 7JZ
Tel: 01769 580345
Fax: 01769 580262

Superb mid-Devon accommodation, ideal location for your country break. Situated between Dartmoor, Exmoor and the stunning Devon coastline. Two refurbished bars and 16 en suite bedrooms, individually decorated, with stylish antique furniture. The hotel offers attractive grounds, a restaurant and excellent local food. Children are welcome. Fishing is available on the River Taw, as well as seasonal rough shooting, clay shooting and horse riding. A unique hotel in a beautiful location.

e-mail: relax@foxandhoundshotel.co.uk • www.foxandhoundshotel.co.uk

FULLY LICENSED. 16 BEDROOMS, ALL WITH PRIVATE BATHROOMS. CHILDREN AND WELL BEHAVED DOGS WELCOME. CONFERENCE FACILITIES. CIVIL WEDDING CEREMONIES. CHULMLEIGH 4 MILES. D££/£££.

Prices

Normal Bed & Breakfast rate per person
(single room)

PRICE RANGE	CATEGORY
Under £40	S£
£40-£55	S££
£56-£70	S£££
Over £70	S££££

Normal Bed & Breakfast rate per person
(sharing double/twin room)

PRICE RANGE	CATEGORY
Under £40	D£
£40-£55	D££
£56-70	D£££
Over £70	D££££

This is meant as an indication only and does not show prices for Special Breaks, Weekends, etc. Guests are therefore advised to verify all prices on enquiring or booking.

FULLY LICENSED. 8 BEDROOMS, ALL EN SUITE. NON-SMOKING ACCOMMODATION AVAILABLE.
PETS WELCOME. CONFERENCE FACILITIES. TAVISTOCK 8 MILES. S££££, D££££ (DB&B).

Hope Cove, Kingsbridge, South Devon TQ7 3HJ
Tel: 01548 561555 • Fax: 01548 561455
info@hopecove.com • www.hopecove.com

The Cottage Hotel, in the same family since 1973, sits above a secluded beach in a beautiful village on the rugged South Devon coastline. It offers all that is best in a traditional British holiday - superb accommodation, excellent cuisine, a relaxing atmosphere, and a style of service you thought had disappeared forever.

- De luxe balcony rooms, double/twin rooms (some with balcony), family and single rooms. • Most have sea views
- Three comfortable lounges • Cocktail bar
- Five course Dinner menu, changes daily
- Table tennis, play area for children • Laundry • Baby listening
- Exeter, Plymouth, Torbay and Dartmoor approx. one hour's drive
- Within easy reach of golf, tennis, riding, fishing, nature reserves

FULLY LICENSED. 35 BEDROOMS, 26 WITH PRIVATE BATHROOMS.
CHILDREN AND PETS WELCOME. CONFERENCE FACILITIES. CIVIL. S£/££, D££/£££/££££.

LANGDON COURT HOTEL & RESTAURANT

Langdon, Wembury Cove, Plymouth, Devon PL9 0DY
Tel: 01752 862358 • Fax: 01752 863428
www.langdoncourt.com • e-mail: enquiries@langdoncourt.com

Set in 10 acres of private woodland and 17th century old walled garden, this beautiful Grade II* Listed Tudor Manor is set in the South Hams of Devon, close to the scenic grandeur of Dartmoor. Historically fascinating, the house was once owned by Henry VIII, and later became the home of his last wife Katherine Parr. The air of traditional hospitality offered by the resident owners is particularly evident in the bar which boasts a wide selection of freshly prepared meals and real ales, and in the award-winning restaurant, where the finest cuisine is complemented by friendly and efficient service. Accommodation is of an equally high standard, the well-appointed bedrooms affording views over fields and woodland.

OPEN ALL YEAR. FULLY LICENSED. 18 BEDROOMS, ALL WITH PRIVATE BATHROOMS.
CHILDREN WELCOME. CONFERENCE FACILITIES. CIVIL WEDDING CEREMONIES. PLYMOUTH 5 MILES.

The Lifton Hall Hotel and Village Inn Lifton, Devon PL16 0DR

Tel: 01566 784863 • Fax: 01566 784770 • relax@liftonhall.co.uk • www.liftonhall.co.uk

A family-run hotel where old-fashioned values of service, style and comfort can still be enjoyed. On the Devon/Cornwall border, ½ mile off the A30, it offers the perfect opportunity to explore the West Country. The tastefully furnished bedrooms have en suite bath or shower and a full range of amenities; there is also a light and airy residents' lounge, a stylish dining room and a cosy bar with open fire. Meals are an essential part of the Lifton Hall experience, with something to suit every taste and appetite, using only the best quality local produce. A carefully chosen and reasonably priced wine list provides the perfect accompaniment.

OPEN ALL YEAR. FULLY LICENSED. 10 BEDROOMS, ALL WITH PRIVATE BATHROOMS.
CHILDREN AND PETS WELCOME. LAUNCESTON 4 MILES. S££££, D££.

A charming 18th century country house, with a wealth of history and character, Brendon House nestles in a hidden wooded valley beneath the rolling moors. Sample excellent Devonshire cooking with a generous four-course evening meal served often with organic vegetables fresh from the garden, accompanied by a good selection of fine wines from across the world. All the recently refurbished bedrooms have private facilities, television, tea/coffee and stunning Exmoor views. This is a perfect base for walking, fishing, riding – or just to unwind. Please ring for a brochure and details of weekly discounts and special breaks.

BRENDON HOUSE

Brendon, Lynton, Devon EX35 6PS
Tel: 01598 741206 • e-mail: brendonhouse4u@aol.com
www.brendonhouse4u.com

OPEN ALL YEAR. LICENSED. 5 BEDROOMS, ALL WITH PRIVATE BATHROOMS. LYNTON 3 MILES

FREE or REDUCED RATE entry to Holiday Visits and Attractions – see our **READERS' OFFER VOUCHERS** on pages 149-172

For Hotels which offer

• Conference facilities • Leisure facilities • Civil Wedding Ceremonies

See the Special supplements on pages 143-148

❖ COUNTISBURY LODGE ❖

Countisbury Hill, Lynmouth EX35 6NB
www.countisburylodge.co.uk

A former Victorian vicarage with magnificent views over the Lyn Valley and sea. Extremely quiet and peaceful yet within 5 minutes' walk of the picturesque village of Lynmouth. Licensed bar. All our bedrooms are centrally heated and en suite. Private parking. Pets welcome free of charge.

❖ ALSO SELF CATERING COTTAGE AND APARTMENT AVAILABLE ❖

Brochure/Tariff with pleasure from Pat & Paul Young (01598 752388)

RESIDENTIAL LICENCE. 4 BEDROOMS, ALL WITH PRIVATE BATHROOMS. CHILDREN AND PETS WELCOME. LYNTON 2 MILES MILES. S£, D£.

A useful index of towns/counties appears on pages 173-174

Beautifully situated with impressive views over Torbay, close to all beaches and a short stroll to the town centre. The spacious bedrooms are all en suite, with colour TV and tea/coffee making facilities and full central heating. Ground floor bedrooms are available, some rooms with sea views and balconies, as well as a honeymoon suite. Cosy bar lounge, beautiful garden.

THE ROSCREA HOTEL
2 Alta Vista Road, Paignton, Devon TQ4 6BZ
Tel & Fax: 01803 558706
www.roscreahotel.co.uk

Seasonal entertainment is provided, including a special Christmas programme. Generous reductions for off-season breaks. Reductions for children. We are well renowned for our excellent food. Kindly write or telephone for our brochure.

OPEN ALL YEAR. LICENSED. ALL BEDROOMS WITH PRIVATE BATHROOMS. CHILDREN AND PETS WELCOME. TORQUAY 3 MILES.

www.sunnymeade.co.uk
Tel: 01271 863668
Fax: 01271 866061

- ***Friendly, comfortable Country Hotel***
- ***Lovely countryside views***
- ***Centrally placed close to Woolacombe's dog-friendly beach, Ilfracombe and Exmoor***
- ***Off-season special breaks***
- ***4 ground floor bedrooms***
- ***Deaf accessible BSL signed***
- ***Award-winning home-cooked food***
- ***Pets welcome – dogs are free***
- ***Lots of lovely walks from the front door***

LICENSED. 12 BEDROOMS, MOST WITH PROVATE BATHROOM. PETS WELCOME. BARNSTAPLE 9 MILES.

FHG Guides

publish a large range of well-known accommodation guides.
We will be happy to send you details or you can use the order form at the back of this book.

EXMOOR SANDPIPER INN *(on facing page)*

FULLY LICENSED. 10 BEDROOMS, ALL WITH PRIVATE BATHROOMS. CHILDREN AND PETS WELCOME. LYNTON 2 MILES.

The Exmoor Sandpiper Inn

is a romantic Coaching Inn dating in part back to the 13th century, with low ceilings, blackened beams, stone fireplaces and a timeless atmosphere of unspoilt old world charm. Offering visitors great food and drink, a warm welcome and a high standard of accommodation.

The inn is set in an imposing position on a hilltop on Exmoor in North Devon, a few hundred yards from the sea, and high above the twin villages of Lynmouth and Lynton, in an area of oustanding beauty.
The spectacular scenery and endless views attract visitors and hikers from all over the world.

We have 16 en suite bedrooms, comfortable sofas in the bar and lounge areas, and five fireplaces, including a 13th century inglenook. Our extensive menus include local produce wherever possible, such as locally reared meat, amd locally caught game and fish, like Lynmouth Bay lobster; specials are featured daily. We also have a great choice of good wines, available by the bottle or the glass, and a selection of locally brewed beers, some produced specially for us.

Stay with us to relax, or to follow one of the seven circular walks through stunning countryside that start from the Inn. Horse riding for experienced riders or complete novices can be arranged. Plenty of parking. Dogs (no charge), children and walkers are very welcome!

The Exmoor Sandpiper Inn

Countisbury, Lynmouth, Devon EX35 6NE

01598 741263

www.exmoorsandpiper.co.uk • www.exmoorsandpiper.com

Dorset

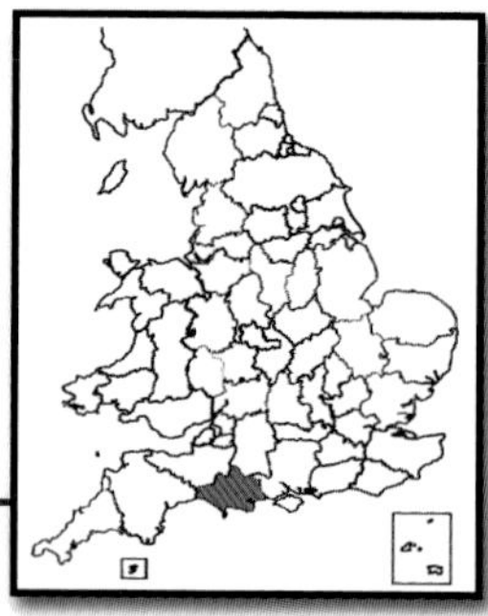

The Country House Hotel in Bournemouth

Built by Edward VII as a Lovenest for Lillie Langtry. A rare gem of a hotel where the building, food, service and history blend to form something quite exceptional. Four posters, Jacuzzi's, complimentary leisure club and award-winning restaurant. Midweek and weekend breaks. As featured on BBC Holiday Show.

"Best Hotel in Bournemouth" - The Guardian

Best Small Hotel *Bournemouth Tourism*

Derby Road, East Cliff, Bournemouth BH1 3QB

Tel: (01202) 553887 www.langtrymanor.co.uk

OPEN ALL YEAR. FULLY LICENSED. 20 BEDROOMS, ALL WITH PRIVATE BATHROOMS. PETS WELCOME. LEISURE FACILITIES. CONFERENCE FACILITIES. CIVIL WEDDING CEREMONIES. SOUTHAMPTON 24 MILES. S££££, D££££.

Visit the FHG website

www.holidayguides.com

for details of the wide choice of accommodation

featured in the full range of FHG titles

CROMWELL HOUSE HOTEL *(on facing page)*

FULLY LICENSED. 25 BEDROOMS, 22 WITH PRIVATE BATHROOM. CHILDREN AND PETS WELCOME. WOOL 4 MILES. S£££, D££.

• • Lulworth Cove • •
Cromwell House Hotel

Catriona and Alistair Miller welcome guests to their comfortable family-run hotel, set in secluded gardens with spectacular sea views. Situated 200 yards from Lulworth Cove, with direct access to the Jurassic Coast.

Accommodation is in 20 en suite bedrooms, with TV, direct-dial telephone, and tea/coffee making facilities; most have spectacular sea views. There is disabled access and a room suitable for disabled guests.

- Self-catering flat and cottage available.
- Restaurant, bar wine list.
- A heated swimming pool is available for guests' use from May to October.

B&B from £40. Two nights DB&B (fully en suite) from £120 pp. Off-peak mid week breaks all year except Christmas.

Cromwell House Hotel,
Lulworth Cove BH20 5RJ
Tel: 01929 400253/400332
Fax: 01929 400566

www.lulworthcove.co.uk

Set in a delightful and secluded garden west of historic Lyme Regis, this is just the place to get away from it all and wind down. This homely, non-smoking retreat offers a warm welcome from owners, Sue and Paul Wightman, dedicated to providing mouthwatering fare – and those breakfasts! Brightly furnished bedrooms have en suite showers and/or bathrooms, colour TV and tea and coffee-makers; one ground floor room.

The Orchard Country Hotel

Picturesque walks abound nearby and many species of birds are attracted to the garden. For the occasional rainy spell, there is a sitting room, a television room, small bar and books and board games.

A gem.

AA ◆◆◆◆

Rousdon, Near Lyme Regis, Dorset DT7 3XW
Tel: 01297 442972
Fax: 01297 443670
e-mail: orchardrousdon@aol.com
www.orchardcountryhotel.com

RESIDENTIAL LICENCE. 11 BEDROOMS, ALL WITH PRIVATE BATHROOMS.
NON-SMOKING ACCOMMODATION AVAILABLE. CHILDREN OVER EIGHT YEARS WELCOME.
LYME REGIS 3 MILES. S££, D££.

"Welcome to one of the most beautiful places in England. I can't take credit for the glorious views and the beaches. But I am proud to provide a comfortable and relaxing hotel with good food and attentive but informal service, to give you the break you deserve."

Andrew Purkis

Manor House Hotel, Studland, Dorset, BH19 3AU • T - 01929 450288
• W - www.themanorhousehotel.com • E - info@themanorhousehotel.com

LICENSED. 21 BEDROOMS, ALL WITH PRIVATE BATHROOMS. CHILDREN OVER 5 YEARS AND PETS WELCOME.
SWANAGE 3 MILES. ££££ (DB&B).

KEMPS HOTEL

East Stoke, Wareham, Dorset BH20 6AL
Tel: 01929 462563 • Fax: 01929 405287
e-mail: stay@kempshotel.com • www.kempshotel.com

AA ★★

Small and welcoming, Kemps is situated in unspoilt Dorset countryside. Facing south, the hotel overlooks the Frome valley and the Purbeck Hills beyond. Once a Victorian rectory, the house provides a comfortable and relaxed atmosphere. Real log fires burn in the grates in the winter months. During the summer, the garden terrace is ideal for an aperitif. Dining in the award-winning Restaurant and Conservatory has long been considered a special treat. The spacious bedrooms are set out in three locations: the Main House; the Garden Wing, where all the rooms are at ground floor level; and the Old Coach House. Rooms have excellent views of the surrounding countryside. Superior rooms have whirlpool baths, and one room has a traditional four-poster bed.

RESIDENTIAL LICENCE. 15 BEDROOMS, ALL WITH PRIVATE BATHROOMS. CHILDREN WELCOME, PETS BY ARRANGEMENT. CONFERENCE FACILITIES. WAREHAM 3 MILES. S££££, D££.

Gloucestershire

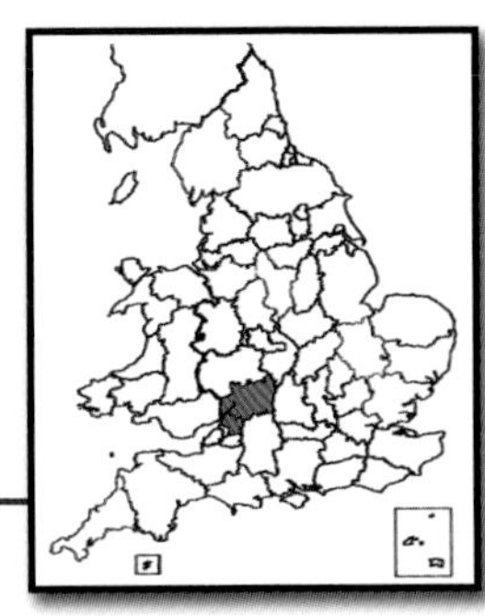

FREE or REDUCED RATE entry to Holiday Visits and Attractions – see our **READERS' OFFER VOUCHERS** on pages 149-172

This is an Elizabethan house of great charm and character with elegant and spacious rooms graced by antiques and warmed by log fires in winter. Formal gardens and paddocks surround the house which is renowned for its hospitality, immaculate and attentive service and for the quality of its food. All guest rooms have bathrooms en suite, remote-control colour television, radio, direct-dial telephone and several other thoughtful practicalities. A number of activities can be organised including clay pigeon shooting, horse riding, golf and wonderful walks.

Shurdington, Cheltenham, Gloucs GL51 4UG
Tel: 01242 862352 • Fax: 01242 862780

e-mail: info@thegreenway.co.uk • www.thegreenway.co.uk **AA ★★★ and Two Rosettes**

OPEN ALL YEAR. FULLY LICENSED. 21 BEDROOMS, ALL WITH PRIVATE BATHROOMS.
ALL ACCOMMODATION NON-SMOKING. CHILDREN AND PETS WELCOME. CIVIL WEDDING CEREMONIES.
CHELTENHAM 3 MILES. S££££, D££££.

Corse Lawn House HOTEL

Corse Lawn, Gloucestershire GL19 4LZ
Tel: 01452 780771 • Fax: 01452 780840
e-mail: enquiries@corselawn.com

There is a refreshing vitality about this elegant Queen Anne Listed building which lies in 12 enchanting acres complete with large ornamental pond. Seemingly remote yet only six miles from the M5 and M50, it is also wonderfully placed for the Cotswolds, Malverns and numerous sporting locations. The atmosphere is relaxed and the services of an enthusiastic young staff is an added bonus.

Superbly appointed guest rooms each have a private bathroom, satellite colour television, radio, direct-dial telephone and tea and coffee-making facilities; some rooms with four-poster beds are available. The noteworthy restaurant is another reason for choosing to stay here, imaginative dishes being supported by expertly chosen wines. There is also a popular bistro situated in the bar area.

OPEN ALL YEAR. FULLY LICENSED. 19 BEDROOMS, ALL WITH PRIVATE BATHROOMS.
NON-SMOKING ACCOMMODATION AVAILABLE. CHILDREN AND PETS WELCOME. LEISURE FACILITIES.
CONFERENCE FACILITIES. CIVIL WEDDING CEREMONIES. S££££, D£££.

THE Old Stocks Hotel

The Square, Stow-on-the-Wold GL54 1AF
Tel: 01451 830666 • Fax: 01451 870014
e-mail: fhg@oldstockshotel.co.uk

Ideal base for touring this beautiful area. Tasteful guest rooms in keeping with the hotel's old world character, yet with modern amenities. Mouth-watering menus offering a wide range of choices. Special bargain breaks also available.

HETB/AA ★★

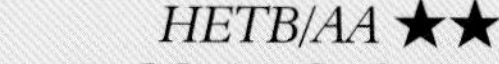

www.oldstockshotel.co.uk

OPEN ALL YEAR. FULLY LICENSED. 18 BEDROOMS, ALL WITH PRIVATE BATHROOMS. CHILDREN AND PETS WELCOME. CHIPPING NORTON 8 MILES. S££, D££.

FULLY LICENSED. 189 BEDROOMS, ALL WITH PRIVATE BATHROOMS.
CHILDREN WELCOME. LEISURE FACILITIES. CONFERENCE FACILITIES. CIVIL WEDDING CEREMONIES. STROUD 9 MILES. S££££, D££££.

Gloucestershire — The Cotswolds

Think of your favourite images of the English countryside....sleepy villages with flower adorned cottages, country pubs with excellent food, antique shops, market towns and impressive churches.....you're already thinking of the Cotswolds ! Here in an area bounded by Bath, Oxford and Stratford– upon –Avon is a warm and appealing countryside, with some of the finest landscape in England. Two things above all give the Cotswolds their special warmth and richness: the soft mellow limestone which gives cottages and manor houses alike such an appealing hue, and the wealth of the wool trade in medieval England, which has left an historic legacy, particularly in some of the churches founded at that time.

The Cotswolds area is hugely enjoyable at any time of year. Winter can be enjoyed in some of the finest hotels in Britain – and if you can't manage a full stay, why not book a tea or dinner ? A pre- dinner drink in front of an open fire in an elegant and relaxing country house hotel must be one of the joys of life. The area also has an impressive collection of pubs – such as The Trouble House bear Cirencester and The Plough at Ford. Spring and summer bring the great gardens of the area, such as Hidcote, to the fore, and there are many smaller private gardens open under the charitable "National Gardens Scheme". There are some delightful attractions in this area, farm parks, high quality museums, and artists and craftspeople. Autumn has its own glories, including autumnal colours at two arboretums, Westonbirt and Batsford. Activities include cycling, walking, riding and campsites.

Treasured towns and villages include Stow-on-the-Wold, the Slaughters, Bibury, Chipping Campden, Cirencester, Winchcombe and Painswick. In his English Journey in 1933, J.B Priestley described the Cotswolds as "the most English and the least spoiled of all our countrysides" and today it is still regarded as quintessentially English. Much of the landscape is a designated Area of Outstanding Natural Beauty. The famous drystone walls of the area represent not only the history of the area but are an important conservation feature. The construction of the walls is a matter of skill, with no mortar involved to hold them together, thus the name.

Don't forget that besides the allure of the countryside and the villages, Cheltenham can provide a great base for touring. Cheltenham Tourism have devised two touring routes under the title "The Romantic Road" which begin and end in this elegant Regency town, and take in some of the loveliest villages en route. In addition Cheltenham has some great places to eat, and an interesting programme of events through the year, including National Hunt racing in March, a Jazz Festival in May, a Festival of Classical Music in July, and the Festival of Literature in October.

Somerset

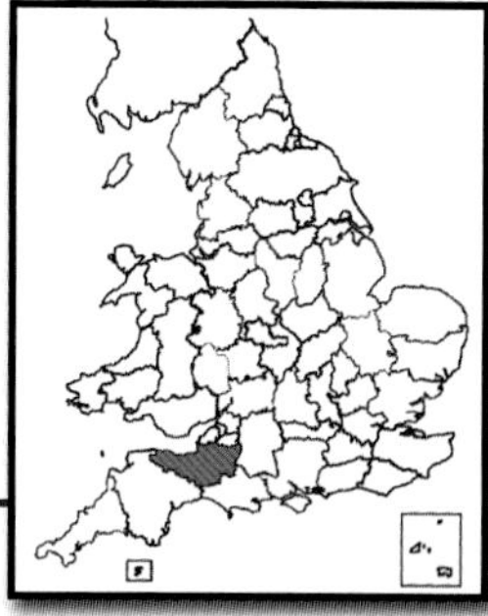

Best Western
THE CLIFFE HOTEL
Crowe Hill, Limpley Stoke, Near Bath
Somerset BA2 7FY

Tel: 01225 723226 • Fax: 01225 723871
e-mail: cliffe@bestwestern.co.uk • www.bw-cliffehotel.co.uk

Only a short distance from the historic city of Bath, this ultra-comfortable, early-Victorian house lies in landscaped gardens of 3½ acres with breathtaking views. The house is both elegant and well-appointed; each en suite guest room is equipped with colour TV, radio, hairdryer, iron, ironing board, trouser press and tea and coffee-making facilities and there are several superior rooms, two with a traditional four-poster bed and one with a whirlpool bath. A varied à la carte menu is on offer in the brightly decorated, award-winning restaurant and early supper arrangements for children and room service are available. **ETC ★★★ AA**

OPEN ALL YEAR. FULLY LICENSED. 11 BEDROOMS, ALL WITH PRIVATE BATHROOMS.
NON-SMOKING ACCOMMODATION AVAILABLE. CHILDREN AND PETS WELCOME. LEISURE FACILITIES.
BATH 3½ MILES. D£££.

Prices

Normal Bed & Breakfast rate per person
(single room)

PRICE RANGE	CATEGORY
Under £40	S£
£40-£55	S££
£56-£70	S£££
Over £70	S££££

Normal Bed & Breakfast rate per person
(sharing double/twin room)

PRICE RANGE	CATEGORY
Under £40	D£
£40-£55	D££
£56-70	D£££
Over £70	D££££

This is meant as an indication only and does not show prices for Special Breaks, Weekends, etc. Guests are therefore advised to verify all prices on enquiring or booking.

TOWN & COUNTRY LODGE HOTEL

A38 Bridgwater Road, Bristol BS13 8AG
Tel: 01275 392441
Fax: 01275 393362

In a rural setting on the A38 midway between the city centre and Bristol Airport, this comfortably appointed hotel has attractions for tourists and business folk.

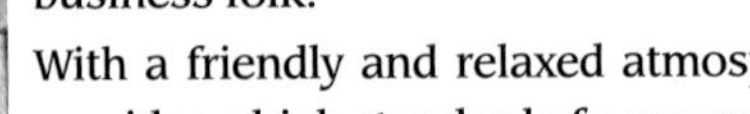

With a friendly and relaxed atmosphere, it provides a high standard of accommodation in rooms with bathrooms en suite, satellite television, telephone and tea and coffee-making facilities, and at terms that reflect real value for money.

★★ HOTEL

Also featured is the renowned Brooms Restaurant and Bar with its interesting international cuisine and tasty grills, offering the choice of menus from pub-style lunches to full à la carte dinners.

e-mail: reservations@tclodge.co.uk
www.tclodge.co.uk

OPEN ALL YEAR. FULLY LICENSED. 36 BEDROOMS, ALL WITH PRIVATE BATHROOMS. CHILDREN WELCOME. BRISTOL AIRPORT 4 MILES. S£££, D£.

Woodlands COUNTRY HOUSE HOTEL

Hill Lane, Brent Knoll, Highbridge, Somerset TA9 4DF
Tel: 01278 760232 • Fax: 01278 769090

At the foot of verdant Brent Knoll and only a couple of miles from the waters of Bridgwater Bay, this elegant, creeper-clad Victorian house appears a haven of peace and serenity, standing in four acres of lovely wooded parkland with panoramic views towards the distant Quantocks. The centrally heated guest rooms are attractively furnished and include a splendid and spacious four-poster room, a de luxe Bridal Suite and a de luxe super king room with whirlpool bath. A delightful restaurant sets a high standard of imaginative cuisine. There is a sheltered swimming pool and sun terrace and footpaths lead directly into the surrounding countryside. Choice of golf courses within easy reach. All rooms are non-smoking, but guests may smoke in the bar.

AA ★★

e-mail: info@woodlands-hotel.co.uk • www.woodlands-hotel.co.uk

LICENSED. ALL BEDROOMS HAVE PRIVATE BATHROOM. CONFERENCE FACILITIES. CIVIL WEDDING CEREMONIES.

The Castle Hotel

Porlock, Somerset TA24 8PY • Tel: 01643 862504
e-mail: info@castleporlock.co.uk • www.castleporlock.co.uk

The Castle Hotel is a small, fully refurbished, fully licensed family-run hotel in the centre of the lovely Exmoor village of Porlock. It is an ideal holiday location for those who wish to enjoy the grandeur of Exmoor on foot or by car. The beautiful villages of Selworthy and Dunster with its castle are only a short distance away. We have 9 en suite bedrooms, all centrally heated. The Hotel has a well stocked bar with real ales, draught Guinness and cider. A full range of bar meals is available all day until 9.30pm, or dine in our spacious restaurant. Traditional roasts are served all day until 8pm on Sundays. Children and well behaved pets are most welcome.

✤ ✤ *Special Breaks available* ✤ *Extremely low rates* ✤✤

OPEN ALL YEAR. FULLY LICENSED. 9 BEDROOMS, ALL WITH PRIVATE BATHROOMS. CHILDREN AND PETS WELCOME. S£, D££.

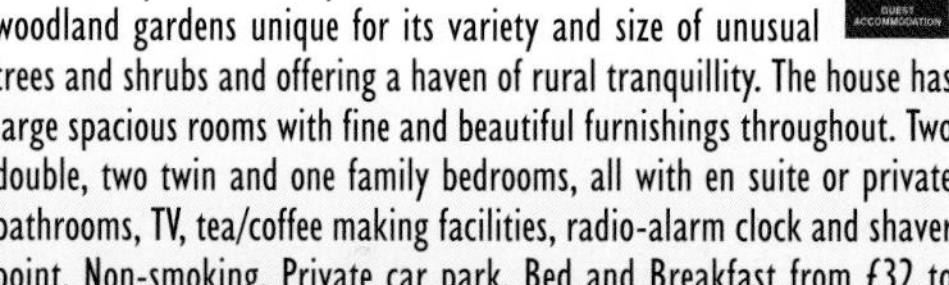

Imposing country house in Exmoor National Park on the wooded slopes of West Porlock commanding exceptional sea views of Porlock Bay and countryside. Set in five acres of beautiful woodland gardens unique for its variety and size of unusual trees and shrubs and offering a haven of rural tranquillity. The house has large spacious rooms with fine and beautiful furnishings throughout. Two double, two twin and one family bedrooms, all with en suite or private bathrooms, TV, tea/coffee making facilities, radio-alarm clock and shaver point. Non-smoking. Private car park. Bed and Breakfast from £32 to £34.50 per person. Credit cards accepted. Sorry, no pets.

West Porlock House
01643 862880

Margery and Henry Dyer, West Porlock House,
West Porlock, Near Minehead TA24 8NX
e-mail: westporlockhouse@amserve.com

5 BEDROOMS, ALL WITH PRIVATE BATHROOMS. CHILDREN OVER SIX YEARS WELCOME. PORLOCK 1 MILE. D£.

The Lynch Country House

Somerton, Somerset TA11 7PD
Tel: 01458 272316 • Fax: 01458 272590
www.thelynchcountryhouse.co.uk

Set in the heart of the lush Somerset countryside on the edge of the delightful medieval market town of Somerton, The Lynch is a perfect base from which to explore a whole range of interesting places, and the area is ideal for walking, touring, and fishing.

B&B is offered, and there are several excellent places to eat locally, to suit every taste and every pocket. This Grade II Listed house is surrounded by an idyllic landscape including a lake which is the home of black swans, numerous exotic ducks and a variety of fish. There are 5 bedrooms, each with bathroom en suite, colour TV and telephone; the separate Coach House has another 4 bedrooms, each with en suite shower room, and exactly the same access to the gardens and lake as the main house.

OPEN ALL YEAR. RESIDENTIAL LICENCE.9 BEDROOMS, ALL WITH PRIVATE BATHROOMS. CHILDREN AND PETS WELCOME. ILCHESTER 4 MILES. S£££, D£/££.

FARTHINGS HOTEL & RESTAURANT
Hatch Beauchamp, Taunton TA3 6SG
Tel: 01823 480664 • Fax: 01823 481118
www.farthingshotel.co.uk
e-mail: info@farthingshotel.co.uk

Welcome to 'Farthings', an elegant Georgian hotel situated in the heart of the Somerset countryside in the historic village of Hatch Beauchamp. Set in three acres of peaceful gardens and overlooking the village green, it enjoys an enviable reputation for hospitality, comfort, pure relaxation and superb cuisine. All ten bedrooms are individual, spacious and en suite, tastefully decorated and furnished, with the usual tea/coffee making facilities, including chilled fresh milk.

The hotel is an ideal base for visiting the many attractions just a short drive away. Within 30 minutes you can visit Wells Cathedral, Bath, Cheddar Gorge, Wookey Hole, the Mendips, Exmoor and both the North and South Devon coasts. Many National Trust and other heritage sites are also within easy reach.

OPEN ALL YEAR. LICENSED. 10 BEDROOMS, ALL WITH PRIVATE BATHROOMS; SELF CATERING APARTMENTS. CHILDREN AND PETS WELCOME. CONFERENCE FACILITIES. CIVIL WEDDING CEREMONIES. TAUNTON 5 MILES. S££, D£££.

BATCH COUNTRY HOTEL
LYMPSHAM, NEAR WESTON-SUPER-MARE
SOMERSET BS24 0EX
Tel: 01934 750371 • Fax: 01934 750501

★ Family-run Hotel with friendly atmosphere and excellent food ★ Fully licensed Lounge Bar ★ Own grounds with unlimited parking, spacious lawns ★ All bedrooms en suite with colour TV, tea/coffee making facilities ★ Golfers most welcome ★ Reduced terms for children ★ Credit cards accepted ★ Easy access from M5 motorway

Weston, Burnham, Brean and Worlebury Golf Courses all within 10 minutes' drive

www.batchcountryhotel.co.uk AA ★★

Weston-Super-Mare Hotels and Restaurants Merit Award

OPEN ALL YEAR. FULLY LICENSED. 11 BEDROOMS, ALL WITH PRIVATE BATHROOM. NON-SMOKING ACCOMMODATION. CHILDREN WELCOME. CONFERENCE FACILITIES. CIVIL WEDDING CEREMONIES. BRISTOL 18 MILES. S£££, D££.

Hampshire

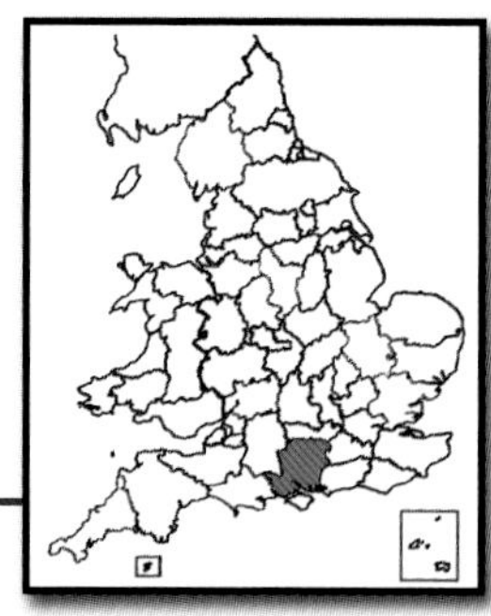

Woodlands Lodge
a new forest hotel ★★★

AA ★★★ Hotel

for somewhere to stay

A little piece of luxury in the heart of the New Forest

The traditional character of our country house offers the perfect opportunity to relax in comfort surrounded by the natural beauty of the New Forest. All of our rooms are en-suite with whirlpool baths. For that special occasion, why not book one of our four poster bedrooms. You deserve to be spoilt! Pets Welcome.

Bartley Road, Woodlands, New Forest, Southampton Hampshire SO40 7GN
Tel: +44 (23) 8029 2257 • Web: www.woodlands-lodge.co.uk • Email: reception@woodlands-lodge.co.uk • Fax: +44 (23) 8029 3090

OPEN ALL YEAR. FULLY LICENSED. 16 BEDROOMS, ALL WITH PRIVATE BATHROOMS. CHILDREN AND PETS WELCOME. CONFERENCE FACILITIES. CIVIL WEDDING CEREMONIES. TOTTON 3 MILES. S£££, D£££.

NEW PARK MANOR HOTEL, SPA & EQUESTRIAN CENTRE

Lyndhurst Road, Brockenhurst, Hampshire SO42 7QH
Tel: 01590 623467 • Fax: 01590 622268

AA ★★★ HOTEL

Set in New Forest parkland midway between Lyndhurst and Brockenhurst, this fine country house hotel was formerly a Royal Hunting Lodge. Luxury suites and bedrooms, some with four-poster beds, enjoy a full range of amenities and the latest communication and entertainment facilities. Based on seasonal produce and local specialities, food here is described as 'modern English' and is served in the charming, candlelit Stags Restaurant. For the ultimate in pampering and relaxation the award-winning Bath House Spa is uniquely positioned to enjoy the beautiful countryside. The hotel also has its own splendid equestrian centre catering for riders of all ages and abilities.

www.newparkmanorhotel.co.uk • e-mail: info@newparkmanorhotel.co.uk

OPEN ALL YEAR. FULLY LICENSED. 24 BEDROOMS, ALL WITH PRIVATE BATHROOMS.
CHILDREN AND PETS WELCOME. LEISURE FACILITIES. CONFERENCE FACILITIES. CIVIL WEDDING CEREMONIES.
LYNDHURST 4 MILES.

FREE or REDUCED RATE entry to Holiday Visits and Attractions – see our **READERS' OFFER VOUCHERS** on pages 149-172

Bramble Hill Hotel

Bramshaw, New Forest, Hampshire SO43 7JG
Telephone: 023 80 813165
www.bramblehill.co.uk

Peacefully located in tranquil surroundings, this country house hotel is only three miles from Junction 1 of the M27 and is set in ancient woodland with 30 acres of glades, lawns and shrubbery to enjoy. Ideal for country walks and horse riding. A short drive from many places of interest including Salisbury, Stonehenge, Winchester and Beaulieu. All bedrooms have en suite bathrooms and some have antique four-poster beds. Cosy public bar and restaurant. Snooker room. A warm friendly welcome and good home cooking assured.

Three day special breaks, weekly terms, daily rates — please phone for details.

FULLY LICENSED. 8 BEDROOMS, ALL WITH PRIVATE BATHROOMS. CHILDREN AND PETS WELCOME. CONFERENCE FACILITIES. CADNAM 2 MILES. S££, D££.

Tyrrells Ford Manor House Country Inn

Avon, Near Ringwood, New Forest,
Hampshire BH23 7BH
Tel: 01425 672646 • Fax: 01425 672262
e-mail: info@tyrrellsfordcountryinn.co.uk
www.tyrrellsford.co.uk

This elegant and handsomely furnished 18th Century Country House is set in 8 acres of beautiful grounds on the edge of the New Forest. The public and private rooms exhibit a wealth of fine panelling, especially in Tyrrells Bar and the sumptuous Tattersalls Restaurant where the worth of the chef inspired à la carte and table d'hôte cuisine is proclaimed far and wide. Guest rooms are charming, all have en suite facilities, colour television, radio alarm, direct-dial telephone and tea and coffee making facilities. There are prime opportunities for golf, fishing, riding and walking in the vicinity and the delightful and diverse attractions of Bournemouth may be reached in 15 minutes.

A jewel of a hotel well worth a visit.

OPEN ALL YEAR. FULLY LICENSED. 16 BEDROOMS, ALL WITH PRIVATE BATHROOMS.
NON-SMOKING ACCOMMODATION AVAILABLE. CHILDREN WELCOME.
CIVIL WEDDING CEREMONIES. RINGWOOD 4 MILES. S£££, D££££.

In the heart of the New Forest

THE WATERSPLASH HOTEL

The Rise, Brockenhurst SO42 7ZP • Tel: 01590 622344

Family-run hotel in two acres of grounds, located in the New Forest village of Brockenhurst with shops, pubs and amenities. Families find that they are particularly welcome here and guests return year after year to enjoy the country house atmosphere and the very high standards of accommodation, service and good food. There are 23 en suite bedrooms of varying sizes, including two four-poster rooms, four large family rooms with baby listening service; cots and high chairs available on request. There are also three ground floor rooms suitable for disabled guests. There is a range of leisure facilities in the surrounding area, including walking, golf and horseriding, and south coast beaches are also easily reached. **AA ★★**

e-mail: bookings@watersplash.co.uk • www.watersplash.co.uk

23 BEDROOMS, ALL WITH PRIVATE BATHROOM. CHILDREN AND PETS WELCOME. LYNDHURST 4 MILES.

MARWELL HOTEL

Thompsons Lane, Colden Common, Winchester, Hampshire SO21 1JY

Tel: 01962 777681 • Fax: 01962 777625

AA ★★★ HOTEL

e-mail: info@marwellhotel.co.uk
www.marwellhotel.co.uk

They say its a jungle out there! Well, adjacent to this superb hotel is the next best thing, the world-renowned 100-acre Marwell Zoological Park, dedicated to the conservation of endangered species, and where guests can enjoy preferential rates. The hotel, itself, has an enchanting woodland setting and organises special Zoofari Getaways and Golf Breaks, the latter by arrangement with nearby East Horton Golf Centre. Popular with business travellers, conference delegates and holidaymakers alike, the hotel exudes a warm welcome to guests of all ages, children being subject to significant reductions. Each splendidly furnished bedroom has a bathroom en suite, satellite television with video on request, radio, telephone, iron and ironing board, hairdryer and hospitality tray.

Conforming to the romantic theme of 'Out of Africa in Hampshire', whether it is cocktails or a cappuccino, the Zanzibar and The Gallery is the place to meet and relax, and a meal at the Zavanna Restaurant with its contemporary menus could be the highlight of any stay, although the superb Leisure Club, with its heated swimming pool, gym and body-toning equipment, vies strongly for this accolade. The purpose-built facilities for conferences are some of the finest in the country and are backed by the hotel's team of dedicated professionals.

OPEN ALL YEAR. FULLY LICENSED. 66 BEDROOMS, ALL WITH PRIVATE BATHROOMS. NON-SMOKING ACCOMMODATION AVAILABLE. CHILDREN AND PETS WELCOME. LEISURE FACILITIES. CONFERENCE FACILITIES. CIVIL WEDDING CEREMONIES. WINCHESTER 4 MILES. S££££, D££££.

Isle of Wight

"Truly unbeatable value for money". This lovely country house hotel is set in a beautiful quiet two-acre garden on the seaward side of the olde worlde village of Bonchurch. Run by the same family for over 40 years, the hotel offers first class food and service, all in a relaxed and friendly atmosphere. All rooms are en suite, with tea/coffee facilities and TV, and are decorated in the "Laura Ashley" style.

Lake Hotel

We can offer an Isle of Wight car ferry inclusive price of just £185.00 for four nights' half board during March/April/May and October, and we really do believe that you will not find better value on our beautiful island.

Shore Road, Lower Bonchurch, Isle of Wight PO38 1RF
Tel: 01983 852613
e-mail: fhg@lakehotel.co.uk • www.lakehotel.co.uk

RESIDENTIAL LICENCE. 20 BEDROOMS, ALL WITH PRIVATE BATHROOMS.
TOTALLY NON-SMOKING ACCOMMODATION. CHILDREN FROM THREE YEARS AND PETS WELCOME.
VENTNOR 1 MILE. S££, D££.

FARRINGFORD HOTEL

ONCE THE HOME OF TENNYSON

'Situated just one mile from Freshwater Bay Golf Course'

Once the home of Tennyson, the Farringford is set in 35 Acres of mature parkland with 18 en suite rooms, including two with four-poster beds. Dine in the AA Rosette awarded Downs Restaurant overlooking Afton Down. Par 3 nine hole golf course, outdoor heated swimming pool, croquet, bowls, children's play area. 29 two-bedroom self-catering cottages also available.

SPRING AND AUTUMN 'MINI BREAKS' THEMED WEEKENDS – MURDER MYSTERY, PAINTING AND WRITING. CHRISTMAS AND NEW YEAR PACKAGES AVAILABLE ON REQUEST.

Farringford Hotel, Freshwater Bay, Isle of Wight PO40 9PE
For colour brochure Tel: 01983 752500 Fax: 01983 756515
e-mail: enquiries@farringford.co.uk www.farringford.co.uk

OPEN ALL YEAR. FULLY LICENSED. 19 BEDROOMS, ALL WITH PRIVATE BATHROOMS.
CHILDREN WELCOME. LEISURE FACILITIES. CONFERENCE FACILITIES.
TOTLAND 1 MILE. S£/£££, D£/£££.

PRIORY BAY HOTEL *(on facing page)*

LICENSED. 18 BEDROOMS, ALL WITH PRIVATE BATHROOMS AND 7 SELF-CATERING COTTAGES.
NON-SMOKING ACCOMMODATION AVAILABLE. CHILDREN AND PETS WELCOME. LEISURE FACILITIES.
CONFERENCE FACILITIES. RYDE 2 MILES. S££££, D££££.

LICENSED. 16 BEDROOMS, ALL WITH PRIVATE BATHROOMS.
NON-SMOKING ACCOMMODATION AVAILABLE. PETS WELCOME. YARMOUTH 3 MILES. S£££. D£££.

Prices

Normal Bed & Breakfast rate per person
(single room)

PRICE RANGE	CATEGORY
Under £40	S£
£40-£55	S££
£56-£70	S£££
Over £70	S££££

Normal Bed & Breakfast rate per person
(sharing double/twin room)

PRICE RANGE	CATEGORY
Under £40	D£
£40-£55	D££
£56-70	D£££
Over £70	D££££

This is meant as an indication only and does not show prices for Special Breaks, Weekends, etc. Guests are therefore advised to verify all prices on enquiring or booking.

OPEN ALL YEAR. 25 BEDROOMS, ALL WITH PRIVATE FACILITIES. CHILDREN AND PETS WELCOME. LEISURE FACILITIES. SHANKLIN 3 MILES.

Isle of Wight

The Isle of Wight has several award-winning beaches, including Blue Flag winners, all of which are managed and maintained to the highest standard. Sandown, Shanklin and Ryde offer all the traditional delights; or head for Compton Bay where surfers brave the waves, fossil hunters admire the casts of dinosaur footprints at low tide, kitesurfers leap and soar across the sea and paragliders hurl themselves off the cliffs

Newport is the commercial centre of the Island with many famous high street stores and plenty of places to eat and drink. Ryde has a lovely Victorian Arcade lined with shops selling books and antiques. Cowes is great for sailing garb and Godshill is a treasure chest for the craft enthusiast. Lovers of fine food will enjoy the weekly farmers' markets selling home-grown produce and also the Garlic Festival held annually in August to celebrate the Island's position as a major producer and exporter of this pungent bulb.

Many attractions are out of doors to take advantage of the Island's milder than average temperatures. However, if it should rain, there's plenty to choose from. There are vineyards offering wine tasting, cinemas, theatres and nightclubs as well as sports and leisure centres, a bowling alley and an ice skating rink, home to the Island's very own ice hockey team – the Wight Raiders.

The Island's diverse terrain makes it an ideal landscape for walkers and cyclists of all ages and abilities. Pony trekking and beach rides are also popular holiday pursuits and the Island's superb golf courses, beautiful scenery and temperate climate combine to make it the perfect choice for a golfing break.

With up to 350 daily ferry crossings, the Isle of Wight has to be the UK's most accessible Island, and once there, it's easy to get around. There's a comprehensive bus network and a regular train service, which operates between Ryde and Shanklin and connects with the Isle of Wight Steam Railway.

Kent

Ashford Road, St Michaels
Tenterden, Kent TN30 6HX

• Set in 97 acres of beautiful Wealden countryside, one mile from Tenterden • Parkland golf course • 26-bedroom hotel • 3 large function rooms • Superb restaurant • Spike bar • 20 mins from Ashford Terminal • 40 mins from Channel Ports

Best Western | AA ★★★ | RAC ★★★ Hotel

Tel: 01580 766279 • Fax: 01580 763884
e-mail: enquiries@londonbeach.com • www.londonbeach.com

OPEN ALL YEAR. FULLY LICENSED. 26 BEDROOMS, ALL WITH PRIVATE BATHROOMS. LEISURE FACILITIES. CONFERENCE FACILITIES. CIVIL WEDDING CEREMONIES.ASHFORD 10 MILES. S££££, D££/£££.

Collina House Hotel
East Hill, Tenterden, Kent TN30 6RL
Tel: 01580 764852/764004 • Fax: 01580 762224
www.collinahousehotel.co.uk
e-mail: enquiries@collinahousehotel.co.uk

This charming hotel is quietly situated in the country town of Tenterden, yet is only a few minutes' walk from the Town Centre. There are many National Trust properties and places of interest in the area, including Sissinghurst Castle, Leeds Castle, Scotney Castle Gardens and the Kent and East Sussex steam engines. Personal attention is assured by the Swiss-trained owners of this comfortable hotel, who provide home cooking of the highest standard, enhanced by the use of home-grown produce. All the well-appointed bedrooms, including five family rooms, have private bathrooms, central heating, colour television, direct-dial telephones, tea-making facilities, and hairdryers. Further details on request.

FULLY LICENSED. 14 BEDROOMS, ALL WITH PRIVATE BATHROOMS. CHILDREN WELCOME, PETS BY ARRANGEMENT. CONFERENCE FACILITIES. ASHFORD 10 MILES. S££, D£/££.

Oxfordshire

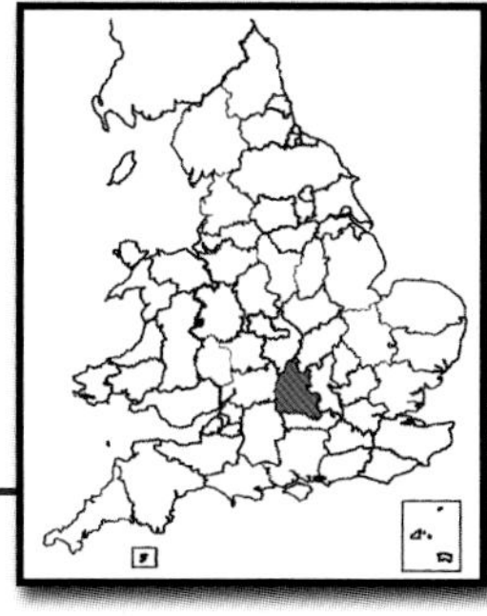

Utterly charming, this lovely, thatched, 17th century country house, built in honeyed local stone, is set in one of the Cotswolds' most picturesque villages. Bedrooms are furnished in classic English style and many thoughtful conveniences are provided, all have en suite facilities and some four-poster rooms are available. This is a welcoming and hospitable hotel with a well known reputation for fine cuisine; one may dine by candlelight in an intimate restaurant with old-world atmosphere captured by original oak beams, inglenooks, horse brasses and pewter. Skilfully prepared dishes feature local produce and are supported by well-chosen wines.

VisitBritain/AA ★★★

WROXTON HOUSE HOTEL Wroxton St Mary, Near Banbury OX15 6QB
Tel: 01295 730777 • Fax: 01295 730800 • www.wroxtonhousehotel.com
e-mail: reservations@wroxtonhousehotel.com

OPEN ALL YEAR. FULLY LICENSED. 32 BEDROOMS, ALL WITH PRIVATE BATHROOMS.
CHILDREN AND PETS WELCOME.
CONFERENCE FACILITIES. CIVIL WEDDING CEREMONIES. BANBURY 3 MILES. S££££, D£££.

Oxfordshire

Oxfordshire is a fascinating blend of rolling countryside, bustling market towns and over 6000 years of history. Whether you are looking for a relaxing stay in the country, a cruise on the Oxford Canal or the shoppers' paradise of Bicester Village, there is something for everyone.

The Oxfordshire Cotswolds is a designated Area of Outstanding Natural Beauty, ideal for an activity break, whether walking, cycling or horse riding. There are miles of way-marked routes for whole day expeditions or gentle afternoon strolls.

For a touch of cosmopolitan city culture visit Oxford, city of dreaming spires. The streets, houses, colleges, churches and chapels of the city represent a carefully documented catalogue of English history, with over 900 buildings of architectural or historic interest, including the Bodleian Library, one of the world's greatest collections of books, with over 5 million volumes. Opera, ballet, pantomime, musicals and major concerts are among a wide variety of performing arts taking place, often in historic settings such as the Sheldonian Theatre, Christ Church Cathedral, and the Holywell Music Room.

Market towns such as Banbury, famous for its landmark Cross, and Bicester are an exciting blend of traditional history and heritage and lively shopping and entertainment. Antique centres, local artists' studios and farm shops mix with quality high street shopping - and don't miss the traditional markets offering a range of produce and products unique to the area.

East Sussex

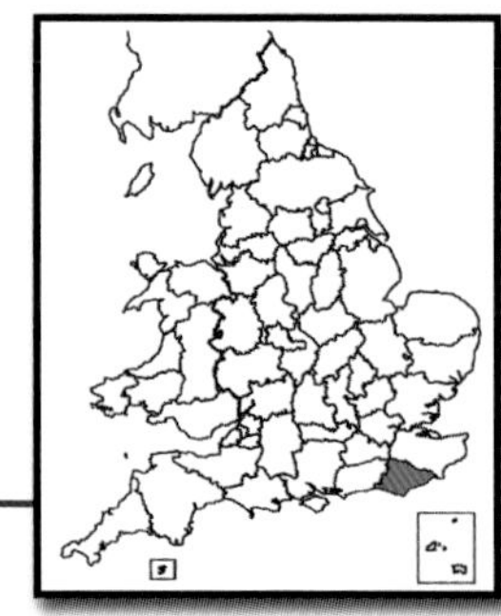

Bolebroke Castle

Henry VIII's hunting lodge, Bolebroke Castle is set on a beautiful 30 acre estate with lakes, woodlands and views to Ashdown Forest, where you will find 'Pooh Bridge'. Antiques and beamed ceilings add to the atmosphere. 4-poster suite available. Explore the Castle's secrets with the audio tour. Please call for our brochure.

In the heart of "Winnie the Pooh" country.

www.bolebrokecastle.co.uk

Bolebroke Castle, Hartfield, East Sussex TN7 4JJ
Tel: 01892 770061

OPEN ALL YEAR. FULLY LICENSED. 5 BEDROOMS, ALL WITH PRIVATE BATHROOMS. CHILDREN WELCOME. CONFERENCE FACILITIES. EAST GRINSTEAD 6 MILES. S££, D£.

★★★ AA & VB ★★★
VB Gold Award • RAC Dining Award
Recommended by Condé Nast Johansens, Signpost and designated a *'Best Loved Hotel of the World'*

"A little Gem of an Hotel"

RYE LODGE

Luxury, elegance and charm in a relaxed atmosphere – Delicious candlelit dinners in the elegant, marbled floored Terrace Restaurant, fine wines and really caring service. Indoor Swimming Pool, Spa and Sauna, plus all the delights of the Ancient Cinque Port of Rye with its picturesque cobbled streets, historic buildings, antique shops, art galleries and old inns.

Short break package: 2 nights dinner, room and breakfast from £139

RYE LODGE HOTEL

'One of the finest small luxury hotels in the country'

HILDER'S CLIFF, RYE, EAST SUSSEX

Tel: 01797 223838 • Fax: 01797 223585

www.ryelodge.co.uk

OPEN ALL YEAR. FULLY LICENSED. 18 BEDROOMS, ALL WITH PRIVATE BATHROOMS. CHILDREN AND PETS WELCOME. LEISURE FACILITIES. HASTINGS 9 MILES. S££££, D£££.

Dale Hill HOTEL & GOLF CLUB

Dale Hill

Situated in 350 acres of beautiful countryside, the newly refurbished Dale Hill is an impressive modern hotel and is home to the Ian Woosnam designed golf course. Our guests can expect a warm and friendly welcome, excellent service, award-winning cuisine, the challenge of two golf courses and the latest fitness facilities, all in a quiet rural location. From elegantly furnished public rooms and en suite bedrooms, to panoramic views over the Kentish Weald, the four-star Dale Hill Hotel is perfect for a relaxing and enjoyable break. Just an hour's drive from London and easily accessible from the M25.

Ticehurst, Wadhurst, East Sussex TN5 7DQ • 01580 200112 • Fax: 01580 201249
e-mail: info@dalehill.co.uk • www.dalehill.co.uk

OPEN ALL YEAR. FULLY LICENSED. 35 BEDROOMS, ALL WITH PRIVATE BATHROOMS.
CHILDREN WELCOME. LEISURE FACILITIES. CONFERENCE FACILITIES. CIVIL WEDDING CEREMONIES.
WADHURST 3 MILES. S££££, D££££.

West Sussex

SPRINGWELLS HOTEL

9 High Street, Steyning, West Sussex BN44 3GG

Once a Georgian merchant's town house, now an elegant ten-bedroom Bed and Breakfast hotel. All rooms have telephones and television; two have four-poster beds. The bar and adjoining conservatory lead to a patio and walled garden with outdoor heated swimming pool. At the front of the hotel there is a sunny dining room and elegant lounge.

ETC/AA/RAC ◆◆◆◆ • *RAC Sparkling Diamond*

Tel: 01903 812446 • Fax: 01903 879823
contact@springwells.co.uk • www.springwells.co.uk

RESIDENTIAL LICENCE. 11 BEDROOMS, 9 WITH PRIVATE BATHROOMS.
CHILDREN WELCOME. LEISURE FACILITIES. WORTHING 6 MILES. S££, D££.

Hertfordshire

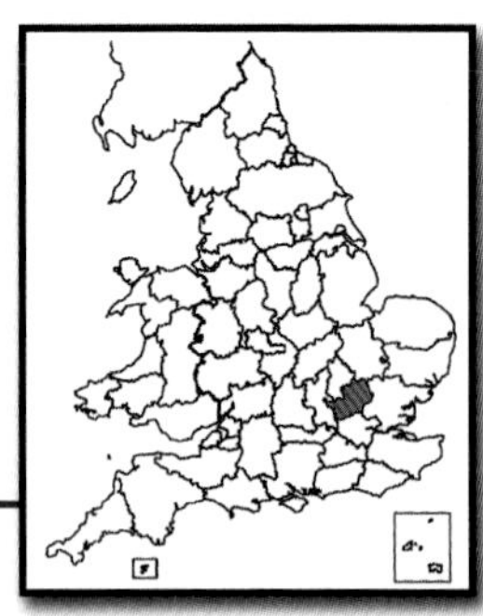

THE PENDLEY MANOR HOTEL

Cow Lane, Tring, Herts HP23 5QY
Tel: 01442 891891 • Fax: 01442 890687
reservations@pendley-manor.co.uk
www.pendley-manor.co.uk ETC/AA ★★★★

Built on the ruins of a 15th century Tudor manor, this elegant Victorian house has been thoughtfully restored to its former glory. The situation, so conveniently placed for London, is an added attraction, not only for tourists but also for those interested in first-rate conference and function facilities, whilst this distinctive and distinguished hotel provides a wonderful range of leisure activities, many of which are sited in magnificent grounds of 35 acres where peacocks roam. Spacious suites and bedrooms are luxuriously appointed and tastefully decorated in harmonious colour schemes to complement comforts of the highest standards; family rooms are available. In the award-winning Oak Restaurant, the imaginative menus are backed by a choice selection of wines.

OPEN ALL YEAR. FULLY LICENSED. 73 BEDROOMS, ALL WITH PRIVATE BATHROOMS.
LEISURE FACILITIES. CONFERENCE FACILITIES. CIVIL WEDDING CEREMONIES. BERKHAMSTED 5 MILES.

Please note

All the information in this book is given in good faith in the belief that it is correct. However, the publishers cannot guarantee the facts given in these pages, neither are they responsible for changes in policy, ownership or terms that may take place after the date of going to press. Readers should always satisfy themselves that the facilities they require are available and that the terms, if quoted, still apply.

Norfolk

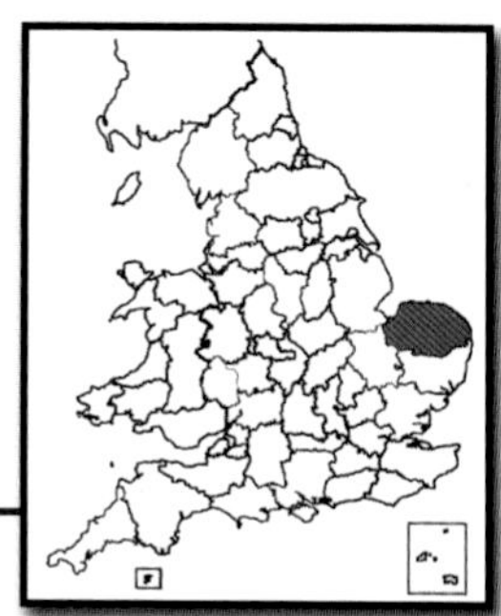

Grove Thorpe

John & Angie welcome you to this 17th century Grade II Listed country house nestling in 10 acres of gardens and grounds, on the edge of the Waveney valley, in tranquil and peaceful surroundings. Recently renovated to the highest standard, but maintaining traditional features, including inglenook fireplaces and a wealth of beams. Tastefully decorated bedrooms, individually furnished with antiques, and with countryside views. All are en suite, with colour TV beverage tray, radio alarm, towelling robes, hairdryer. Ground floor 'Garden Cottage' with separate access. Private fishing lake for guests' use - with barbless hooks. Centrally situated for touring Norfolk and Suffolk. Excellent country inns and restaurants located within 2 miles. *No Smoking • No Pets • No children under 12 years.*

Gold
GOLD AWARD
★★★★★
GUEST ACCOMMODATION

Angela & John Morrish, Grove Thorpe, Grove Road, Brockdish, Norfolk IP21 4JR
Tel: 01379 668305 • www.grovethorpe.co.uk • e-mail: grovethorpe@btinternet.com

OPEN ALL YEAR. RESIDENTIAL LICENCE. 3 BEDROOMS, ALL WITH PRIVATE BATHROOMS.
DISS 5 MILES. D£/££.

Prices

Normal Bed & Breakfast rate per person
(single room)

PRICE RANGE	CATEGORY
Under £40	S£
£40-£55	S££
£56-£70	S£££
Over £70	S££££

Normal Bed & Breakfast rate per person
(sharing double/twin room)

PRICE RANGE	CATEGORY
Under £40	D£
£40-£55	D££
£56-70	D£££
Over £70	D££££

This is meant as an indication only and does not show prices for Special Breaks, Weekends, etc. Guests are therefore advised to verify all prices on enquiring or booking.

Elderton Lodge HOTEL

Thorpe Market, Cromer, Norfolk NR11 8TZ

In the heart of beautiful countryside and only four miles from the coast, this Grade II Listed building is surrounded by six acres of mature gardens and lies adjacent to the 800-acre Gunton Hall Estate with its herds of deer.

Many original features of the house remain and the guest rooms are tastefully appointed to the highest modern standards. With an emphasis on fresh local produce from farm and sea, the superb cuisine in the Langtry Restaurant is well supported by an extensive wine list.

★★★

Tel: 01263 833547 • Fax: 01263 834673

e-mail: enquiries@eldertonlodge.co.uk

www.eldertonlodge.co.uk

THE STUART HOUSE HOTEL

35 Goodwins Road, King's Lynn, Norfolk PE30 5QX
Tel: 01553 772169 • Fax: 01553 774788

It would be hard to find a more pleasant place to stay at any time of year than the Stuart House Hotel, which manages to be both quiet and restful in its own grounds, and very central. It has comfortable and well-equipped bedrooms, including a honeymoon suite which boasts a romantic four-poster bed and a jacuzzi. There are two pleasant reception areas, an excellent CAMRA *Good Beer Guide* Listed bar, and the Stuart House Restaurant where the emphasis is on superb quality and good value. The town of King's Lynn has many attractions, and Royal Sandringham, Burnham Thorpe (Nelson's birthplace) and the fine Norfolk beaches and countryside are all an easy drive away.

e-mail: reception@stuarthousehotel.co.uk • www.stuart-house-hotel.co.uk

OPEN ALL YEAR. FULLY LICENSED. 18 BEDROOMS, ALL WITH PRIVATE BATHROOMS. NON-SMOKING ACCOMMODATION. CHILDREN WELCOME. CONFERENCE FACILITIES. NORWICH 40 MILES. S££, D£.

Surrounded by tranquil countryside 4 miles south of King's Lynn, this picturesque Georgian hotel retains its old-world charm thanks to sympathetic refurbishment. It offers delightfully appointed accommodation in beautifully colour co-ordinated rooms, all of which have full en suite facilities, TV, direct-dial telephone and beverage-makers. An extra special bedroom with jacuzzi can be booked for a touch of luxury. The fully licensed restaurant and bar are also open to non-residents, and offer tempting menus with regular specials. This is a popular venue for weddings and other functions.

ANDEL LODGE

HOTEL & RESTAURANT

48 Lynn Road, Tottenhill Norfolk PE33 0RH
Tel: 01553 810256
Fax: 01553 811429
reservations@andellodge.co.uk
www.andellodge.co.uk

★★★★ GUEST ACCOMMODATION

FULLY LICENSED. ALL BEDROOMS WITH PRIVATE BATHROOM. CHILDREN WELCOME. KINGS LYNN 4 MILES.

ELDERTON LODGE HOTEL *(on facing page)*

OPEN ALL YEAR. FULLY LICENSED. 11 BEDROOMS, ALL WITH PRIVATE BATHROOMS. CHILDREN WELCOME. CONFERENCE FACILITIES. CIVIL WEDDING CEREMONIES. CROMER 4 MILES. S£££, D£££.

Suffolk

Horringer, Bury St Edmunds, Suffolk IP29 5QE
Tel: 01284 735350 • Fax: 01284 736300
e-mail: info@ickworthhotel.com • www.ickwothhotel.co.uk

Surrounded by some 1800 acres of glorious parkland and gardens, this elegant 18th century house presents the opportunity for guests of all ages to live in the grand style for a while, and for youngsters to create a lifetime of memories. One may choose to lord it in the Marquess' bedchamber or snuggle up in the Butler's cosy retreat. All the stunning bedrooms are individual entities and offer luxury and comfort in traditional and contemporary styles. An impressive restaurant offers a superb cuisine and wines; for less formal fare, the Cafe Inferno is popular with family parties. Despite its apparent grandeur, the house has a warm and relaxing atmosphere that parents and children appreciate. Indeed, the little (and not-so-little) ones will have the time of their young lives. For guests of all ages, there is a fine indoor pool and opportunities in the grounds for a variety of sports as well as qualified coaching. To sample all the wonderful things at this magical never-never-land, it would take a break of extraordinary lengths - but it would be fun trying!

★★★★ HOTEL

AA ★★★★ HOTEL

27 BEDROOMS, ALL WITH PRIVATE BATHROOM. 11 APARTMENTS. CHILDREN WELCOME. LEISURE FACILITIES. CONFERENCE FACILITIES. IPSWICH 23 MILES.

A beautiful Tudor mansion set in the heart of the Suffolk countryside, this outstanding country hotel gazes out over sweeping lawns to a picturesque lake. For an invigorating break from routine, this has it all: peerless accommodation, a magnificent cuisine, style, and a captivating aura of living history. Pretty fabrics and tasteful decor set off contemporary luxuries to maximum advantage, and en suite guest rooms of all sizes are superbly appointed. In the dining room exquisitely prepared dishes are presented amidst a setting of glassware, gleaming silver and spotless napery, with a mouth-watering vegetarian selection also on offer. The Courtyard Leisure Club, set inside the adjacent Tudor tithe barn, includes a large swimming pool and fully equipped gymnasium.

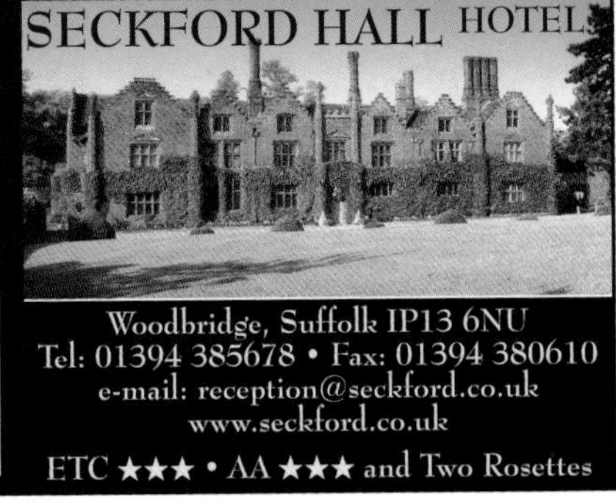

Woodbridge, Suffolk IP13 6NU
Tel: 01394 385678 • Fax: 01394 380610
e-mail: reception@seckford.co.uk
www.seckford.co.uk

ETC ★★★ • AA ★★★ and Two Rosettes

OPEN ALL YEAR (EXCEPT CHRISTMAS DAY). FULLY LICENSED. 32 BEDROOMS, ALL WITH PRIVATE BATHROOMS. CHILDREN AND DOGS WELCOME. LEISURE FACILITIES. CONFERENCE FACILITIES. CIVIL WEDDING CEREMONIES. IPSWICH 8 MILES. S££££, D££££.

Derbyshire

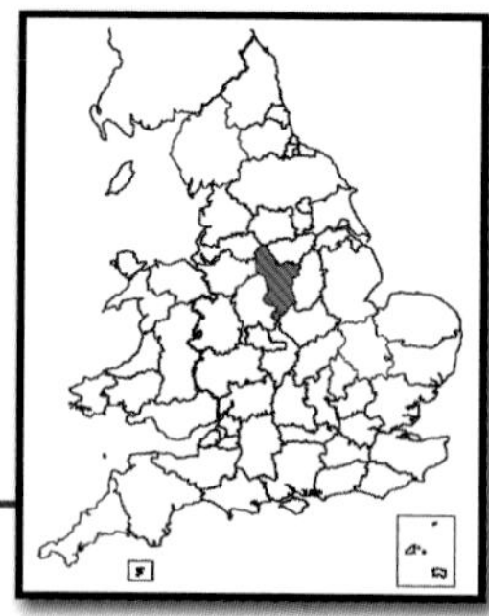

BIGGIN HALL

Tranquilly set 1000ft up in the White Peak District National Park, 17th century Grade II* Listed Biggin Hall – a country house hotel of immense character and charm where guests experience the full benefits of the legendary Biggin Air – has been sympathetically restored, keeping its character while giving house room to contemporary comforts. Rooms are centrally heated with bathrooms en suite, colour television, tea-making facilities, silent fridge and telephone. Those in the main house have stone arched mullioned windows, others are in converted 18th century outbuildings. Centrally situated for stately homes and for exploring the natural beauty of the area. Return at the end of the day to enjoy your freshly cooked dinner alongside log fires and personally selected wines.

Biggin-by-Hartington, Buxton, Derbyshire SK17 0DH
Tel: 01298 84451
Fax: 01298 84681
www.bigginhall.co.uk

OPEN ALL YEAR. LICENSED. 20 BEDROOMS, ALL EN SUITE. CHILDREN OVER 12 YEARS WELCOME. ASHBOURNE 9 MILES. S£££, D££.

Please note

All the information in this book is given in good faith in the belief that it is correct. However, the publishers cannot guarantee the facts given in these pages, neither are they responsible for changes in policy, ownership or terms that may take place after the date of going to press. Readers should always satisfy themselves that the facilities they require are available and that the terms, if quoted, still apply.

Leicester & Rutland

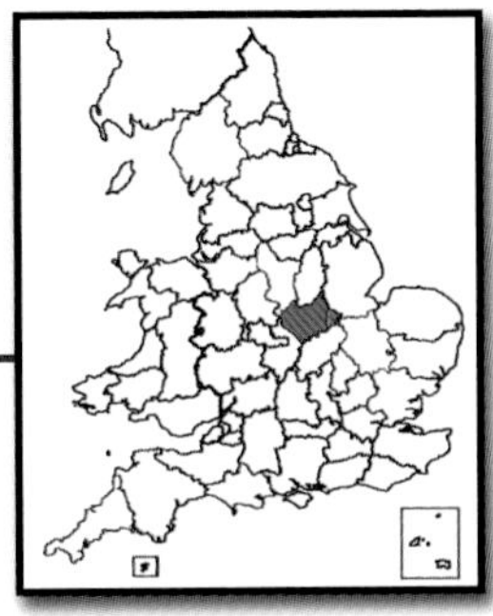

BARNSDALE LODGE HOTEL

A delightful, welcoming country house hotel situated between the north shore of Rutland Water and The Earl of Gainsborough's Exton Park Estate. An ideal base to visit Geoff Hamilton's Barnsdale Gardens, Belton House (National Trust), Burghley House and the historic market towns of Stamford and Oakham with all the attractions of Rutland Water; sailing, windsurfing, fishing, cycling and beautiful scenic walks. A bistro menu based on locally sourced produce is served in relaxed surroundings of the dining room, conservatory or courtyard garden. Viciente beauty treatment room now open. This excellent accommodation comprises rooms with en suite bathrooms, Sky television, broadband, radio alarms, and tea/coffee making facilities. Children's menu - cots available. Pets welcome. Private gardens.

The Avenue, Rutland Water, North Shore, Near Oakham, Rutland LE15 8AH
Tel: 01572 724678 • Fax: 01572 724961 • e-mail: enquiries@barnsdalelodge.co.uk
www.barnsdalelodge.co.uk *ETC ★★★ and Silver Award • AA ★★★*

OPEN ALL YEAR. FULLY LICENSED. 44 BEDROOMS, ALL EN SUITE. CHILDREN AND PETS WELCOME.
BEAUTY TREATMENT ROOM, CONFERENCE FACILITIES.
CIVIL WEDDING CEREMONIES. MELTON MOWBRAY 9 MILES. *S££££, D££.*

Prices

Normal Bed & Breakfast rate per person
(single room)

PRICE RANGE	CATEGORY
Under £40	S£
£40-£55	S££
£56-£70	S£££
Over £70	S££££

Normal Bed & Breakfast rate per person
(sharing double/twin room)

PRICE RANGE	CATEGORY
Under £40	D£
£40-£55	D££
£56-70	D£££
Over £70	D££££

This is meant as an indication only and does not show prices for Special Breaks, Weekends, etc. Guests are therefore advised to verify all prices on enquiring or booking.

HAMBLETON HALL

Hambleton, Oakham, Rutland LE15 8TH

The county of Rutland is verdant, undulating, and largely unspoilt, making it an ideal place to spend a tranquil vacation. No better venue for such an excursion exists than this fine hotel, perched in the very centre of man-made Rutland Water. The superb cuisine exhibits flair and refreshing originality, with the emphasis very much on seasonal, freshly sourced ingredients. Beautifully furnished in subtle shades, elegant and profoundly comfortable, with 17 individually and lavishly decorated bedrooms. Hambleton is within easy reach of numerous places of historic interest, wonderful gardens and antique shops. On-site tennis, outdoor heated swimming pool and croquet lawn, and within a short drive, horse riding, golf, sailing, fishing and boating.

Michelin Star

AA ★★★

Tel: 01572 756991
Fax: 01572 724721
hotel@hambletonhall.com
www.hambletonhall.com

OPEN ALL YEAR. FULLY LICENSED. 17 BEDROOMS, ALL WITH PRIVATE BATHROOMS. NON-SMOKING ACCOMMODATION AVAILABLE. CHILDREN AND PETS WELCOME. LEISURE FACILITIES. CONFERENCE FACILITIES. CIVIL WEDDING CEREMONIES. OAKHAM 3 MILES. S££££, D££££.

Please mention **Recommended Country Hotels** when making enquiries about accommodation featured in these pages

For Hotels which offer

• Conference facilities • Leisure facilities • Civil Wedding Ceremonies

See the Special supplements on pages 143-148

Lincolnshire

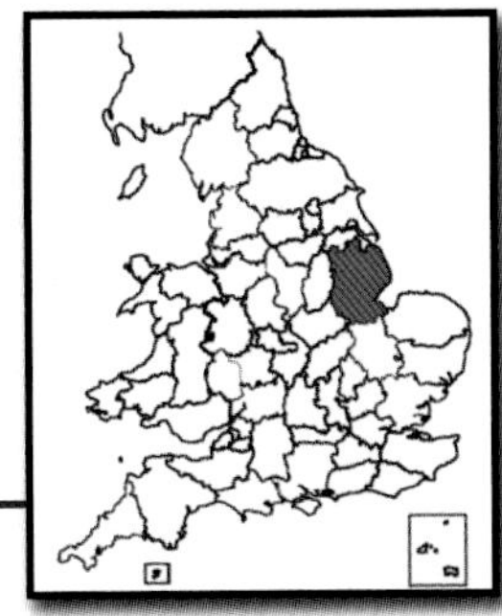

- 50 En-suite Bedrooms
- Lakeside Restaurant
- Leisure Facilities
- Conference Facilities
- Wedding Specialists
- Open to Non Residents

Only 5 minutes drive from Historic Lincoln, our beautiful hotel dates back to 1885 and is set in 88 acres of wooded parkland and lakes.

A venue for all seasons...

Lincoln Road, Branston, Lincoln, LN4 1PD

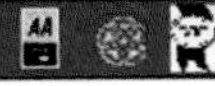

Telephone: 01522 793305

OPEN ALL YEAR. FULLY LICENSED. 50 BEDROOMS, ALL WITH PRIVATE BATHROOMS.
CHILDREN WELCOME. LEISURE FACILITIES. CONFERENCE FACILITIES. CIVIL WEDDING CEREMONIES. LINCOLN 4 MILES. S££££, D££/££££.

Stixwould Road, Woodhall Spa LN10 6QG
Tel: 01526 352411 • Fax: 01526 353473
reception@petwood.co.uk • www.petwood.co.uk

Originally built in the early 1900s The Petwood Hotel stands in 30 acres of mature woodland and gardens. During World War II, 617 Squadron, known as the "Dambusters", used the hotel as their Officers' Mess. Today it is a country house hotel of unique charm, offering a high standard of comfort and hospitality in elegant surroundings. All bedrooms are fully equipped to meet the needs of today's discerning guests, and the highly recommended Tennysons Restaurant offers the very best of English and Continental cuisine. There are ample leisure opportunities available locally as well as tranquil villages and historic market towns to explore.

AA ★★★ ETC

OPEN ALL YEAR. FULLY LICENSED. 53 BEDROOMS, ALL WITH PRIVATE BATHROOMS.
CHILDREN AND PETS WELCOME. CONFERENCE FACILITIES. CIVIL WEDDING CEREMONIES.
LINCOLN 18 MILES. S££££, D££££.

A useful index of towns/counties appears on pages 173-174

Nottinghamshire

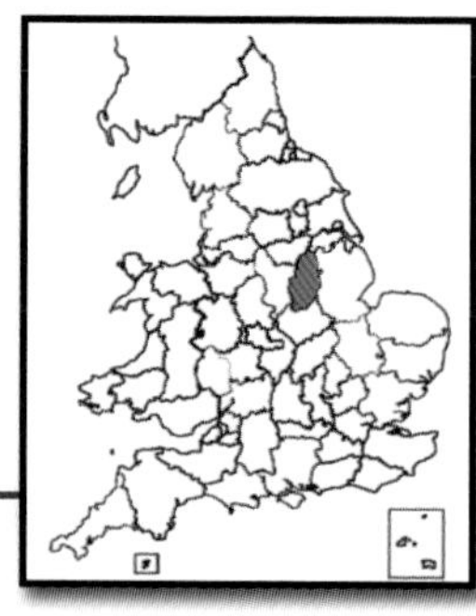

OPEN ALL YEAR. FULLY LICENSED. 10 BEDROOMS, ALL WITH PRIVATE BATHROOMS. NON-SMOKING ACCOMMODATION. CHILDREN AND PETS WELCOME. CONFERENCE FACILITIES. CIVIL WEDDING CEREMONIES. NOTTINGHAM 12 MILES. S££££, D££££.

Prices

Normal Bed & Breakfast rate per person
(single room)

PRICE RANGE	CATEGORY
Under £40	S£
£40-£55	S££
£56-£70	S£££
Over £70	S££££

Normal Bed & Breakfast rate per person
(sharing double/twin room)

PRICE RANGE	CATEGORY
Under £40	D£
£40-£55	D££
£56-70	D£££
Over £70	D££££

This is meant as an indication only and does not show prices for Special Breaks, Weekends, etc. Guests are therefore advised to verify all prices on enquiring or booking.

Shropshire

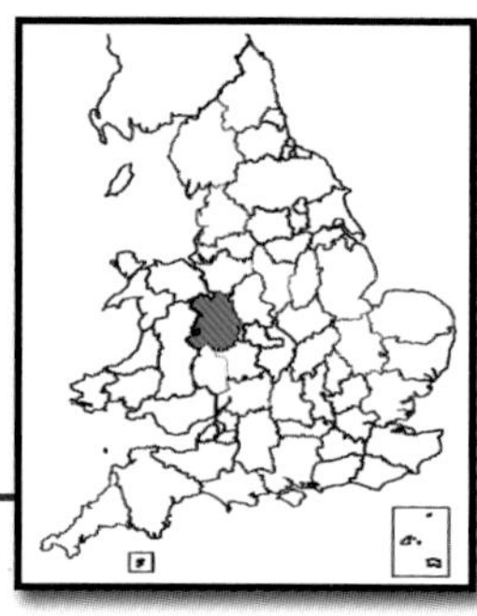

CHURCH STRETTON
SHROPSHIRE SY6 6AG
Tel: 01694 722244
Fax: 01694 722718
info@longmynd.co.uk
www.longmynd.co.uk

Perched high above the pleasant town of Church Stretton in grounds of ten acres, this fine hotel enjoys sweeping views over the beautiful Welsh border country.

The modern well furnished rooms all have en suite facilities.

Facilities also include an outdoor swimming pool, 9-hole pitch and putt course, and sauna. Riding, fishing, shooting and gliding may also be arranged nearby.

The cuisine is noteworthy for its excellence and variety and there are superb facilities for conferences and other functions.

There are also self-catering lodges in the hotel grounds.

LICENSED. 50 BEDROOMS, ALL WITH PRIVATE BATHROOMS PLUS SELF-CATERING LODGES. LEISURE FACILITIES. CONFERENCE FACILITIES. SHREWSBURY 12 MILES. S££/£££, D££/£££.

Soulton Hall

The Ashton family look forward to welcoming you to this historic house, with its pillared courtyard and mature trees. In the main house there are four well appointed double rooms, three of which are en suite, and the Coach House offers two spacious en suite ground floor bedrooms, one with adjoining sitting room.

• Oak-beamed bar • Elegant dining room serving excellent home cooking, with the emphasis on fresh and home-grown produce. • Leisure pursuits such as coarse fishing can be arranged. • Three well equipped self-catering cottages also available.

Soulton Hall, Near Wem, Shropshire SY4 5RS
Tel: 01939 232786 • Fax: 01939 234097
e-mail: enquiries@soultonhall.co.uk
www.soultonhall.co.uk

LICENSED. 7 BEDROOMS, SIX EN SUITE, ONE WITH PRIVATE BATHROOM. NON-SMOKING ACCOMMODATION. CHILDREN WELCOME, PETS BY ARRANGEMENT. SHREWSBURY 10 MILES, TELFORD 12 MILES.

Warwickshire

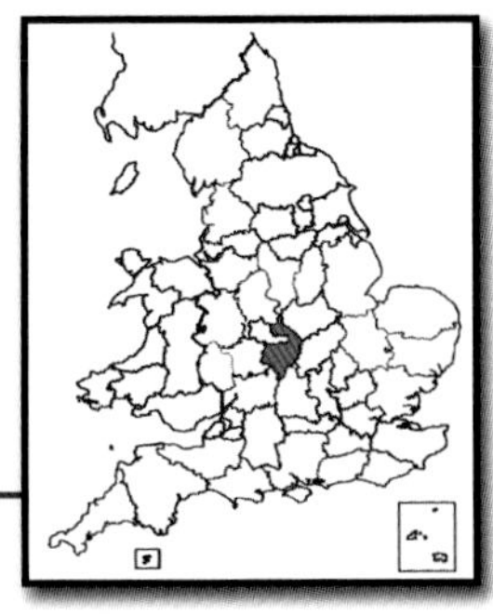

Leamington Town Hall, headquarters of Warwick District Council

ARDENCOTE MANOR *(on facing page)*

(on facing page)

FULLY LICENSED. 76 BEDROOMS, ALL WITH PRIVATE BATHROOMS.
NON-SMOKING HOTEL. CHILDREN WELCOME. LEISURE FACILITIES. CONFERENCE FACILITIES.
CIVIL WEDDING CEREMONIES. HENLEY-IN-ARDEN 4 MILES, WARWICK 4. S££££, D£££.

ARDENCOTE MANOR

HOTEL, COUNTRY CLUB & SPA

Near Warwick

is a premier hotel and leisure-break venue. Located in countryside just 5 minutes from the M40/M42 motorways, this privately owned independent 4 star venue offers unrivalled amenities.

The 76 bedrooms are comfortable and well appointed, many having fine views of the lake and grounds. The Hotel's award winning lakeside restaurant offers superb dining for all the family in a relaxed, informal setting.

Unparalleled leisure facilities include indoor heated pool and jacuzzi, sauna and steam rooms, outdoor heated whirlpool, gyms, squash, tennis, dance studio and 9 hole golf course.

ARDENCOTE
MANOR HOTEL

Local attractions include Shakespeare Country, Warwick & Kenilworth Castles, Hatton Country World, theatres and race courses of Stratford-upon-Avon and Warwick, and shopping in Stratford-upon-Avon, Leamington Spa and Solihull's Touchwood Centre.

The luxurious Ardencote Spa offers a superb selection of individual spa treatments, pamper days and spa breaks.

For full details contact Ardencote Manor on ***01926 843111***
e-mail hotel@ardencote.com *or visit the websites on*
www.ardencote.com *and* ***www.ardencotespa.com***

ARDENCOTE MANOR HOTEL, COUNTRY CLUB & SPA, LYE GREEN ROAD, CLAVERDON, WARWICK CV35 8LT

Worcestershire

Brockencote Hall

COUNTRY HOUSE HOTEL

Chaddesley Corbett
Near Kidderminster
Worcs DY10 4PY
Tel: 01562 777876
Fax: 01562 777872

In beautifully landscaped grounds of seventy acres with an impressive lake, Brockencote Hall presents a gracious style of living in the best English tradition under the knowledgeable auspices of owners, Alison and Joseph Petitjean. The atmosphere is relaxed and informal and the service efficient and willing. Among many attractions is the superb cuisine where authentic French influences are allied to a most impressive wine list in the award-winning restaurant. The well-proportioned guest rooms are delightfully equipped; each bedroom has a private bathroom (some with a jacuzzi), television, direct-dial telephone and hair dryer and also enjoys an outstanding outlook. From the picturesque village of Chaddesley Corbett it is only a 30-minute journey to the centre of Birmingham and the NEC, with many places of interest within easy reach, including Stratford-upon-Avon and the Cotswolds.

ETC ★★★
AA ★★★ and Two Rosettes
Johansens
'Tastes of Worcestershire'
Restaurant of the Year Award 2003/4

e-mail: info@brockencotehall.com
www.brockencotehall.com

OPEN ALL YEAR. FULLY LICENSED. 17 BEDROOMS, ALL WITH PRIVATE BATHROOMS. NON-SMOKING ACCOMMODATION AVAILABLE. CHILDREN WELCOME. LEISURE FACILITIES. CONFERENCE FACILITIES. CIVIL WEDDING CEREMONIES. KIDDERMINSTER 4 MILES. S££££, D££££.

For Hotels which offer

• Conference facilities • Leisure facilities • Civil Wedding Ceremonies

See the Special supplements on pages 143-148

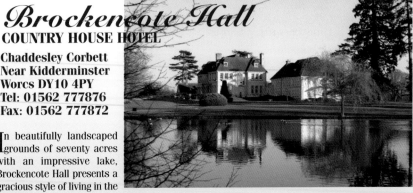

A friendly, family-managed Hotel & Country Club, set in a private estate and nature reserve in rural Worcestershire, just a few minutes' drive from Tenbury Wells. Facilities include a picturesque but challenging 9-hole golf course, indoor swimming pool and leisure facilities, bowls and two fishing lakes (Trout and Coarse).
The hotel provides a warm welcome with a homely atmosphere, an excellent choice of daily menus and 14 en suite bedrooms. AA ★★

Berrington Green, Tenbury Wells, Worcs WR15 8TQ
Telephone & Fax: 01584 810044
e-mail: info@cadmorelodge.co.uk
www.cadmorelodge.co.uk

FULLY LICENSED. 14 BEDROOMS, ALL WITH PRIVATE BATHROOMS.
CHILDREN WELCOME. LEISURE FACILITIES.
CONFERENCE FACILITIES. TENBURY WELLS 2½ MILES. S£££, D££.

East Yorkshire

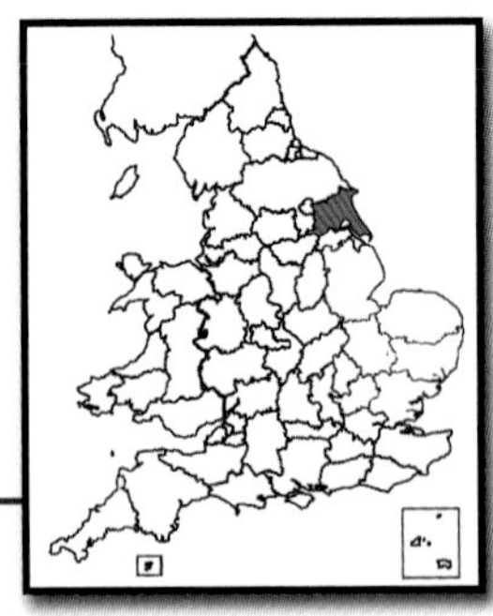

Wentworth House Hotel

12 Seaside Road, Aldbrough, Near Hull HU11 4RX
Telephone & Fax: 01964 527246
e-mail: ww@eduktion.co.uk
www.wentworthhousehotel.com

Family-run hotel set in spacious gardens, offering delightful accommodation. In the attractive licensed dining room the emphasis is placed on good home cooking, and special/medical diets can be catered for..

* CONFERENCE FUNCTION ROOM * GAMES ROOM
* ALL DOUBLE ROOMS EN SUITE, ONE WITH PRIVATE LOUNGE
* BEDROOMS HAVE COLOUR TV, TELEPHONE AND RADIO ALARM CLOCK
* BAR AREA WITH SELECTION OF WINES, SPIRITS & BEERS * CAR PARK

OPEN ALL YEAR. FULLY LICENSED. 8 BEDROOMS, 7 WITH PRIVATE BATHROOMS. CHILDREN AND PETS WELCOME. LEISURE FACILITIES. CONFERENCE FACILITIES. CIVIL CEREMONIES. HORNSEA 6 MILES. *S£/££, D££/£££.*

Prices

Normal Bed & Breakfast rate per person
(single room)

PRICE RANGE	CATEGORY
Under £40	S£
£40-£55	S££
£56-£70	S£££
Over £70	S££££

Normal Bed & Breakfast rate per person
(sharing double/twin room)

PRICE RANGE	CATEGORY
Under £40	D£
£40-£55	D££
£56-70	D£££
Over £70	D££££

This is meant as an indication only and does not show prices for Special Breaks, Weekends, etc. Guests are therefore advised to verify all prices on enquiring or booking.

North Yorkshire

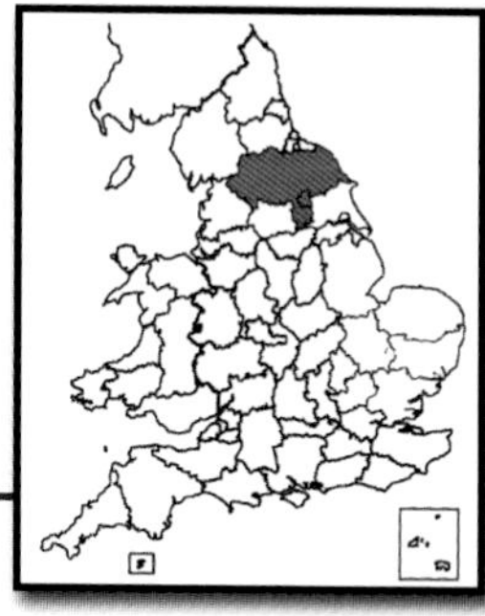

Experience the unique atmosphere and traditional hospitality at...

Set in magnificent countryside near the market town of Hawes, Simonstone Hall is a beautifully restored country house hotel with spectacular views over the dale and surrounding fell.

- Outstanding Bar Meals and Sunday Lunches served in the Game Tavern and Orangery, our Restaurant provides an elegant setting for our wide selection of fine foods and wines.
- An excellent base for walking and exploring the Dales.
- Pets welcome in most rooms.

A relaxed, friendly establishment with open fires, four-poster beds and experienced staff to look after all your needs.

Telephone: 01969 667255 • Fax: 01969 667741
e-mail: email@simonstonehall.demon.co.uk
www.simonstonehall.co.uk AA ★★

OPEN ALL YEAR. FULLY LICENSED. 18 BEDROOMS, ALL WITH PRIVATE BATHROOM. CHILDREN AND PETS WELCOME. CONFERENCE FACILITIES. CIVIL WEDDING CEREMONIES. KIRKBY STEPHEN 4 MILES. S££££, D££/£££/££££.

Licensed Country House Hotel & Restaurant overlooking magnificent Wensleydale
23 Quality en Suite Bedrooms (some with private conservatories opening onto gardens)
Delicious food & fine wines
The Perfect Venue for a relaxing break deep in the heart of the Yorkshire Dales.
Dogs genuinely welcome
Short Breaks available now

Sedbusk, Hawes, North Yorkshire DL8 3PT
Tel: 01969 667571 • Fax: 01969 667720
www.stonehousehotel.com

RESIDENTIAL AND TABLE LICENCE. 23 BEDROOMS, ALL WITH PRIVATE BATHROOMS. NON-SMOKING ACCOMMODATION AVAILABLE. CHILDREN AND PETS WELCOME. HEALTH AND BEAUTY TREATMENTS. KIRKBY STEPHEN 4 MILES. S££, D££.

FULLY LICENSED. 7 BEDROOMS, ALL WITH PRIVATE BATHROOMS.
HELMSLEY 3 MILES, YORK 26 MILES. S££, D£.

OPEN ALL YEAR. FULLY LICENSED. 52 BEDROOMS, ALL WITH PRIVATE BATHROOMS.
CHILDREN AND PETS WELCOME. LEISURE FACILITIES. CONFERENCE FACILITIES. CIVIL WEDDING CEREMONIES.
ROBIN HOOD'S BAY 3 MILES. S££, D££.

Please mention **Recommended Country Hotels**
when making enquiries about accommodation featured in these pages

BECK HALL *MALHAM BD23 4DJ*

18th century B&B on the Pennine Way, log fires and huge breakfasts.

Midweek and 4-night specials.

Ideal for exploring the Yorkshire Dales.

Tel: 01729 830332

e-mail: simon@beckhallmalham.com

www.beckhallmalham.com

MOST BEDROOMS WITH PRIVATE BATHROOM. CHILDREN AND PETS WELCOME. HARROGATE 20 MILES.

THE CONISTON HOTEL

Coniston Cold, Skipton, North Yorkshire BD23 4EB

Situated on the A65 Skipton to Kendal Road, the Hotel provides an ideal base for guests wishing to explore the Yorkshire Dales or just get away from it all. Set in a stunning 1400-acre estate with 24-acre lake. the hotel offers 50 en suite bedrooms, a restaurant, with a bar and orangery for more informal meals. Ten luxury bedrooms now open!

Clay Pigeon Shooting, Off-Road Driving, Archery, Driving Range, Falconry and Fishing available on site. Exceptional location for conferences and weddings. Special rates for Leisure Breaks and family rooms.

AA ★★★

Silver

Tel: 01756 748080 • Fax: 01756 749487

e-mail: sales@theconistonhotel.com • www.theconistonhotel.com

LICENSED. 50 BEDROOMS, ALL WITH PRIVATE BATHROOMS. NON-SMOKING ACCOMMODATION AVAILABLE. CHILDREN AND PETS WELCOME. LEISURE FACILITIES. CONFERENCE FACILITIES. CIVIL WEDDING CEREMONIES. SKIPTON 6 MILES. S££££, D££££.

Golden Fleece

Market Place, Thirsk YO7 1LL
Tel: 01845 523108 • Fax: 01845 523996

This characterful old Coaching Inn offers good food and up to date facilities. All rooms are en suite, with satellite TV, phone, trouser press, hairdryer. On site parking. Perfect for Dales and Moors touring and walking or shopping in York or Harrogate.

www.goldenfleecehotel.com
reservations@goldenfleecehotel.com

ETC ★★
Silver Award
AA ★★ 75%

OPEN ALL YEAR. FULLY LICENSED.23 BEDROOMS, ALL EN SUITE..
CONFERENCE FACILITIES. CIVIL WEDDING CEREMONIES. NORTHALLERTON 8 MILES. S£££/££££, D££££.

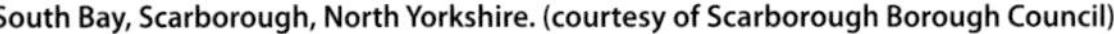

South Bay, Scarborough, North Yorkshire. (courtesy of Scarborough Borough Council)

Durham

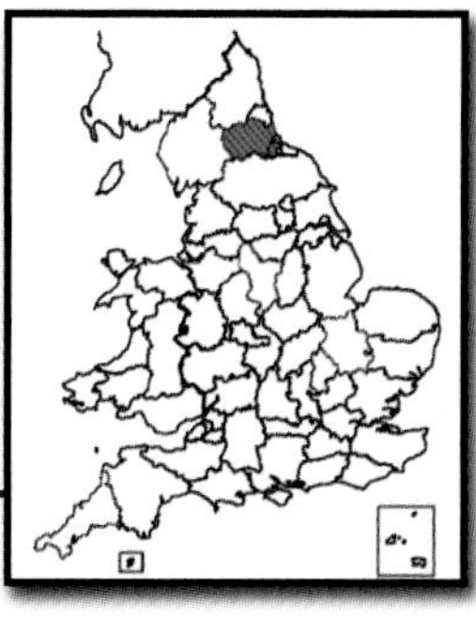

BEAMISH HALL

www.beamish-hall.co.uk

Steeped in local history and set in 24 acres of scenic grounds, the hotel is located close to the historic city of Durham. Beamish Hall provides the perfect setting for civil marriages and wedding receptions, conferences and corporate events and all types of parties and functions. It is also an ideal base for holiday breaks, and golf can be arranged at the adjacent course. Beamish, The North of England Open Air Museum is another local attraction.

36 elegant bedrooms - Classic, De Luxe, Premier and Suites - all with antiques, fine furnishings and modern-style bathrooms. Premier rooms have jacuzzis.

Beamish Hall Country House Hotel
Beamish, Stanley, Co Durham DH9 OYB
Tel: 01207 233733 Fax: 01207 299220
info@beamish-hall.co.uk

OPEN ALL YEAR. FULLY LICENSED. 36 BEDROOMS, ALL WITH PRIVATE BATHROOMS. CONFERENCE FACILITIES. CIVIL WEDDING CEREMONIES. STANLEY 2 MILES.

Hardwicke Hall Manor Hotel

Hesleden, Hartlepool TS27 4PA
Tel: 01429 836326 • Fax: 01429 837676
e-mail: enquiries@hardwickehallmanor.co.uk
www.hardwickehallmanor.co.uk

The superb rural setting of Hardwicke Hall with its beautiful lawns and woodland background give it an air of tranquillity and relaxation. As expected in a Grade II Listed Manor House, many original features have been retained, such as open stone

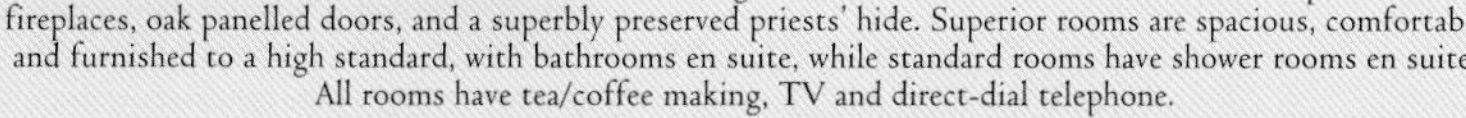

fireplaces, oak panelled doors, and a superbly preserved priests' hide. Superior rooms are spacious, comfortable and furnished to a high standard, with bathrooms en suite, while standard rooms have shower rooms en suite. All rooms have tea/coffee making, TV and direct-dial telephone.

The comfortable Lounge And Bar are ideal for a pre-dinner drink, and the elegant Wedgwood Suite and intimate Bistros offer traditional and contemporary menus.

The hotel is ideally situated for exploring the area, with Durham and Newcastle within a short drive.

OPEN ALL YEAR. FULLY LICENSED. 15 BEDROOMS, ALL WITH PRIVATE BATHROOMS. CHILDREN AND PETS WELCOME. CONFERENCE FACILITIES. CIVIL WEDDING CEREMONIES. PETERLEE 2 MILES. S£££, D£££.

FREE or REDUCED RATE entry to Holiday Visits and Attractions
– see our **READERS' OFFER VOUCHERS** on pages 149-172

Northumberland

OPEN ALL YEAR. FULLY LICENSED.8 BEDROOMS, ALL EN SUITE. CHILDREN AND PETS WELCOME. ALNWICK 4 MILES. S££, D££.

Please note

All the information in this book is given in good faith in the belief that it is correct. However, the publishers cannot guarantee the facts given in these pages, neither are they responsible for changes in policy, ownership or terms that may take place after the date of going to press. Readers should always satisfy themselves that the facilities they require are available and that the terms, if quoted, still apply.

Waren Mill, Belford, Near Bamburgh,
Northumberland NE70 7EE
Tel: 01668 214581 • Fax: 01668 214484
e-mail: enquiries@warenhousehotel.co.uk
www.warenhousehotel.co.uk

Set in six acres of mature wooded grounds, Waren House has been reborn under the talented and loving hands of owners, Anita and Peter Laverack. Beautifully presented food is served in the elegant dining room, and the wine list is a most fascinating read. Probably the icing on the cake is that the beauty of this uncrowded Heritage Coast makes it much like the Lake District was 40 years ago, before it was well and truly discovered.

Please do "discover" Waren House – it will be a choice you will never regret.

LICENSED. 13 BEDROOMS, ALL WITH PRIVATE BATHROOMS. NON-SMOKING ACCOMMODATION. BERWICK-UPON-TWEED 14 MILES. S££££, D££££.

Riverdale Hall Hotel

Bellingham, Northumberland
NE48 2JT
01434 220254
www.riverdalehallhotel.co.uk
reservations@riverdalehallhotel.co.uk

The Cocker Family's 29th year

A Victorian country hotel, overlooking the North Tyne River. All bedrooms are en suite, some with four-poster beds. The popularity of Riverdale Hall, one of the county's foremost country house hotels, is largely due to the hotel restaurant (the only one in Northumberland with the Les Routiers Gold Plate Award), and the many varied walks, including the Pennine Way, Hadrian's Wall and Kielder Water. Northumberland's best moorland golf course is opposite. Indoor pool with sauna, salmon and sea trout beats, cricket field. 5

Special Offer for FHG Readers
2 night break in superior bedroom from £63pppn DB&B. Free room on 3rd night.
Self-catering apartments also available.

Iben (Head Chef) and John Cocker receive the Les Routiers Gold Plate Award from Clarissa Dickson Wright (Two Fat Ladies) and Sir John Scott.

OPEN ALL YEAR. FULLY LICENSED. 33 BEDROOMS, ALL WITH PRIVATE BATHROOMS. CHILDREN AND PETS WELCOME. LEISURE FACILITIES. CONFERENCE FACILITIES. CIVIL WEDDING CEREMONIES. NEWCASTLE UPON TYNE 20 MILES. S££/£££, D£££.

THE **TANKERVILLE ARMS** HOTEL WOOLER, NORTHUMBERLAND NE71 6AD

A charming 17th century coaching inn with a relaxing and cosy atmosphere, situated in the heart of the Northumbrian countryside. It is an ideal base for the unspoilt attractions of Bamburgh, Holy Island, the Cheviot Hills and the Scottish Borders. Fine food, excellent service, and quality bedrooms are combined with a strong desire to make your stay both enjoyable and memorable. The Tankerville Arms Hotel is situated just off the A697.

Tel: 01668 281581
Fax: 01668 281387

enquiries@tankervillehotel.co.uk • www.tankervillehotel.co.uk

OPEN ALL YEAR. FULLY LICENSED. 16 BEDROOMS, ALL WITH PRIVATE BATHROOMS.
NON-SMOKING ACCOMMODATION. CHILDREN WELCOME.
CONFERENCE FACILITIES. CIVIL WEDDING CEREMONIES. ALNWICK 15 MILES. S££, D££.

Tyne & Wear

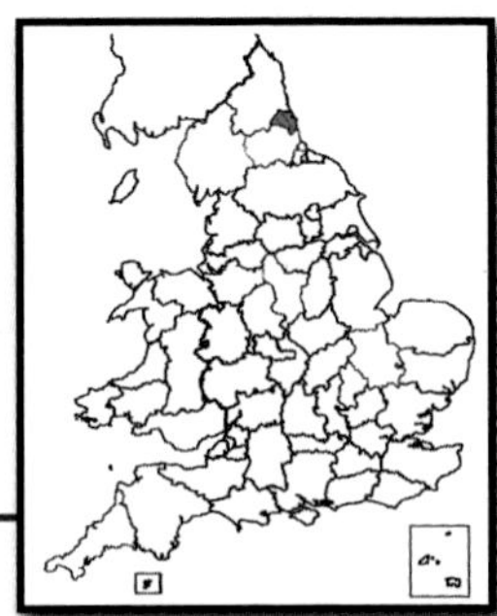

Hedgefield House Hotel

Stella Road, Ryton on Tyne NE21 4LR
Tel/Fax: 0191 413 7373 • Mobile: 07958 304942
e-mail: david@hedgefieldhouse.co.uk
www.hedgefieldhouse.co.uk

A stunning Georgian mansion standing in four acres of fabulous wooded gardens, on the edge of the Northumbrian countryside, yet only minutes away from Newcastle city centre and its lively quayside and nightlife.

Friendly personal service • Beautiful period, en suite rooms, including a four-poster suite
Sauna, gym & relaxation area • Aromatherapy/Swedish massage available
Conference facilities • Secure on-site parking
Close to Newcastle, Gateshead & the Metro Centre, and Hadrian's Wall

OPEN ALL YEAR. 5 BEDROOMS, ALL WITH PRIVATE BATHROOMS. CHILDREN WELCOME.
LEISURE FACILITIES. NEWCASTLE 6 MILES. S££, D££.

Cheshire

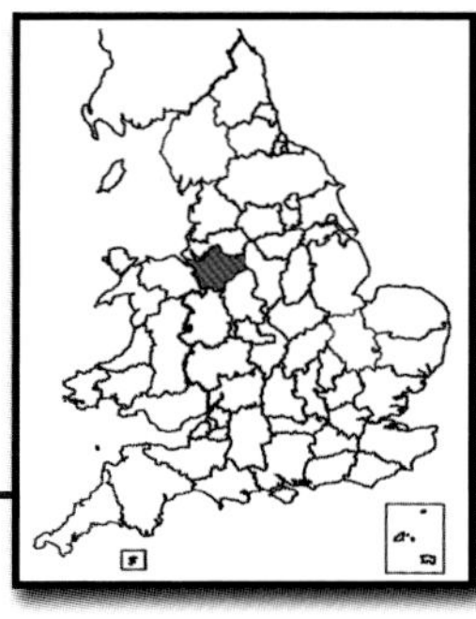

OPEN ALL YEAR. RESIDENTIAL LICENCE. 8 BEDROOMS, ALL WITH PRIVATE BATHROOMS. NON-SMOKING ACCOMMODATION AVAILABLE. CHILDREN AND PETS WELCOME. CIVIL WEDDING CEREMONIES. CHESTER 12 MILES. S££££, D££££.

HIGHER HUXLEY HALL

Huxley, Chester,
Cheshire CH3 9BZ
Tel: 01829 781484
info@huxleyhall.co.uk
www.huxleyhall.co.uk

In a lush valley between the wooded Cheshire hills and the Welsh mountains, this comfortable retreat dates, in part, from before the 13th century and its historic features are set off by numerous antiques. The dining room is situated in the oldest part of the house.

Perhaps the most intriguing feature is the late Elizabethan staircase, fashioned out of ships' timbers salvaged from remnants of the Spanish Armada.

Contemporary comforts of high order exist in the beamed guest rooms, including baths or showers en suite, telephone, colour television and tea and coffee-making facilities. A non-smoking house, Higher Huxley has an attractive sun room. Free wireless internet access.

OPEN ALL YEAR. RESIDENTIAL LICENCE. 5 BEDROOMS, ALL WITH PRIVATE BATHROOMS.
CHILDREN OVER 15 WELCOME. TARPORLEY 3 MILES. S££, D££.

THE CHIMNEY HOUSE HOTEL

This half-timbered Tudor-style hotel is situated in its own eight acres of peaceful woodland in the heart of the Cheshire countryside, yet offers easy access from the M6. There are 48 comfortable bedrooms. The excellent Patio Restaurant and conservatory offer views of the gardens.

The hotel is well placed for the Potteries to the south and the Peak District to the east; Crewe main line rail station offers direct links to Manchester and London.

You will experience high quality service in a refreshing and friendly atmosphere.

Congleton Road, Sandbach, Cheshire CW11 4ST • Tel: 0870 609 6164 • Fax: 01270 768916
www.foliohotels.com/chimneyhouse • e-mail: chimneyhouse@foliohotels.com

OPEN ALL YEAR. LICENSED. 48 BEDROOMS, ALL WITH PRIVATE BATHROOMS.
NON-SMOKING ACCOMMODATION AVAILABLE. CHILDREN WELCOME. CONFERENCE FACILITIES.
CREWE 5 MILES.

ROOKERY HALL Hotel & Spa

Worleston, Near Nantwich, Cheshire CW5 6DQ
Tel: 08450 727533 • Fax: 08450 727534
rookeryhall@handpicked.co.uk • www.handpicked.co.uk

With many rich features of architectural interest, this Grade II Listed Building stands resplendent in some 38 acres of landscaped gardens and woods alongside which runs the River Weaver. Although Georgian in origin, this fine country house was subsequently transformed into a baronial chateau in the late 19th century. Today, under Hand Picked Hotels ownership, it has the reputation for being one of the best regarded hotels in the country for cuisine, comfort and service. The spacious bedrooms are opulently furnished and beautifully decorated. Internationally acclaimed, the cuisine is modern European in style and augmented by an impressive wine list. The luxurious health club and spa offers a full range of pampering treatments, guaranteed to relax and de-stress.

OPEN ALL YEAR. FULLY LICENSED. 70 BEDROOMS, ALL WITH PRIVATE BATHROOMS.
CHILDREN WELCOME. LEISURE FACILITIES. CONFERENCE FACILITIES. CREWE 3 MILES.

Cumbria

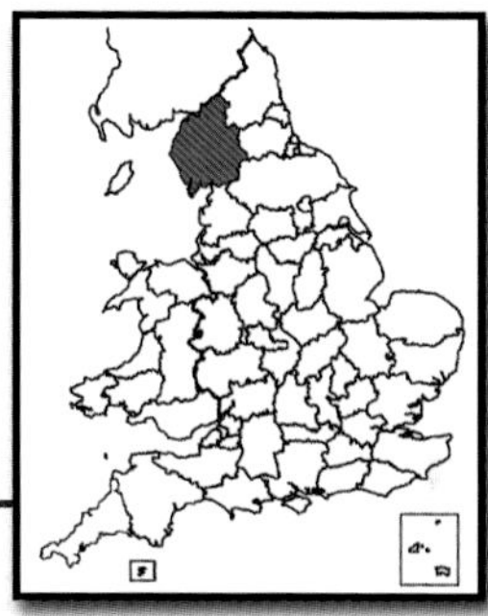

ARMATHWAITE HALL COUNTRY HOUSE HOTEL
Bassenthwaite Lake, Keswick CA12 4RE
Tel: 017687 76551 • Fax: 017687 76220
www.armathwaite-hall.com
e-mail: reservations@armathwaite-hall.com

The romance of the Lake District is encapsulated to perfection in this magnificent, one-time stately home adjacent to the serenity of Bassenthwaite Lake, with lofty Skiddaw gazing down on a vista of beauty and peace. Bedrooms and suites are superbly appointed and the cuisine is a connoisseur's dream. Promoting healthy appetites to do justice to the splendid fare, the Spa Leisure Club has outstanding facilities that include a swimming pool, gym, sauna, and beauty salon.

OPEN ALL YEAR. FULLY LICENSED. 42 BEDROOMS, ALL WITH PRIVATE BATHROOMS.
CHILDREN AND PETS WELCOME. LEISURE FACILITIES. CONFERENCE FACILITIES. CIVIL WEDDING CEREMONIES.
COCKERMOUTH 7 MILES. S££££, D££££.

MARY MOUNT HOTEL

Set in 4½ acres of gardens and woodlands on the shores of Derwentwater. 2½ miles from Keswick in picturesque Borrowdale. Superb walking and touring. All rooms en suite with colour TV and tea/coffee making facilities. Licensed. *Brochure on request.*

BORROWDALE, NEAR KESWICK CA12 5UU
017687 77223
e-mail: mawdsley1@aol.com • www.marymounthotel.co.uk

★★ HOTEL

LICENSED. ALL BEDROOMS WITH PRIVATE BATHROOM. CHILDREN WELCOME. KESWICK 2½ MILES.

BRIDGE HOTEL AA ★★★ ETC

Buttermere, Lake District, Cumbria CA13 9UZ

Tel: 017687 70252
Fax: 017687 70215

e-mail: enquiries@bridge-hotel.com • www.bridge-hotel.com

A leading, award-winning, privately owned Three Star Lakeland hotel.
A jewel in the heart of the Lake District.

• 21 refurbished en suite bedrooms • Traditional four-posters
• Two fully licensed bars and patio • Dogs welcome

CAMRA, Which?, Les Routiers & Good Hotel Guide Recommended

SPECIAL BREAKS ALL YEAR
Superb Unrestricted Walking
Painting – Photography – Fishing – Birdwatching

OPEN ALL YEAR. LICENSED. 21 BEDROOMS, ALL WITH PRIVATE BATHROOM. CHILDREN WELCOME. KESWICK 15 MILES, COCKERMOUTH 10.

AYNSOME MANOR HOTEL

Cartmel, Near Grange-over-Sands LA11 6HH
Tel: 015395 36653 • Fax: 015395 36016

Beckoning the discriminating country lover, particularly those who appreciate superb home cooking, Aynsome Manor has a happy and informal air and enjoys a tranquil setting in a sheltered valley just four miles from Lake Windermere. Rooms are delightfully furnished and bedroom amenities include private bathroom, colour television, tea/coffee making facilities and direct-dial telephone. Central heating and cheerful log fires ensure added comfort for those taking Spring or Autumn holidays. The Varley family personally supervise the well-being of guests and, assisted by a friendly and efficient staff, present a highly regarded cuisine. Dining is by candlelight in elegant surroundings, and tariffs include five-course dinner.

AA ★★ HOTEL

www.aynsomemanorhotel.co.uk • e-mail: aynsomemanor@btconnect.com

RESIDENTIAL LICENCE. 12 BEDROOMS, ALL WITH PRIVATE BATHROOMS. CHILDREN AND PETS WELCOME. NEWBY BRIDGE 4 MILES. S££££, D£££.

Sun Hotel & 16th Century Inn

A superbly located 10-bedroom hotel designed to overlook the village and enjoy panoramic mountain views. With a large private garden, patio, comfortable lounge, and extensive restaurant menu and wine list, the hotel offers comfortable en suite accommodation in a peaceful and informal setting. All bedrooms have been recently refurbished, with a relaxing night's sleep as good as promised! Better still, when built (in 1902), the hotel was attached to the end of a 16th century pub! It is now a freehouse with real ales and real fires in a classic Lakeland setting of beamed ceiling, flagged floor and an old range.

★★ HOTEL

Coniston LA21 8HQ • Tel: 015394 41248
Fax: 015394 41219 • info@thesunconiston.com
www.thesunconiston.com

10 BEDROOMS, ALL WITH PRIVATE BATHROOM. FREE HOUSE WITH REAL ALE. CHILDREN AND PETS WELCOME. RESTAURANT MEALS. NON-SMOKING AREAS. AMBLESIDE 6 MILES. S££, D££.

The Borrowdale Gates Hotel

Grange, Cumbria CA12 5UQ
Tel: 017687 77204
Fax: 017687 77254
e-mail: hotel@borrowdale-gates.com
www.borrowdale-gates.com

Nestling peacefully in two acres of wooded gardens, the hotel is superbly situated on the edge of the ancient hamlet of Grange-in-Borrowdale, amidst breathtaking scenery.

The personally-run hotel occupies an enviable position in what many regard as the best valley for walking in The Lakes. Comfortable lounges, log fires and antiques will welcome you, whilst all our 26 bedrooms will ensure a great night's sleep after a hard day walking, cycling, touring, climbing or relaxing! Indulge yourself in award-winning gastronomic food, cooked by talented chefs using many local products, coupled with an excellent and diverse wine list.

OPEN ALL YEAR. RESIDENTIAL LICENCE. 26 BEDROOMS, ALL WITH PRIVATE BATHROOMS. NON-SMOKING ACCOMMODATION AVAILABLE. CHILDREN WELCOME. CONFERENCE FACILITIES. KESWICK 4 MILES. S££££, D££££.

Prices

Normal Bed & Breakfast rate per person

(single room)

PRICE RANGE	CATEGORY
Under £40	S£
£40-£55	S££
£56-£70	S£££
Over £70	S££££

Normal Bed & Breakfast rate per person

(sharing double/twin room)

PRICE RANGE	CATEGORY
Under £40	D£
£40-£55	D££
£56-70	D£££
Over £70	D££££

This is meant as an indication only and does not show prices for Special Breaks, Weekends, etc. Guests are therefore advised to verify all prices on enquiring or booking.

Woodlands

COUNTRY HOUSE & COTTAGE
Ireby, Cumbria CA7 1EX

A delightful Victorian country house with seven well-equipped en suite bedrooms, offering high quality food and wine, and a very warm welcome. Relax in our comfortable lounge or cosy bar and snug, and enjoy the peace and quiet. We are ideally situated to explore the unspoilt beauty of the Western Lakes, the Northern Fells, and the Solway coast – an Area of Outstanding Natural Beauty. Although only half an hour's drive from Keswick, we are well away from the crowds. There is wheelchair access and ample free parking. The house is non-smoking. Four-course country house dinner and coffee is available. A charming two-bedroom self-catering stable conversion is also available.

VB ★★★★

Tel: 016973 71791 • Fax: 016973 71482 • stay@woodlandsatireby.co.uk • www.woodlandsatireby.co.uk

RESIDENTIAL LICENCE. 7 BEDROOMS, ALL WITH PRIVATE BATHROOMS. CHILDREN AND PETS BY ARRANGEMENT. WIGTON 6 MILES. S££, D£/££.

Overwater Hall

Overwater, Ireby, Near Keswick, Cumbria CA7 1HH • 017687 76566
welcome@overwaterhall.co.uk
www.overwaterhall.co.uk

Elegant, family-run Country House Hotel offering you the best in traditional comforts, award-winning food and friendly hospitality. Peacefully secluded yet within only a short drive of the popular centres of the Lake District, this is the ideal place for a real break. 18 acres of grounds to explore, ideal for dog walking. Special breaks available all year.

Please telephone for a brochure or visit our website for further information.

OPEN ALL YEAR. RESTAURANT AND RESIDENTIAL LICENCE. 11 BEDROOMS, ALL WITH PRIVATE BATHROOMS. CHILDREN AND PETS WELCOME. WIGTON 6 MILES. D£££.

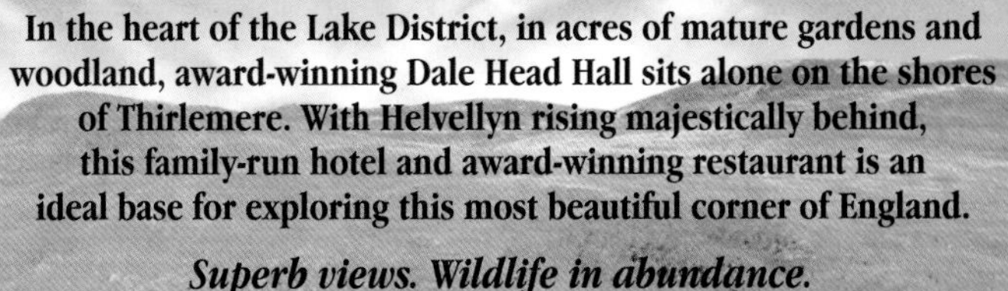

Dale Head Hall Lakeside Hotel

and luxury self-catering suites

Lake Thirlmere, Keswick CA12 4TN • Tel: 017687 72478 • Fax: 017687 71070
e-mail: onthelakeside@daleheadhall.co.uk www.daleheadhall.co.uk

LICENSED. OPEN ALL YEAR. 12 BEDROOMS, ALL WITH PRIVATE BATHROOM. CHILDFEN WELCOME. PENRITH 16 MILES.

THE LINTHWAITE HOUSE HOTEL & RESTAURANT

Crook Road, Windermere, Cumbria LA23 3JA
Tel: 015394 88600
Fax: 015394 88601

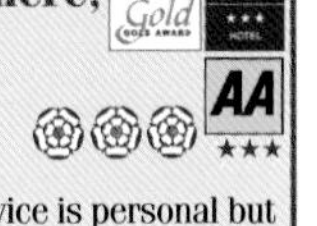

"A different kind of hotel." If one word were to sum up our hotel it would be 'unstuffy'. Our service is personal but informal, our staff are professional but unpretentious. Bedrooms are decorated in both contemporary and traditional styles, with 12-channel TV, CD hi-fi and modem point; there are also two de luxe suites and a ground floor bedroom with separate exterior access and ramp. Whether taking lunch on the terrace or dining in the Mirror Room, the food is an absolute delight, using the best local produce to prepare imaginative dishes. Special occasions can be catered for. Linthwaite House and the Lake District are an all-weather destination offering a host of pastimes and activities. • **e-mail: stay@linthwaite.com • www.linthwaite.com**

OPEN ALL YEAR. FULLY LICENSED. 27 BEDROOMS, ALL WITH PRIVATE BATHROOMS.
CHILDREN WELCOME, PETS IN KENNELS IN GROUNDS ONLY . CONFERENCE FACILITIES. CIVIL WEDDING CEREMONIES. KENDAL 7 MILES. S££££, D££££.

A useful index of towns/counties appears on pages 173-174

CHILDREN AND PETS WELCOME. CONFERENCE FACILITIES. CIVIL WEDDING CEREMONIES. WINDERMERE 3 MILES. S££, D££.

Cumbria - The Lake District

Cumbria - The Lake District is often described as the most beautiful corner of England. and it's easy to see why 15 million visitors head here every year. It is a place of unrivalled beauty with crystal clear lakes and bracken-covered mountains which soar into the clouds. There are rolling meadows, peaceful forests where deer roam free, trickling rivers, quiet country roads and miles of stunning coastline. There are welcoming pubs with real fires, houses steeped in legend, and glorious country gardens. In fact, there is something for everyone.

At the heart of Cumbria is the Lake District National Park. Each of the lakes that make up the area has its own charm and personality: Windermere, England's longest lake, is surrounded by rolling hills; Derwentwater and Ullswater are circled by craggy fells; England's deepest lake, Wastwater, is dominated by high mountains including the country's highest, Scafell Pike. For those who want to tackle the great outdoors, Cumbria offers everything from rock climbing to fell walking and from canoeing to horse riding – all among stunning scenery.

Cumbria - the Lake District also has strong literary connections. Visitors can see the sweeping landscapes that inspired the Lake poets, William Wordsworth and Samuel Taylor Coleridge, and the works of writers such as Arthur Ransome and Beatrix Potter. It is an area rich in heritage, with the beautiful ruins of Furness Abbey in the Lake District Peninsula, England's smallest cathedral in Carlisle, Birdoswald Roman Fort and Hadrian's Wall, where the Scots were kept out, and Carlisle Castle where Mary Queen of Scots was imprisoned. South from Carlisle runs the Eden Valley – an area of rolling green landscapes contrasting with the hump-backed open moors of the North Pennines. In the Western Lakes there are the lush and peaceful Ennerdale and Eskdale valleys and the sandstone cliffs of St Bees Head, part of a designated Heritage Coast.

Cumbria has many delightful market towns. There is Alston, the highest market town in England, and Keswick, the jewel of the Northern Lakes, an ideal centre for walkers or for those who just want to relax and browse through the shops. In the south, the cobbled streets of Ulverston have many claims to fame – the birthplace of Quakerism, Stan Laurel and pole vaulting. The Georgian town of Whitehaven was once Britain's third largest port, and further south, Barrow-in-Furness combines a Dock Museum with a modern centre. There are historic houses and beautiful gardens such as Holker Hall with its 25 acres of award-winning gardens. There are many opportunities to sample local produce, such as Cumbrian fell-bred lamb, Cumberland Sausage, and trout and salmon plucked fresh from nearby lakes and rivers.

Cumbria is a county of contrasts with a rich depth of cultural and historical interest in addition to stunning scenery. Compact and accessible, it can offer something for every taste.

Lancashire

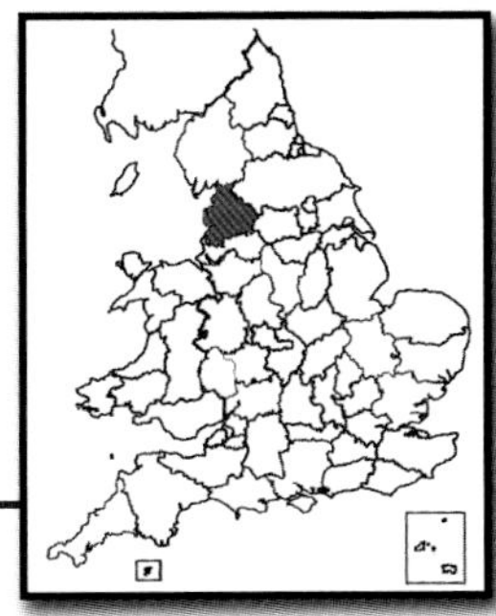

THE BROWN LEAVES COUNTRY HOTEL

**LONGSIGHT ROAD, COPSTER GREEN,
NEAR BLACKBURN BB1 9EU
01254 249523 • Fax: 01254 245240**

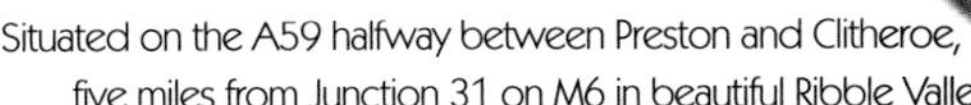

Situated on the A59 halfway between Preston and Clitheroe,
five miles from Junction 31 on M6 in beautiful Ribble Valley.

All rooms ground floor, en suite facilities, satellite TV, tea-making and hairdryer. Guests' lounge and bar lounge. Car parking. Pets by arrangement. All credit cards welcome.

www.brownleavescountryhotel.co.uk

SUMMARY TO FOLLOW

Egerton House Hotel

Relaxed Elegance

A privately owned country house set in 3 acres of beautiful gardens, yet only 3 miles from the centre of Bolton.
A combination of style with relaxed elegance. 29 individual bedrooms with an à la carte restaurant. Over 30 years' experience of hosting wedding receptions (from 45-150 sit down). Menu changes daily.

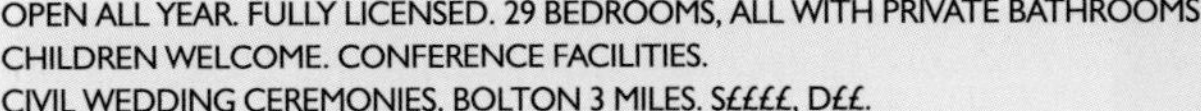

**Blackburn Road, Egerton, Bolton BL7 9LP • Tel: 01204 307171 • Fax: 01204 593030
sales@egertonhouse-hotel.co.uk • www.egertonhouse-hotel.co.uk**

OPEN ALL YEAR. FULLY LICENSED. 29 BEDROOMS, ALL WITH PRIVATE BATHROOMS.
CHILDREN WELCOME. CONFERENCE FACILITIES.
CIVIL WEDDING CEREMONIES. BOLTON 3 MILES. S££££, D££.

Please mention **Recommended Country Hotels**
when making enquiries about accommodation featured in these pages

The Higher Trapp Country House Hotel offers the best in friendly service and good old fashioned hospitality. It is situated on the enchanting Pendle Hillside in over four acres of magnificent terraced gardens that are fortunate enough to enjoy panoramic views over the Lancashire countryside.

The Hotel is as beautiful on the inside as it is on the outside, offering 29 en suite bedrooms, complete with telephone, colour television, radio, trouser press, hairdryer and tea/coffee making facilities. All of our rooms are furnished to a high standard, offering everything you would expect from a quality hotel, and our three four-poster bedrooms overlooking the gardens are ideal for a romantic occasion.

The Higher Trapp Country House Hotel, Trapp Lane, Simonstone, Near Burnley BB12 7QW
Tel: 01282 772781 • Fax: 01282 772782 • e-mail: reservations@highertrapphotel.co.uk
www.lavenderhotels.co.uk/highertrapp

OPEN ALL YEAR. FULLY LICENSED. 29 BEDROOMS, ALL WITH PRIVATE BATHROOMS. CHILDREN WELCOME. PETS BY ARRANGEMENT. CONFERENCE FACILITIES. CIVIL WEDDING CEREMONIES. MANCHESTER 22 MILES. S£££, D££££.

Merseyside

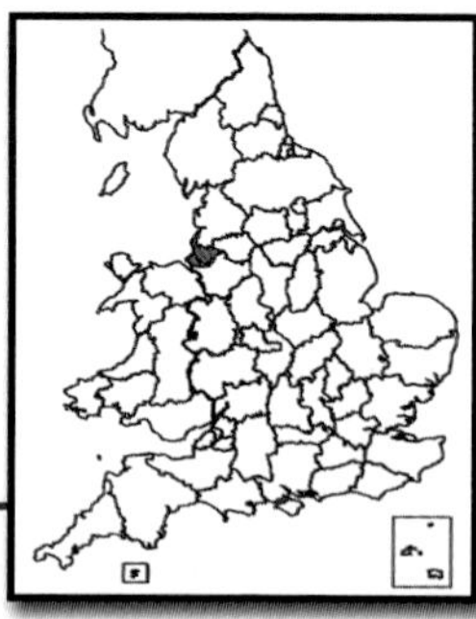

Tree Tops

www.treetopsformby.co.uk ETC/AA ★★★

COUNTRY HOUSE RESTAURANT & HOTEL

In a tranquil setting between Liverpool and Southport and within easy reach of sandy beaches and several golf courses, this is a delightful retreat for holidaymakers and business folk. Superbly appointed accommodation is provided in lodges situated in the five acres of wooded grounds. All rooms are en suite with TV, radio, direct-dial telephone and tea and coffee-makers. The restaurant and conservatory offer outstanding à la carte and table d'hôte cuisine, whilst a snack menu is available during the day. In summertime meals may be served on the lawns or on the swimming pool patio.

Southport Old Road, Formby, Near Southport L37 0AB • Tel: 01704 572430
Fax: 01704 573011 • e-mail: sales@treetopsformby.fsnet.co.uk

FULLY LICENSED. 11 BEDROOMS, ALL WITH PRIVATE BATHROOMS. CHILDREN WELCOME. LEISURE FACILITIES. CONFERENCE FACILITIES. CIVIL WEDDING CEREMONIES. LIVERPOOL 11 MILES. S££££, D££££.

Scotland

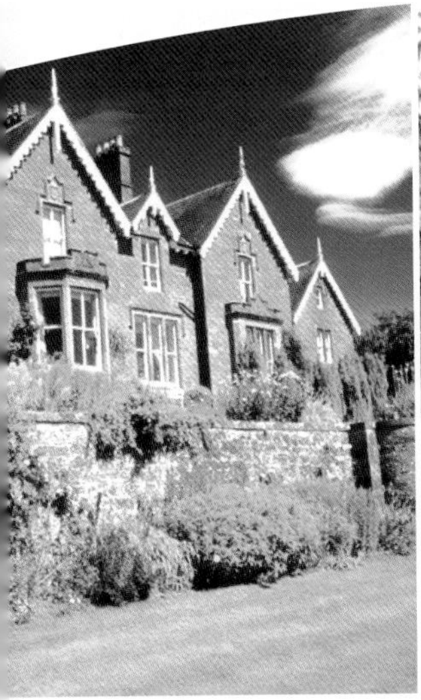

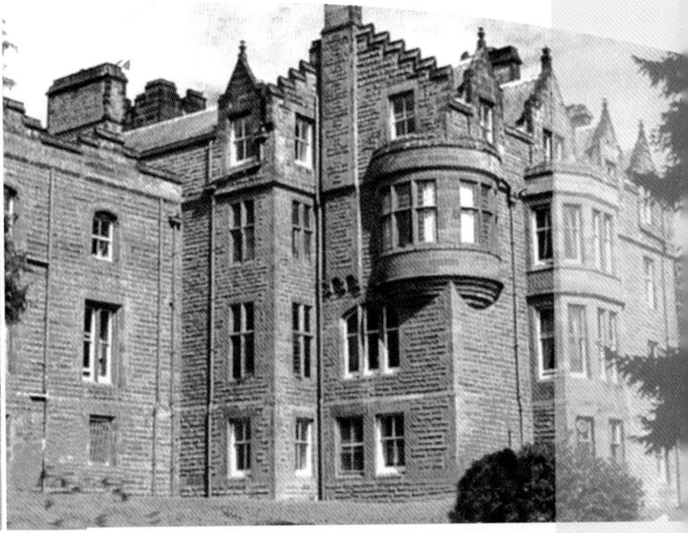

Scotland • Regions

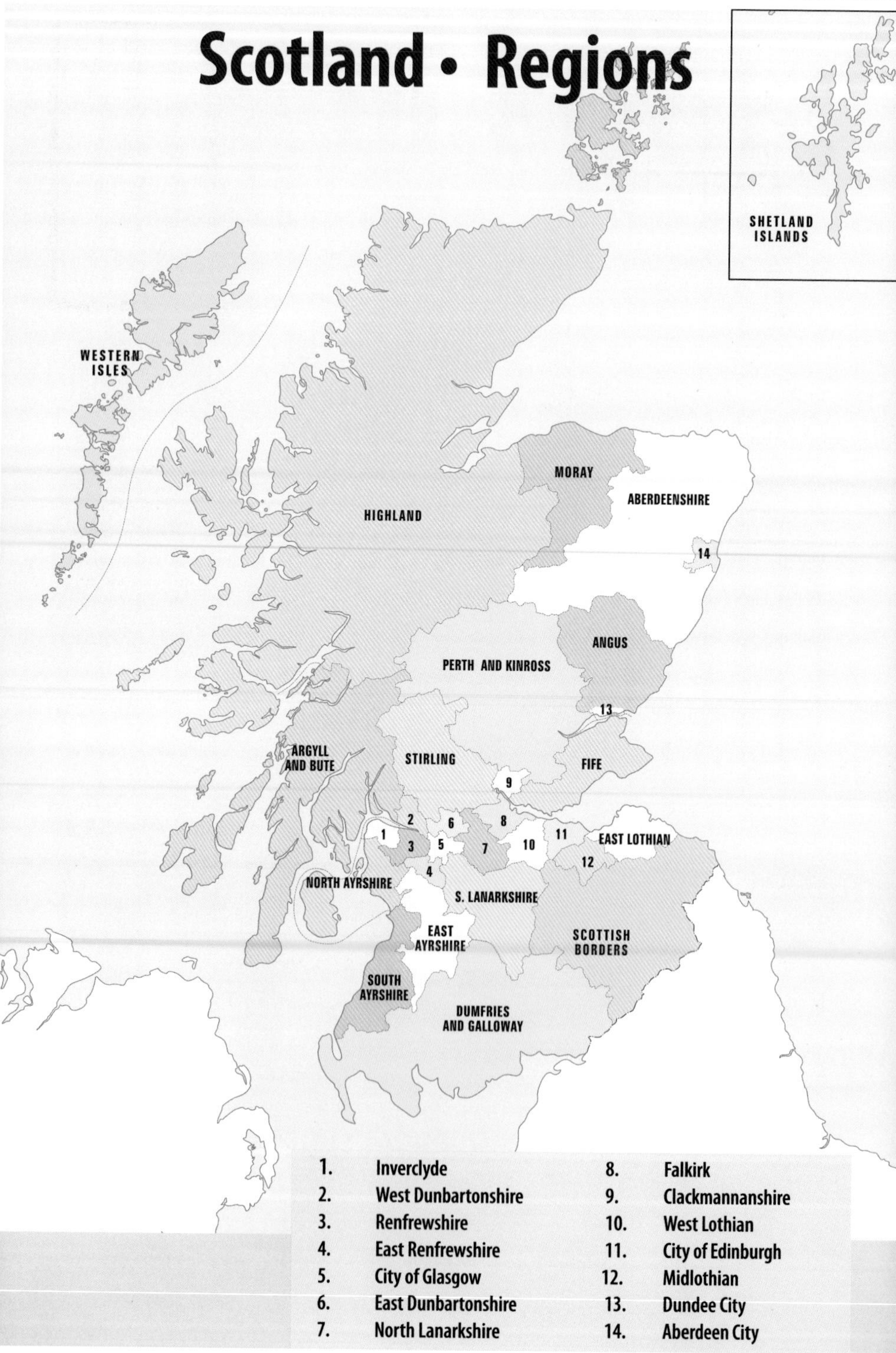
SHETLAND ISLANDS
WESTERN ISLES
HIGHLAND
MORAY
ABERDEENSHIRE
14
ANGUS
PERTH AND KINROSS
13
FIFE
ARGYLL AND BUTE
STIRLING
9
2
6
8
1
3
5
7
10
11
EAST LOTHIAN
12
4
NORTH AYRSHIRE
S. LANARKSHIRE
EAST AYRSHIRE
SCOTTISH BORDERS
SOUTH AYRSHIRE
DUMFRIES AND GALLOWAY
1. Inverclyde
2. West Dunbartonshire
3. Renfrewshire
4. East Renfrewshire
5. City of Glasgow
6. East Dunbartonshire
7. North Lanarkshire
8. Falkirk
9. Clackmannanshire
10. West Lothian
11. City of Edinburgh
12. Midlothian
13. Dundee City
14. Aberdeen City

Aberdeen, Banff & Moray

CAMBUS O'MAY HOTEL

Ballater
Aberdeenshire AB35 5SE
Tel & Fax: 013397 55428
www.cambusomayhotel.co.uk

This family-run country house hotel is situated four miles east of Ballater overlooking the River Dee and its environs. The hotel prides itself on the old-fashioned standards of comfort and service it offers to its guests. Excellent food is available from the table d'hôte menu which changes daily and can be complemented by fine wines from the cellar. The 12 bedrooms have en suite facilities and the hotel is centrally heated throughout.

The area affords a wealth of interests such as hill walking, golf, fishing, and shooting, and there are many historic sites including Balmoral Castle.

OPEN ALL YEAR. FULLY LICENSED. 12 BEDROOMS, ALL WITH PRIVATE BATHROOMS. CHILDREN AND PETS WELCOME. BALLATER 4 MILES. S£, D£.

Built as a coaching inn in the 16th century and graduating into an elegant Georgian manor house, Banchory Lodge stands in lovely wooded surroundings beside the River Dee, world-famous for its salmon. It is natural therefore that angling enthusiasts are attracted by its hospitable atmosphere, to say nothing of its high standards of service, cuisine and accommodation. Log fires, fresh flowers, traditional furnishings and original paintings add to the air of tranquillity. There is also ample scope nearby for golf, as well as numerous forest walks and nature trails. The best of fresh local produce features on the imaginative menus presented in the spacious dining room.

Banchory, Kincardineshire AB31 5HS • Tel: 01330 822625 • Fax: 01330 825019
www.banchorylodge.co.uk • e-mail: enquiries@banchorylodge.co.uk

OPEN ALL YEAR. FULLY LICENSED. 22 BEDROOMS, ALL WITH PRIVATE BATHROOMS. NON-SMOKING ACCOMMODATION AVAILABLE. CHILDREN AND PETS WELCOME. CONFERENCE FACILITIES. CIVIL WEDDING CEREMONIES. ABERDEEN 18 MILES. S££££, D£££.

FREE or REDUCED RATE entry to Holiday Visits and Attractions
– see our **READERS' OFFER VOUCHERS** on pages 149-172

LEARNEY ARMS HOTEL

Torphins, Banchory AB31 4GP

Overlooking the peaceful village of Torphins, the Learney Arms lies within easy reach of two of Scotland's most famous salmon rivers and only 22 miles from Aberdeen. There are some excellent golf courses nearby.

There are 10 bedrooms with en suite facilities, all individually and comfortably furnished. Good food is served in the Craigmyle Dining Room, which enjoys views over the landscaped gardens, and also in the Golfer's Return lounge bar, along with real ales and a wide selection of whiskies. Families welcome.

info@learneyarmshotel.com
www.learneyarmshotel.com
Tel: 013398 82202
Fax: 013398 82123

Scottish Tourist Board ★★ HOTEL

OPEN ALL YEAR. FULLY LICENSED. 12 BEDROOMS, 10 EN SUITE. CHILDREN WELCOME. BANCHORY 6 MILES. S££, D£.

Idyllically set in 3,500 acres of parkland and forest in beautiful Royal Deeside, but only 20 minutes from Aberdeen Airport and within easy reach of the city centre. The elegant reception rooms are filled with antiques, paintings and flowers, and the beautiful Oval Dining Room is the perfect setting for a leisurely dinner. The 20 bedrooms have every facility for the discerning guest; ground floor rooms are available. In the grounds are many beautiful walks, a Par 3 9-hole golf course, an all-weather tennis court and a summer croquet lawn.

The area is renowned for its golf and fishing, and there are many wonderfully romantic castles to visit.

Raemoir House Hotel & Restaurant

Raemoir, Banchory, Royal Deeside AB31 4ED • Tel: 01330 824884
Fax: 01330 822171 • e-mail: relax@raemoir.com • www.raemoir.com

OPEN ALL YEAR. FULLY LICENSED. 20 BEDROOMS, ALL WITH PRIVATE BATHROOMS. NON-SMOKING ACCOMMODATION AVAILABLE. CHILDREN AND PETS WELCOME. LEISURE FACILITIES. CONFERENCE FACILITIES. CIVIL WEDDING CEREMONIES. ABERDEEN 16 MILES. S£££, D££/£££.

MACDONALD PITTODRIE HOUSE *(on facing page)*

FULLY LICENSED. 27 BEDROOMS, ALL WITH PRIVATE BATHROOM. CHILDREN WELCOME. LEISURE FACILITIES. CONFERENCE FACILITIES. CIVIL WEDDING CEREMONIES. ABERDEEN 14 MILES.

Macdonald Pittodrie House

One of Scotland's most historic and picturesque hotels, originally built in 1480, still stands amidst the 2500 acre Pittodrie estate, nestling at the foot of the spectacular Bennachie. Stunning views, extensive private gardens and a reputation for culinary excellence and impecccable service combine to ensure your stay will be perfect in every way.

Turrets, spiral staircases, period furniture and ancestral portraits

Make yourself at home in our comfortable surroundings. Dining Room, Drawing Room, Orangery and Patio, Library, Billiard Room, Ballroom, Snug Bar. Log fires in winter, Victorian walled garden.

Luxury accommodation in each unique bedroom

27 rooms/suites, all with private facilities, radio, satellite television, direct dial telephone, wireless broadband internet access, trouser press, iron and ironing board, tea & coffee making facilities, hairdryer, dressing gown and slippers; newspaper deliveries, laundry and dry-cleaning service.

An impressive range of activities around the Estate

Individually tailored – from purely social to teambuilding, from a couple of hours to a whole day, including off-road driving, clay pigeon shooting, archery, shooting, quad-biking, one-man hovercraft, fly casting, family fun days.

Golf, fishing and deer stalking available locally. Also several interesting walks around the Pittodrie estate.

Savour the taste of Scottish country house cooking

Food and drink of the very highest quality in "The Mither Tap" Restaurant, prepared by our award-winning chef, incorporating the freshest of seasonal ingredients. Exceptional international list of over 200 wines, and over 140 malt whiskies on offer in the bar.

Wedding, Conference and Banqueting facilities

Full of period character, and with Bennachie as a backdrop, Pittodrie House is the perfect setting for a truly romantic wedding. Call our management team on 01467 681 744 and arrange to look round the hotel and experience the facilities.

MACDONALD
PITTODRIE HOUSE

Chapel of Garioch, Near Inverurie, Aberdeenshire AB51 5HS

Tel: 01467 681744 • Fax: 01467 681648 • E-mail: pittodrie@macdonald-hotels.co.uk

www.macdonaldhotels.co.uk/pittodrie

Angus & Dundee

Rosely Country House Hotel
Forfar Road, Arbroath DD11 3RB
Tel/Fax: 01241 876828
www.theroselyhotel.co.uk
enq@theroselyhotel.co.uk

A beautiful Victorian residence surrounded by four acres of lawns and mature trees on the edge of rural Angus, and only five minutes from Arbroath.

- All rooms en suite, with TV and tea/coffee making.
- Licensed bar and restaurant.
- Traditional home-made food.
- Great emphasis on fresh local produce.
- Ironing and hairdrying facilities.
- Close to many golf courses.

OPEN ALL YEAR. FULLY LICENSED. 11 BEDROOMS, ALL WITH PRIVATE BATHROOMS. CHILDREN AND PETS WELCOME. CIVIL WEDDING CEREMONIES. DUNDEE 15 MILES. S££, D£££.

Guthrie Castle

By Forfar, Angus DD8 2TP

The perfect location for romantic, fairytale weddings, private family celebrations, or a base for short holidays spent fishing, golfing or walking.

www.guthriecastle.com
e-mail: enquiries@guthriecastle.com
Tel: 01241 828691

LIMITED HOTEL ACCOMMODATION, SELF-CATERING ACCOMMODATION AVAILABLE IN GROUNDS. LEISURE FACILITIES. CONFERENCE FACILITIES. CIVIL WEDDING CEREMONIES. FORFAR 7 MILES.

Angus & Dundee

When you tour Scotland, a visit to the ancient land of Angus and the east coast city of Dundee rewards you with unspoiled highland glens, stunning rugged coastlines and a vibrant and cosmopolitan urban centre. Wherever you stay, your itinerary will easily combine beautiful scenery, world class sport, a unique mix of history and culture, and great hospitality from warm and friendly folk.

The Angus Glens offer a real treasure trove of hill walking and the Cairngorms National Park is within easy reach as its southern boundary incorporates the north of the Angus Glens. If you fancy a change of scenery, the Angus Coastline provides another dimension in walking with miles of sandy beaches or rugged coastlines. Look out for traditional fishing villages like Auchmithie near Arbroath - a perfect place to spend a few quiet hours and discover the home of the Arbroath Smokie!

Angus and Dundee is an area rich in historical and cultural gems. Visit some of the many stunning visitor attractions in this, Scotland's ancient and historic heartland. Discover the country's roots from the early Picts at Pictavia Visitor Centre in Brechin, through to the Scottish Noblemen who marked the Declaration of Independence in 1320 at Arbroath Abbey. Explore the roots of the present day British Royal Family at the ancestral home of Her Majesty the Queen Mother at Glamis Castle.

The area has much to offer in world class sporting and leisure activities, with Championship Golf at Carnoustie, which will again host the Open Championship in 2007, now synonymous with internationally renowned golfing destinations like St Andrews and Gleneagles.

For more details call 01382 527527 or visit www.angusanddundee.co.uk/www.visitscotland.com

Argyll & Bute

Port Appin, Appin, Argyll PA38 4DF
Tel: 01631 730236 • Fax: 01631 730535
e-mail: airds@airds-hotel.com • www.airds-hotel.com

For breathtaking mountain and loch views and a stupendous cuisine that is a gourmet's dream, this neat, tidy and homely hotel is an aesthetic delight. Flowers are everywhere, sitting rooms are hung with romantic, gold-framed prints, books fill alcoves and fires blaze and crackle all day long. Bedrooms are stylishly furnished and possess what can only be described as thoughtful niceties and some of the bathrooms are almost as large as the bedrooms they serve. Through gabled windows, the eye is enchanted by views of the distant mountains of Morvern, seemingly rising out of the sea. Walkers thrill to the possibilities of a varied terrain from rugged paths to strolls through carpets of wild flowers.

LICENSED. 11 BEDROOMS, ALL WITH PRIVATE BATHROOMS, PLUS ONE COTTAGE (2 BEDROOMS).
CHILDREN WELCOME, PETS BY ARRANGEMENT.
CIVIL WEDDING CEREMONIES. OBAN 19 MILES. S££££, D££££.

Cairndow, Argyll PA26 8BN
Tel: 01499 600286 • Fax: 01499 600220
www.cairndow.com

Across the Arrochar Alps at the head of Loch Fyne, this historic coaching inn enjoys a perfect position. All bedrooms are en suite with TV, radio, central heating, tea/coffee and direct-dial phone. Two de luxe bedrooms with king-size beds and two-person spa bath are available. Dine by candlelight in our Stables Restaurant; bar meals and drinks served all day. Ideal centre for touring Western Highlands and Trossachs. Amenities include a loch-side beer garden, sauna, multi-gym, solarium; half-price green fees at Inveraray Golf Course.

Scottish Tourist Board ★★★ INN

LICENSED. 12 BEDROOMS, ALL WITH PRIVATE BATHROOMS. CHILDREN WELCOME. LEISURE FACILITIES.
ARROCHAR 12 MILES, INVERARAY 10. S££, D££.

Rockhill Waterside Country House

Est 1960 **Ardbrecknish, By Dalmally, Argyll PA33 1BH**

Tel: 01866 833218

17th century guest house in spectacular waterside setting on Loch Awe with breathtaking views to Ben Cruachan, where comfort, peace and tranquillity reign supreme.

Small private Highland estate breeding Hanoverian competition horses. 1200 metres free trout fishing. Five delightful rooms with all modern facilities. First-class highly acclaimed home cooking with much home-grown produce. Wonderful area for touring the Western Highlands, Glencoe, the Trossachs and Kintyre. Ideal for climbing, walking, bird and animal watching. Boat trips locally and from Oban (30 miles) to Mull, Iona, Fingal's Cave and other islands.

Dogs' Paradise! ***Also Self-Catering Cottages***

FIVE BEDROOMS. PETS WELCOME. LEISURE FACILITIES. OBAN 30 MILES.

Bay House Hotel

West Bay, Dunoon PA23 7HU

Tel: 01369 704832

A warm welcome awaits you at Bay House Hotel from owners Linda and Rick Murry. The small, non-smoking, family-run hotel is situated on the traffic-free West Bay Promenade with spectacular views of the Firth of Clyde and the islands of Arran, Bute and the Cumbraes.

The Hotel is an ideal base for touring the Cowal Peninsula and surrounding areas. The locality boasts some of the finest scenery in Scotland with ample opportunities for walking, cycling, golf, bowls and sightseeing. The lochs provide more amazing sights, with the mountains providing the striking backdrop.

• 6 bedrooms, all en suite (3 with sea views) • Guest lounge with magnificent views • Dining room serving breakfast • Residential licence

www.bayhousehotel.co.uk • info@bayhousehotel.co.uk

OPEN ALL YEAR. RESIDENTIAL LICENCE. 6 BEDROOMS, ALL WITH PRIVATE BATHROOMS. CHILDREN WELCOME. GOUROCK 4 MILES (BY FERRY). S£, D£.

Enmore Hotel

Dunoon, Argyll PA23 8HH

Tel: 01369 702230 • Fax: 01369 702148

info@enmorehotel.co.uk • www.enmorehotel.co.uk

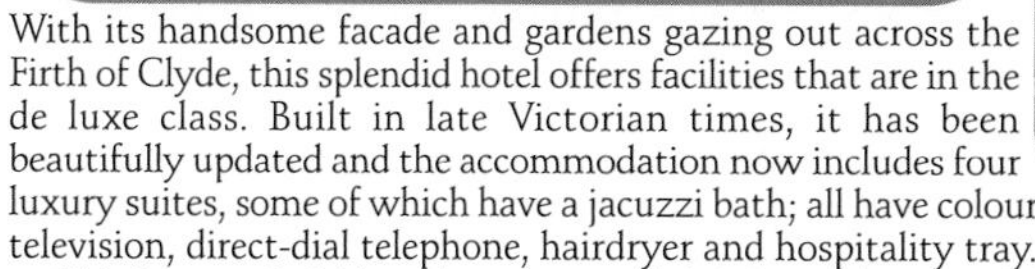

With its handsome facade and gardens gazing out across the Firth of Clyde, this splendid hotel offers facilities that are in the de luxe class. Built in late Victorian times, it has been beautifully updated and the accommodation now includes four luxury suites, some of which have a jacuzzi bath; all have colour television, direct-dial telephone, hairdryer and hospitality tray.

This is a wonderful base for a memorable holiday with so many diversions and activities readily at hand; squash, golf, riding, fishing and sailing, whilst Glasgow can easily be reached by ferry. Also within easy reach are such tourist attractions as Loch Lomond and the Cowal Peninsula.

OPEN ALL YEAR. FULLY LICENSED. 10 BEDROOMS, ALL WITH PRIVATE BATHROOMS. CHILDREN AND PETS WELCOME. CIVIL WEDDING CEREMONIES. GOUROCK 4 MILES (BY FERRY). S£££/££££, D££/££££.

The Falls of Lora Hotel

Connel Ferry, By Oban PA37 1PB

You are sure to receive a warm and friendly welcome at this Victorian hotel, overlooking Loch Etive, and only 5 miles from Oban - 'The gateway to the Highlands and Islands'.

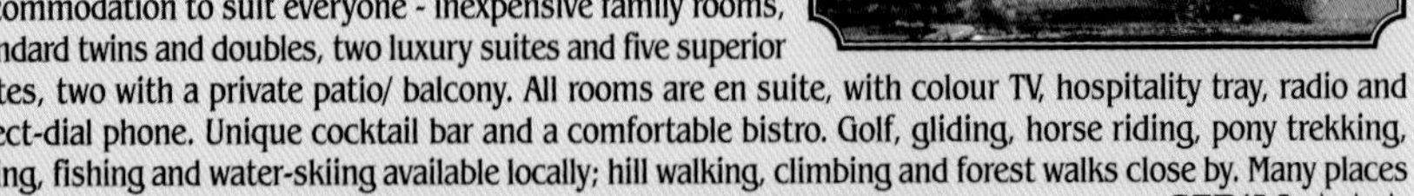

Accommodation to suit everyone - inexpensive family rooms, standard twins and doubles, two luxury suites and five superior suites, two with a private patio/ balcony. All rooms are en suite, with colour TV, hospitality tray, radio and direct-dial phone. Unique cocktail bar and a comfortable bistro. Golf, gliding, horse riding, pony trekking, diving, fishing and water-skiing available locally; hill walking, climbing and forest walks close by. Many places of interest to visit, or you can just relax in the peace and quiet of Connel. **STB/AA ★★★**

Tel: 01631 710483 • Fax: 01631 710694 • e-mail: enquiries@fallsoflora.com • www.fallsoflora.com

FULLY LICENSED. 30 BEDROOMS, ALL WITH PRIVATE BATHROOMS. NON-SMOKING ACCOMMODATION AVAILABLE. CHILDREN AND PETS WELCOME. OBAN 5 MILES. S££/£££, D£/££/£££.

Nestling beside Loch Feochan, this privately owned and family-run hotel offers a warm and friendly atmosphere. All rooms have private facilities and views of the countryside or the loch. There is a well stocked bar, extensive wine list, and fine restaurant. Children are welcome, and well behaved dogs by arrangement.

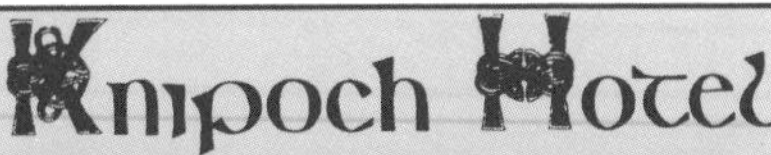

By Oban, Argyll PA34 4QT
Tel: 01852 316251
e-mail: reception@knipochhotel.co.uk
www.knipochhotel.co.uk

There are many delightful walks in the area, and excursions and tours to the outlying islands. Oban is only 6 miles from the hotel. Special Spring and Autumn Breaks available.

FULLY LICENSED. 22 BEDROOMS, ALL WITH PRIVATE BATHROOMS. CHILDREN AND PETS WELCOME. OBAN 6 MILES.

Roineabhal COUNTRY HOUSE

Kilchrenan, Taynuilt, Argyll PA35 1HD
Tel: 01866 833207 • Fax: 01866 833477
e-mail: maria@roineabhal.com • www.roineabhal.com

A luxurious country retreat of original character, set in the magical glens of Argyll, close to the shores of Loch Awe (the longest loch in Scotland) offering much more than Bed and Breakfast in superior country house accommodation with the very best in Scottish/Continental fare. In these secluded surroundings under the care of Roger, Maria and family you will uncover a unique short stay experience. Please visit our website or call for more details.

Scottish TOURIST BOARD ★★★★ B&B

3 BEDROOMS, ALL WITH PRIVATE BATHROOMS. CHILDREN WELCOME. BONAWE 1/2 MILE. S£££/££££, D£££/££££.

Ayrshire & Arran

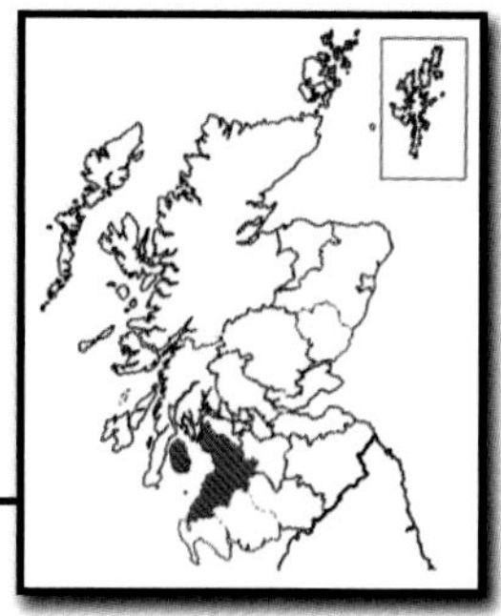

M
Experience for yourself
what has been created here

MOORPARK HOUSE, KILBIRNIE, AYRSHIRE KA25 7LD
TEL: 01505 683503
e-mail: reception@moorparkhouse.co.uk
www.moorparkhouse.co.uk

Recently having undergone a multi-million pound refurbishment, this welcoming country house offers superb amenities in a luxurious setting.

Each individually styled bedroom has the most up-to-date facilities including satellite TV, computer, fax, and luxury bathroom. The emphasis is on fine dining, and the restaurant is open to the public for morning coffee, lunch, afternoon tea and dinner.

All types of functions are catered for, from intimate dinners to weddings and conferences.

OPEN ALL YEAR. FULLY LICENSED. 12 BEDROOMS, ALL WITH PRIVATE BATHROOMS.
CHILDREN AND PETS WELCOME. CONFERENCE FACILITIES. CIVIL WEDDING CEREMONIES.
GLASGOW 30 MINS DRIVE. S££££, D££££.

Ayshire & Arran

Few places can boast a heritage like Ayrshire and Arran. Culzean Castle, designed by the famous architect Robert Adam, sits proudly on the edge of a steep cliff. Dundonald Castle, a little further north, was the ancestral home of the Stewart Kings over 600 years ago, and astunning array of medieval arms and armoury displayed at Dean Castle in Kilmarnock betray a lively and rebellious past, as do the scattering of ruins that punctuate the landscape. The many Heritage Centres, museums and attractions chart the history of the region – the Isle of Arran Heritage Museum portrays island life until the present, the smallest Cathedral in Europe can be visited on the Isle of Cumbrae, and The Burns National Heritage Park celebrates the life and works of Scotland's national poet.

Ayrshire and Arran has always held a special affinity with families and this is reflected in the many fun attractions and activities geared towards children. These include farm parks, theme parks with daring funfair rides, and many sports and leisure centres. Older visitors may enjoy a visit to Ayr Racecourse, enjoy a shopping spree, or treat themselves to a round on one the areas 44 golf courses.

Dumfries & Galloway

The Urr Valley Hotel

A privately owned hotel set in 14 acres of mature woodland and gardens within walking distance of Castle Douglas. Galloway is one of the most beautiful and diverse areas of countryside in Britain - offering everything from golden sandy beaches to grouse moors, and picturesque harbour villages to forest walks. Panelled walls, log fires and a cosy Sportsman's Bar with over 50 whiskies to offer. 17 en suite rooms, with colour TV, tea & coffee making facilities, hairdryer, trouser press and direct dial telephone.

Fabulous Wedding Venue • Conferences
Special Occasions • Holidays,
Short Breaks and Fine Dining.
Open all year.
WIFI Complimentary

Ernespie Road, Castle Douglas,
Dumfries & Galloway DG7 3JG
Tel: 01556 502188 • Fax: 01556 504055
e-mail: info@urrvalleyhotel.com
www.urrvalleyhotel.com

OPEN ALL YEAR. FULLY LICENSED. 17 BEDROOMS, ALL WITH PRIVATE BATHROOMS. CHILDREN WELCOME. CONFERENCE FACILITIES. CIVIL WEDDING CEREMONIES. KIRKCUDBRIGHT 9 MILES. S££, D££.

Set in 45 acres of woodland, Friars Carse, with its magnificent panelled entrance hall and elegant staircase, offers guests a warm welcome. The 21 en suite bedrooms have remote-control TV, telephone, hairdryer and tea/coffee facilities. The Whistle Restaurant serves excellent local cuisine, with an extensive wine list.

- Private fishing on a mile of the River Nith
- Panelled snooker room
- 9-hole putting green
- Golf and cycling can be arranged nearby
- Close to the border between Scotland and England, 6 miles from Dumfries on the A76

Scottish Tourist Board ★★★ Country House Hotel

www.pofr.com

Friars Carse

COUNTRY HOUSE HOTEL

Auldgirth, Dumfries DG2 0SA
Tel: 01387 740388 • Fax: 01387 740550
e-mail: fc@pofr.co.uk

OPEN ALL YEAR. FULLY LICENSED. 21 BEDROOMS, ALL WITH PRIVATE BATHROOMS. CHILDREN,WELCOME, PETS BY ARRANGEMENT. LEISURE FACILITIES. CONFERENCE FACILITIES. CIVIL WEDDING CEREMONIES. DUMFRIES 6 MILES.

GRETNA CHASE HOTEL Sark Bridge, Gretna DG16 5JB

Tel: 01461 337517 • Fax: 01461 337766
e-mail: enquiries@gretnachase.co.uk
www.gretnachase.co.uk

A lure for the romantically minded, this beautifully furnished little hotel is beset by glorious gardens which engender the mood and there are lovely views across the Solway Firth. Everything about the house exudes quality, comfort and a feeling of relaxed togetherness, from the cosy lounges to the spacious bedrooms with their attractive fabrics and selection of brass, half-tester and four-poster beds, the latter in the Bridal Suite. Love is in the air! The hotel has a peerless reputation for its imaginative cuisine, featuring home-grown vegetables and locally caught salmon, meals being served in a sizeable and pleasant dining room. The beginning of a lasting dream for many!

FULLY LICENSED. 20 BEDROOMS, ALL WITH PRIVATE BATHROOMS. CHILDREN WELCOME. CARLISLE 16 MILES. S££££, D££££.

Lockerbie Manor

COUNTRY HOTEL

Set in 78 acres, the hotel is a peaceful place for a relaxed getaway. Indulge yourself in a four poster en suite room. Enjoy the history, shopping and sights of the area. Perfectly situated for easy travel from all over the UK. The hotel is less than two miles from junction 17 of the M74 in Dumfries and Galloway, Southern Scotland. Ideal venue for a Scottish wedding close to Gretna Green or as a base for a golfing break.

BORELAND RD, LOCKERBIE DG11 2RG • Tel: 01576 202610/203939 • Fax: 01576 203046
e-mail: info@lockerbiemanorhotel.co.uk • www.lockerbiemanorhotel.co.uk

FULLY LICENSED. 32 BEDROOMS, ALL WITH PRIVATE BATHROOM. PETS WELCOME. CONFERENCE FACILITIES. CIVIL WEDDING CEREMONIES. CARLISLE 22 MILES. GRETNA 12 MILES.

Creebridge House Hotel

Set in 3 acres of idyllic gardens and woodland, just 2 minutes walk from the town. Golf and fishing nearby. Walkers and cyclists welcome.

Newton Stewart DG8 6NP
01671 402121
e-mail: info@creebridge.co.uk
www.creebridge.co.uk

OPEN ALL YEAR. LICENSED. 18 BEDROOMS, ALL WITH PRIVATE BATHROOMS. CHILDREN WELCOME, PETS BY ARRANGEMENT. WIGTOWN 7 MILES.

Edinburgh & Lothians

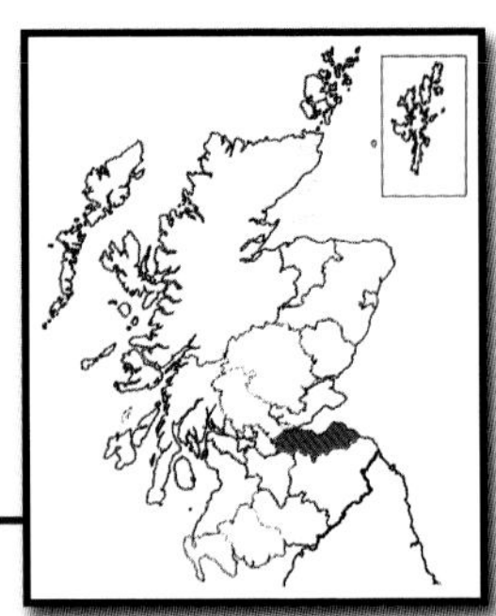

EDINBURGH & LOTHIANS

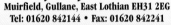

Scotland's Capital is home to a wide range of attractions offering something to visitors of all ages. The annual Festival in August is part of the city's tradition and visitors flock to enjoy the performing arts, theatre, ballet, cinema and music, and of course "The Tattoo" itself. Other festivals and entertainments take place throughout the year, including children's festivals, science festivals, the famous Royal Highland Show and the Hogmanay street party.

East Lothian has beautiful countryside and dramatic coastline, all only a short distance from Edinburgh. Once thriving fishing villages, North Berwick and Dunbar now cater for visitors who delight in their traditional seaside charm. In Midlothian you can step back in time with a visit to Rosslyn Chapel or Borthwick and Crichton Castles, all dating from the 15th century, or seize the chance to brush up on your swing at Melville Golf Range and Course. filler

Fife

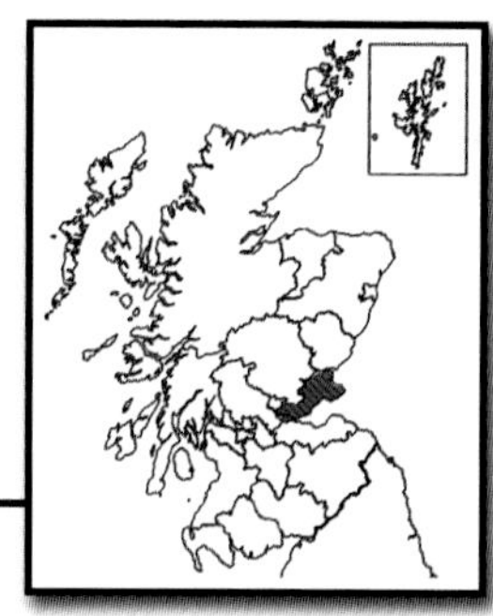

Fernie Castle Hotel

Letham, Near Cupar, Fife KY15 7RU
Tel: 01337 810381 • Fax: 01337 810422

Fernie Castle is superbly situated for golf, shooting and fishing, which can be arranged locally. Edinburgh 40 minutes, Dundee 20 and Perth 30. Set in 17 acres of mature woodland with a private loch, the hotel has excellent, comfortably appointed rooms, all with private bath, and a first-class reputation for food and wine. You can relax over an aperitif in the historic 'Keep Bar' and enjoy dinner in the elegant 'Auld Alliance' dining room.

AA ★★★
RAC ★★★ Hotel

e-mail: mail@ferniecastle.demon.co.uk
www.ferniecastle.demon.co.uk

FULLY LICENSED. 20 BEDROOMS, ALL WITH PRIVATE BATHROOMS.
CHILDREN AND PETS WELCOME. CONFERENCE FACILITIES. CUPAR 4 MILES. S£££, D£££.

Eden House Hotel

2 Pitscottie Road, Cupar, Fife KY15 4HF

The hotel is a Victorian Town House dating from 1876, enjoying a truly superb elevated position overlooking the Haugh Park in the centre of Cupar, one of the oldest burghs in Scotland.
Personal care, attention and the warmest of welcomes awaits.

Tel: 01334 652510
Fax: 01334 652277
mail@edenhousehotel.co.uk
www.edenhousehotel.co.uk

OPEN ALL YEAR. FULLY LICENSED. 11 BEDROOMS, ALL WITH PRIVATE BATHROOMS.
NON-SMOKING ACCOMMODATION AVAILABLE. CHILDREN AND PETS WELCOME.
GLENROTHES 10 MILES. S££, D£.

FREE or REDUCED RATE entry to Holiday Visits and Attractions – see our **READERS' OFFER VOUCHERS** on pages 149-172

Highlands

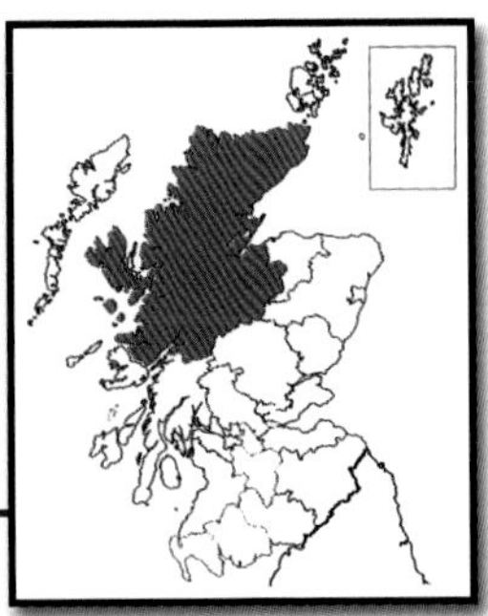

Apart from the stunning scenery, the major attraction of

THE SCOTTISH HIGHLANDS is that there is so much to see and do, whatever the season, Stretching from Fort William in the south, to Wick in the far north, there is a wealth of visitor attractions and facilities. Loch Ness, home of the famous monster, is perhaps the most famous of these attractions and the Loch Ness Visitor Centre also provides a variety of souvenirs, including kilts and whisky, The Clansman Centre, The Rare Breeds Park and The Caledonian Canal Heritage Centre are also worth a visit. Fort William in the Western Highlands is a busy town with a wide range of shops and services, pubs, restaurants and Scottish entertainment. The West Highland Museum in the town illustrates the tale of Bonnie Prince Charlie and the Jacobites. The North West Highlands is home to the Nations first Geopark, underlining the importance of the area's geological past. The famous Inverewe Gardens with its wonderful array of foreign plants, more formal borders and lovely views everywhere is worth a visit at any season. John O'Groats is, of course, the ultimate destination of most travellers as it was for the Norsemen centuries ago, whose heritage is preserved in the Northlands Viking Centre at Auckengill. The main towns in this sparsely populated area are Dornoch, Golspie, Brora and Helmsdale.

Opportunities exist throughout the Highlands for all kinds of water sports, and the Caledonian Canal is ideal for cruising holidays, or yachting. Other activities include walking, cycling, pony trekking and golf, and anglers will find good sea fishing, as well as some great value day permits for fresh water fishing. filler

GLENFINNAN HOUSE HOTEL *(on facing page)*

FULLY LICENSED. 13 BEDROOMS, ALL WITH PRIVATE BATHROOMS.
CHILDREN AND PETS WELCOME. WEDDING CEREMONIES. FORT WILLIAM 15 MILES. S££, D£££.

Glenfinnan House Hotel

The North-West of Scotland is rich in history, legends, myth and magic...
...including the romantic story of Bonnie Prince Charlie

Glenfinnan House Hotel stands just around the bay from the tall monument to him on Loch Shiel, and the famous Glenfinnan viaduct railway bridge is a ten minute walk away through the Glenfinnan Estate, where red deer can often be seen.
The country house hotel is a fine stone mansion dating from 1755, passed down through the family of the original Jacobite owner for many generations, from the time of Culloden.

Today resident managers, Manja and Duncan Gibson, will welcome you into the delightful hall, with its blazing log fire and pine-panelled walls. Attractive public rooms include a Drawing Room and a cheery Bar where traditional music is often played.

The Dining Room offers à la carte dining with a wide choice of speciality signature dishes using local produce.

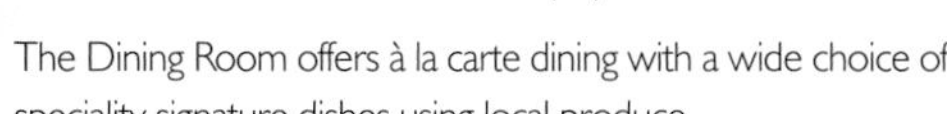

Charming bedrooms, many with a beautiful loch view, are furnished with terrific old mahogany and oak furniture, huge wardrobes and enormous chests of drawers. Select from a choice of Standard, Superior, Family Room, Family Suite (with adjoining bedrooms) or the Four-Poster Room.
You'll find fresh flowers, fruit and tea and coffee in each room.

The perfect venue for quiet breaks or romantic weekends, in the majestic setting of the historic Scottish Highlands.

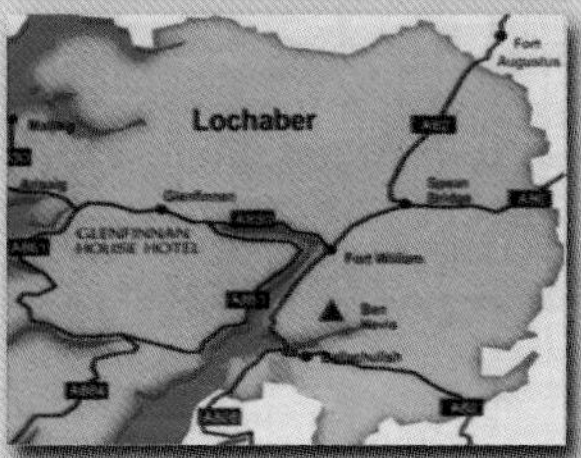

Glenfinnan House Hotel
Glenfinnan, By Fort William
Scottish Highlands PH37 4LT
Tel/Fax: 01397 722235
E-mail: availability@glenfinnanhouse.com
www.glenfinnanhouse.com

Beautifully situated on the shores of Loch Duich 15 miles south of the Skye Bridge.

Our 12 en suite bedrooms have recently been refurbished and most offer stunning views across the Loch.

Lunches, dinners and bar suppers are served daily using only fresh local produce.

Open all year round, ideally located whether you are an enthusiastic walker, or just wishing to enjoy the scenery and have a relaxing break.

FULLY LICENSED. 12 BEDROOMS, ALL WITH PRIVATE FACILITIES.
CHILDREN AND PETS WELCOME. CONFERENCE FACILITIES. KYLE OF LOCHALSH 8 MILES. S££, D££.

We will warmly welcome you and ensure that you enjoy your stay. Here you can combine all the modern comforts of a high quality hotel with the great outdoors of the Scottish Highlands, an Area of Outstanding Natural Beauty.

- *20 bedrooms with en suite bathroom, writing desk, mini-bar, hairdryer, TV, beverage-making facilities.*
- *Sample fine local whiskies, including Inver Lodge's own malt.*
- *Imaginative menus using fresh local produce - fish, meat & game.*
- *Facilities include snooker, billiards, sauna, sunbed, and gift shop.*

Scottish Tourist Board ★★★★ HOTEL

Lochinver, Sutherland IV27 4LU
Tel: 01571 844496 • Fax: 01571 844395
e-mail: stay@inverlodge.com
www.inverlodge.com

AA ★★★★

FULLY LICENSED. 20 BEDROOMS, ALL WITH PRIVATE BATHROOMS..
CHILDREN AND PETS WELCOME. LEISURE FACILITIES. ULLAPOOL 38 MILES. S££££, D££££.

Skerray, Tongue, Sutherland KW14 7TH

Set in a secluded Highland glen by the stunning River Borgie lies Borgie Lodge, where mouthwatering food, fine wine, roaring log fires and a very warm welcome await after a day's fishing, hill walking, pony trekking or walking on the beach. Relax after dinner with a good malt and tales of salmon, trout and deer.

Tel: 01641 521 332
www.borgielodgehotel.co.uk
e-mail: info@borgielodgehotel.co.uk

FULLY LICENSED. 8 BEDROOMS, ALL WITH PRIVATE FACILITIES. NON SMOKING ACCOMMODATION. CHILDREN AND PETS WELCOME. TONGUE 10 MILES. S£££, D££.

Lanarkshire

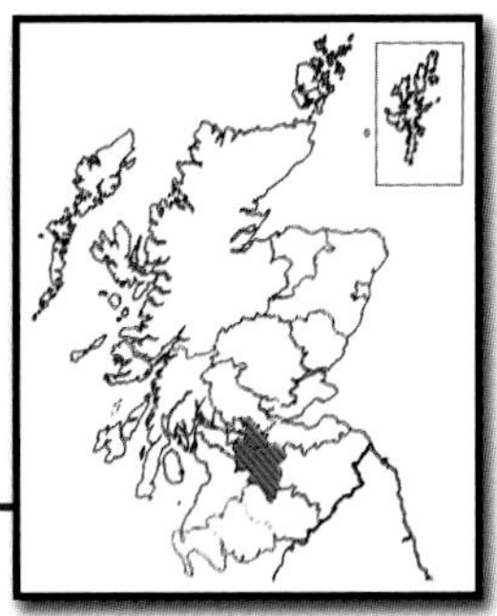

Quothquan, Biggar,
Lanarkshire ML12 6NA

Tel: 01899 220035 • Fax: 01899 221092

Extensively refurbished in recent years with the painstaking attention to detail that is the mark of a truly first-class establishment, Shieldhill has gained a reputation for excellence. 26 bedrooms and suites are available to suit all requirements, all individually decorated in beautiful wallpapers and fabrics and equipped to the highest standards. For that very special occasion, the magnificent Chancellor Suite offers a king-size bed and a double jacuzzi — truly the ultimate in romantic luxury! The generous menu features imaginative combinations of fresh ingredients and is accompanied by an out-of-the-ordinary wine list. All in all, this fine hotel is well worth tracking down.

e-mail: enquiries@shieldhill.co.uk • www.shieldhill.co.uk

OPEN ALL YEAR EXCEPT CHRISTMAS AND NEW YEAR. FULLY LICENSED. 26 BEDROOMS, ALL WITH PRIVATE BATHROOMS. CHILDREN AND PETS WELCOME. CONFERENCE FACILITIES. CIVIL WEDDING CEREMONIES. BIGGAR 13 MILES. S££££, D££££.

Prices

Normal Bed & Breakfast rate per person
(single room)

PRICE RANGE	CATEGORY
Under £40	S£
£40-£55	S££
£56-£70	S£££
Over £70	S££££

Normal Bed & Breakfast rate per person
(sharing double/twin room)

PRICE RANGE	CATEGORY
Under £40	D£
£40-£55	D££
£56-70	D£££
Over £70	D££££

This is meant as an indication only and does not show prices for Special Breaks, Weekends, etc. Guests are therefore advised to verify all prices on enquiring or booking.

Perth & Kinross

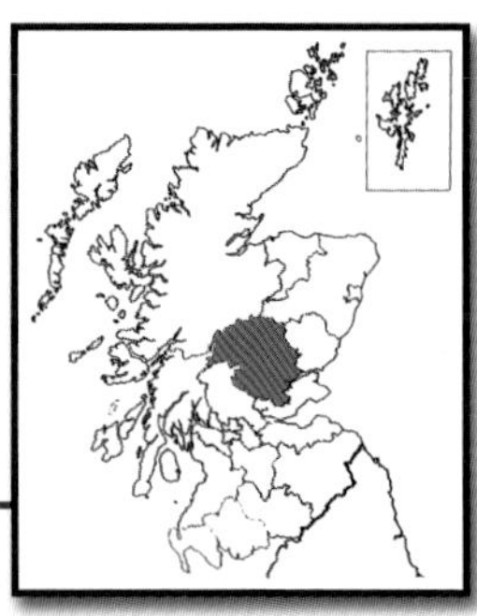

Fortingall Hotel

The award-winning four star Fortingall Hotel is set in the heart of the enchanting thatched village of Fortingall, in stunning Highland Perthshire. From the graceful surroundings of the dining room, to the luxury and comfort of the eleven en suite bedrooms, the Hotel offers 21st century comfort and service, whilst retaining its Victorian style and heritage. Combined with the peace and tranquillity of the area, the friendliness of the staff, and the delicious food, the Fortingall Hotel offers first class facilities in a fabulous setting, ensuring you have a memorable stay.

Fortingall, Aberfeldy, Perthshire PH15 2NQ
Tel/Fax: 01887 830367 e: hotel@fortingallhotel.com www.fortingallhotel.com

FULLY LICENSED. 11 BEDROOMS, ALL WITH PRIVATE BATHROOMS. CHILDREN WELCOME, PETS BY ARRANGEMENT. CIVIL WEDDING CEREMONIES. ABERFELDY 7 MILES. S££££, D££££.

Please note

All the information in this book is given in good faith in the belief that it is correct. However, the publishers cannot guarantee the facts given in these pages, neither are they responsible for changes in policy, ownership or terms that may take place after the date of going to press. Readers should always satisfy themselves that the facilities they require are available and that the terms, if quoted, still apply.

Looking for holiday accommodation?

for details of hundreds of properties
throughout the UK including
comprehensive coverage of all areas of Scotland try:

www.holidayguides.com

LANDS OF LOYAL HOTEL *(on facing page)*

LICENSED. 16 BEDROOMS, ALL WITH PRIVATE BATHROOMS.
CHILDREN WELCOME. CONFERENCE FACILITIES. BLAIRGOWRIE 5 MILES. S££££, D£££.

A tranquil haven of calm and relaxation...

This much respected country house has been a very prominent hotel in the heart of Scotland since 1945

❖ LANDS OF LOYAL HOTEL ❖

Set on a hillside overlooking the Vale of Strathmore to the Sidlaw Hills beyond, lies the Lands of Loyal luxury country house hotel. Built in the 1830s, this impressive Victorian Mansion is surrounded by six acres of tiered gardens.

The great hall, with its grand log fire, warms, welcomes and comforts guests on arrival. Regarded as a second home to our guests for many years, the hotel offers a tranquil haven of calm and relaxation in a hectic world.

Our highly acclaimed restaurant makes full use of local fish and game in a style which is both traditional and imaginative.

For the country sportsman fishing and shooting are available, with salmon and trout fishing in the loch and river. Pheasant and grouse shooting, wild fowling and deer stalking are also available as the seasons permit.

The hotel makes an ideal base for the ambitious golfer with 30 courses within an hour's drive, and is an ideal setting for weddings, meetings and functions.

Lands of Loyal Hotel, Alyth, Perthshire PH11 8JQ
Tel: 01828 633151 ❖ Fax: 01828 633313
e-mail: info@landsofloyal.com ❖ www.landsofloyal.com

The finest lochside Location in the Southern Highlands.

INVESTOR IN PEOPLE

The Four Seasons Hotel
St Fillans, Perthshire PH6 2NF
Tel: 01764 685 333 e-mail: sham@thefourseasonshotel.co.uk

FULLY LICENSED. 18 BEDROOMS, ALL WITH PRIVATE BATHROOMS.
NON-SMOKING ACCOMMODATION AVAILABLE. CHILDREN AND PETS WELCOME. CIVIL WEDDING CEREMONIES.
COMRIE 5 MILES. S£££, D££.

Kinclaven, Stanley PH1 4QN
Tel: 01250 883268
Fax: 01250 883396

Located on its own Perthshire estate, Ballathie House Hotel offers 41 bedrooms, each room elegantly furnished to the highest standards. Lodge-style rooms are also available with the grounds. Under the guidance of the Head Chef, the award-winning restaurant offers the finest Scottish produce in a stylish setting. The hotel is well placed to explore this scenic area, and Perth itself has a theatre, concert hall and specialist shopping.

e-mail: email@ballathiehousehotel.co.uk • www.ballathiehousehotel.co.uk

OPEN ALL YEAR. FULLY LICENSED. 41 BEDROOMS, ALL WITH PRIVATE BATHROOMS.
CHILDREN WELCOME. CONFERENCE FACILITIES. CIVIL WEDDING CEREMONIES. BLAIRGOWRIE 5 MILES.

A useful index of towns/counties appears on pages 173-174

Renfrewshire

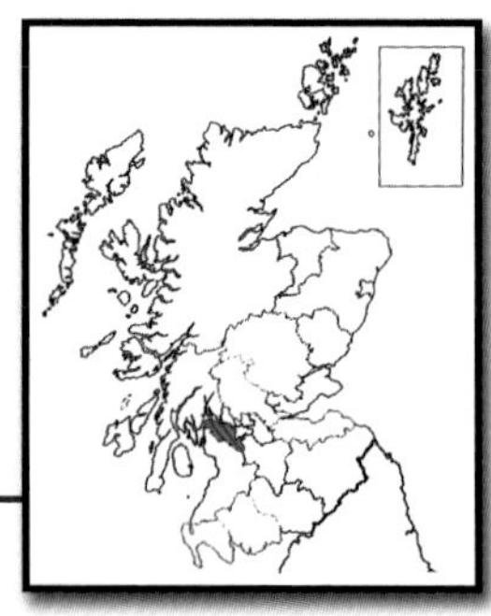

This 19th century Gothic Mansion is only a short drive from Glasgow Airport, Glasgow City Centre and Loch Lomond. 53 individually designed bedrooms and suites allow you to choose accommodation to suit your personal taste, your character and your mood. Each room has all the amenities one would expect of a luxury hotel, including a superb range of Aveda toiletries.

Light snacks and lunches are served in the comfort of the Grand Hall, while The Cristal fine dining restaurant offers the finest Scottish produce.

The hotel's convenient location makes it ideal for business meeting and functions, with 7 rooms able to accommodate 2-120 delegates.

The Aveda Concept Spa has 12 treatment rooms, hair and nail salon, swimming pool, gymnasium and relaxation lounge.

www.marhall.com

MAR HALL

Earl of Mar Estate, Bishopton,
Near Glasgow PA7 5NW
Tel: 0141 812 9999
Fax: 0141 812 9997
sales@marhall.com

OPEN ALL YEAR. FULLY LICENSED. 53 BEDROOMS, ALL WITH PRIVATE BATHROOMS.
LEISURE FACILITIES. CONFERENCE FACILITIES. CIVIL WEDDING CEREMONIES. GLASGOW AIRPORT 6 MILES.

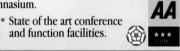

BOWFIELD HOTEL AND COUNTRY CLUB

Howwood, Renfrewshire PA9 1DZ

Tel: 01505 705225 • Fax: 01505 705230

Peacefully situated, yet only 15 minutes from Glasgow Airport, Bowfield offers quiet comfort, superb leisure facilities and an AA Rosette Restaurant, all within a relaxing country club atmosphere.

- Swimming pool, jacuzzi, sauna, steam room, health & beauty spa, squash courts and gymnasium.
- State of the art conference and function facilities.

enquiries@bowfieldcountryclub.co.uk
www.bowfieldcountryclub.co.uk

OPEN ALL YEAR. FULLY LICENSED. 23 BEDROOMS, ALL WITH PRIVATE BATHROOMS.
CHILDREN AND PETS WELCOME. LEISURE FACILITIES. CONFERENCE FACILITIES. CIVIL WEDDING CEREMONIES.
JOHNSTONE 3 MILES. S££££, D££.

Readers are requested to mention this FHG guidebook when seeking accommodation

Stirling & The Trossachs

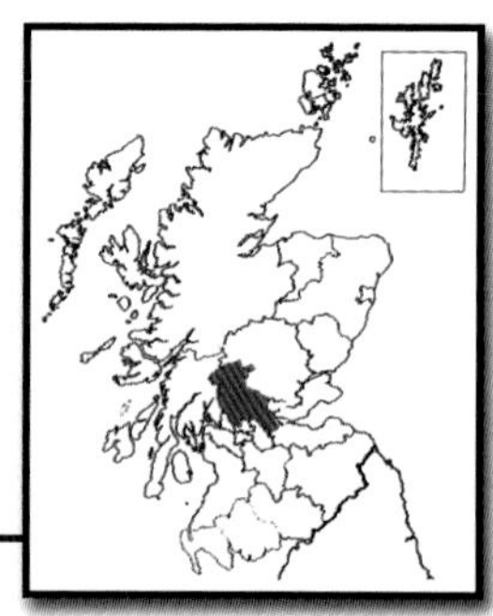

CULCREUCH CASTLE HOTEL & COUNTRY PARK

Fintry, Stirlingshire G63 0LW
Tel: 01360 860228/860555 • Fax: 01360 860556
e-mail: info@culcreuch.com • www.culcreuch.com

Standing four-square amidst beautiful scenery, Culcreuch Castle is a great survivor: built in 1296 it remains in remarkable condition. Part of a 1600-acre estate, it provides elegant accommodation for visitors to picturesque central Scotland and Loch Lomond, Stirling and the Trossachs in particular, whilst Glasgow may be reached in under half an hour.

The views from this fascinating place are breathtaking and within its stout walls are handsome furnished suites and bedrooms, some with four-posters. Some 200 yards from the castle is a new development of eight Scandinavian style holiday lodges. Guests may dine well in either the ornate, panelled Castle Restaurant or in the 700-year old Dungeon Diner in a far happier state of mind than previous occupants!

OPEN ALL YEAR. FULLY LICENSED. 14 BEDROOMS, ALL WITH PRIVATE BATHROOMS. CHILDREN WELCOME. CONFERENCE FACILITIES. CIVIL WEDDING CEREMONIES. BALFRON 5 MILES. S£££, D££££.

Publisher's note

While every effort is made to ensure accuracy, we regret that FHG Guides cannot accept responsibility for errors, misrepresentations or omissions in our entries or any consequences thereof. Prices in particular should be checked.

We will follow up complaints but cannot act as arbiters or agents for either party.

- A sympathetically converted Listed steading at the foot od the stunning Ochil Hills.
- Centrally located for tourists, business travellers or golfers.
- 11 comfortable en suite bedrooms.
- All day dining in colourful courtyard restaurant.

- Conferences, weddings and social functions catered for.
- Marquee can be erected for larger numbers.
- Special D,B&B weekend rates.
- YiFi available.
- Winner of UKFX Tourism Best Hotel 2004 Award.

THE HARVIESTOUN COUNTRY HOTEL & RESTAURANT
Dollar Road, Tillicoultry, Clackmannanshire FK13 6PQ
Tel: 01259 752522 • Fax: 01259 752523
e-mail: harviestounhotel@aol.com • www.harviestouncountryhotel.com

Scottish Tourist Board ★★★ SMALL HOTEL

LICENSED. 11 BEDROOMS, ALL WITH PRIVATE BATHROOM. CONFERENCE FACILITIES. CIVIL WEDDING CEREMONIES. ALLOA 3 MILES.

Prices

Normal Bed & Breakfast rate per person
(single room)

PRICE RANGE	CATEGORY
Under £40	S£
£40-£55	S££
£56-£70	S£££
Over £70	S££££

Normal Bed & Breakfast rate per person
(sharing double/twin room)

PRICE RANGE	CATEGORY
Under £40	D£
£40-£55	D££
£56-70	D£££
Over £70	D££££

This is meant as an indication only and does not show prices for Special Breaks, Weekends, etc. Guests are therefore advised to verify all prices on enquiring or booking.

Scottish Islands

Away from it all in the truest sense, this fine hotel provides a wonderful opportunity to commune with nature in peaceful surroundings and enjoy some of the best loch fishing in Britain and, what is more, the cuisine is really out of this world.
Guest rooms are delightfully furnished; all have en suite facilities, colour TV, direct-dial telephone, tea-makers and appointments that would shame many a 5-star establishment. Standing on the shores of Harray Loch, the emphasis here, naturally enough, is on fishing and many major events are held. Novices are welcomed and boats, outboards and ghillies may be arranged. The views from the hotel are breathtaking and other activities available include golf, squash and rock climbing.

Loch Harray, Orkney KW17 2LF • Tel: 01856 771366 • Fax: 01856 771515
merkister-hotel@ecosse.net • www.merkister.com

FULLY LICENSED. 13 BEDROOMS, ALL WITH PRIVATE BATHROOMS. 3 SUPERIOR TERRACED SUITES. CHILDREN AND PETS WELCOME.
LEISURE FACILITIES. STROMNESS 10 MILES. S££, D££.

GLENVIEW HOTEL

CULNACNOC, STAFFIN, SKYE IV51 9JH

- 01470 562248 -

Traditional island house, ideally situated for exploring North East Skye. Comfortable en suite bedrooms. Restaurant renowned for fresh seafood and traditional home cooking. Pets most welcome.

Which? Best B&B. *IAN STRATTON & DOREEN HARBEN*

e-mail: enquiries@glenviewskye.co.uk • www.glenviewskye.co.uk

OPEN ALL YEAR. FULLY LICENSED. 5 BEDROOMS, ALL WITH PRIVATE BATHROOMS.
NON-SMOKING ACCOMMODATION AVAILABLE. PETS WELCOME. STAFFIN 4 MILES. S££/£££, D£/££.

Wales

Ratings & Awards

For the first time ever the AA, VisitBritain, VisitScotland, and the Wales Tourist Board will use a single method of assessing and rating serviced accommodation. Irrespective of which organisation inspects an establishment the rating awarded will be the same, using a common set of standards, giving a clear guide of what to expect. The RAC is no longer operating an Hotel inspection and accreditation business.

Accommodation Standards: Star Grading Scheme

Using a scale of 1-5 stars the objective quality ratings give a clear indication of accommodation standard, cleanliness, ambience, hospitality, service and food, This shows the full range of standards suitable for every budget and preference, and allows visitors to distinguish between the quality of accommodation and facilities on offer in different establishments. All types of board and self-catering accommodation are covered, including hotels,
B&Bs, holiday parks, campus accommodation, hostels, caravans and camping, and boats.

The more stars, the higher level of quality

★★★★★
exceptional quality, with a degree of luxury

★★★★
excellent standard throughout

★★★
very good level of quality and comfort

★★
good quality, well presented and well run

★
acceptable quality; simple, practical, no frills

VisitBritain and the regional tourist boards, enjoyEngland.com, VisitScotland and VisitWales, and the AA have full details of the grading system on their websites

enjoyEngland.com
★★★★ FARMHOUSE

visitScotland.com
Scottish TOURIST BOARD ★★★ HOTEL

visitWales.com
GWESTY ★★★ HOTEL

AA ★★★ Guest Accommodation
theAA.com

National Accessible Scheme

If you have particular mobility, visual or hearing needs, look out for the National Accessible Scheme. You can be confident of finding accommodation or attractions that meet your needs by looking for the following symbols.

 Typically suitable for a person with sufficient mobility to climb a flight of steps but would benefit from fixtures and fittings to aid balance

 Typically suitable for a person with restricted walking ability and for those that may need to use a wheelchair some of the time and can negotiate a maximum of three steps

 Typically suitable for a person who depends on the use of a wheelchair and transfers unaided to and from the wheelchair in a seated position. This person may be an independent traveller

 Typically suitable for a person who depends on the use of a wheelchair in a seated position. This person also requires personal or mechanical assistance (eg carer, hoist).

Anglesey & Gwynedd

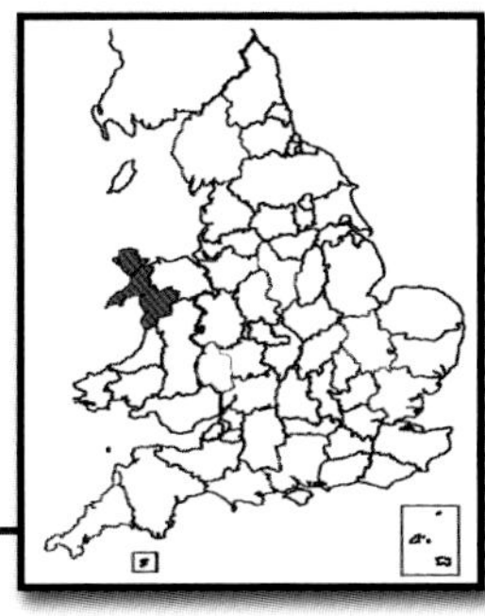

A warm welcome and spectacular scenery awaits you at this former Welsh Manor House, set in 20 acres of mountainside and gardens.

- 11 tastefully decorated bedrooms, all en suite, with tea/coffee making facilities, hairdryers and radio alarms.
- De luxe rooms with extra comforts, plus superb views
- Four-course dinner menu using fresh local produce
- Breakfasts feature a traditional Welsh Grill as well as lighter options.
- Interesting wine list, including two from Wales.
- Cosy bar, new conservatory, TV lounge
- Short walk from the village of Beddgelert in the heart of Snowdonia.

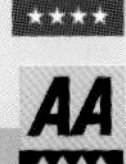

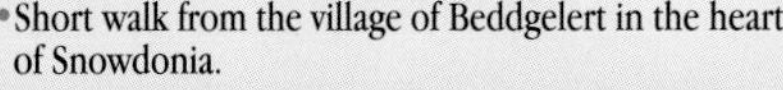

SYGUN FAWR COUNTRY HOUSE • Beddgelert, Gwynedd LL55 4NE
Tel & Fax: 01766 890258 • e-mail: sygunfawr@aol.com • www.sygunfawr.co.uk

RESIDENTIAL LICENCE. 11 BEDROOMS, ALL WITH PRIVATE BATHROOMS.
CHILDREN AND PETS WELCOME. CAERNARFON 12 MILES. S££, D£/££.

Bryn Eglwys Country House Hotel

Beddgelert, Gwynedd LL55 4NB
Tel: 01766 510260 • Fax: 01766 890485

This former Georgian farmhouse stands within Snowdonia National Park, with superb views of the River Glaslyn and Moel Hebog. The en suite bedrooms are comfortable and well equipped, with TV and tea/coffee making. Freshly prepared local produce is served in the restaurant and guests can relax in the comfortable lounge or in the small intimate bar.
With popular walking routes nearby, this is an ideal base for exploring this scenic area.

e-mail: bryneglwys@btinternet.com • www.bryneglwyshotel.co.uk

LICENSED. ALL BEDROOMS WITH PRIVATE BATHROOMS. CHILDREN WELCOME. CAERNARVON 12 MILES.

DOLSERAU HALL
COUNTRY HOUSE HOTEL

- A lovely Victorian Country House Hotel, set in the beautiful hills of Southern Snowdonia.
- Guests are assured of peace and quiet, even in high season, along with old-fashioned service in traditional surroundings. No children under 12 years.
- 15 bedrooms in Main House and 5 in Coach House (pets welcome). Lift to second floor of Main House.
- Bedrooms and public rooms non-smoking.
- Daily-changing dinner menu featuring local meat and produce; special diets can be catered for.

AA ★★★

www.dolserau.co.uk

Resident Proprietors: **Tim & Susan Langdon, Dolserau Hall Hotel, Dolgellau LL40 2AG**

Tel: 01341 422522 • Fax: 01341 422400 • e-mail: welcome@dolserau.co.uk

FULLY LICENSED. 20 BEDROOMS, ALL WITH PRIVATE BATHROOM. TOTALLY NON-SMOKING.
PETS WELCOME. BALA 17 MILES.

Fronoleu Country Hotel

Lounge and bar, both with log fires.
11 well appointed bedrooms, all en suite and some with four-poster beds.
Restaurant offering a wide selection of delicious dishes, lunchtimes and evenings. Only the finest cuts of Welsh lamb, beef and game in season are used, as well as local fish.
Extensive selection of wines.
Traditional breakfast served.

Surrounded by wild Welsh beauty, overlooking the magnificent Mawddach Estuary, combining traditional warmth with modern comfort.

Tabor, Dolgellau LL40 2PS
Tel: 01341 422361 • Fax: 01341 422023
e-mail: fronoleu@fronoleu.co.uk • www.fronoleu.co.uk

LICENSED. 11 BEDROOMS, ALL WITH PRIVATE BATHROOM. CHILDREN AND PETS WELCOME. BALA 17 MILES.

Bryn Artro Country House

Llanbedr, Gwynedd LL45 2LE • Tel: 01341 241619

★★★★ AA ★★★★

Built in a bygone age as a gentleman's country residence, Bryn Artro Country Residence offers a slower pace of life which harks to the days of the stagecoach travelling over uneven roads from villages to towns, dropping off weary travellers for a welcome rest in comfortable surroundings. The guest house itself has been sympathetically restored to retain a friendly and homely atmosphere. Licensed restaurant, bar meals available; vegetarian menu and other dietary requirements catered for. Cyclists, motorcyclists and walkers are welcome; activity weekends can be arranged.

www.llanbedr-brynartro.com/ • e-mail: julie@llanbedr-brynartro.com

OPEN ALL YEAR. RESIDENTIAL LICENCE. 7 BEDROOMS, ALL WITH PRIVATE BATHROOMS.
CHILDREN WELCOME. HARLECH 3 MILES. S££, D£.

Gwesty Minffordd Hotel

Tel: 01654 761665
Fax: 01654 761517

Talyllyn, Tywyn, Gwynedd LL36 9AJ

This 17th century Drovers' Inn offers today's traveller all modern comforts. There is a mixture of old and new style centrally heated bedrooms, and three lounges with log fires for relaxation. The delicious meals on offer use local Welsh produce, organic vegetables, Welsh flavourings and are cooked on an Aga. With the Cader Idris Path starting from the door, this Hotel is ideal for walking, touring or sightseeing. The Talyllyn Lake, Dolgoch Falls and the Centre for Alternative Technology are within five miles. Further afield there are beaches and fishing ports, but whatever your taste you will find a real welcome (or Croeso in Welsh) upon your return.

Perhaps that is why guests return year after year.

GWESTY ★★★ HOTEL

e-mail: hotel@minffordd.com • www.minffordd.com

OPEN ALL YEAR. FULLY LICENSED. 7 BEDROOMS, ALL WITH PRIVATE BATHROOM. MACHYNLLETH 10 MILES. S££, D££.

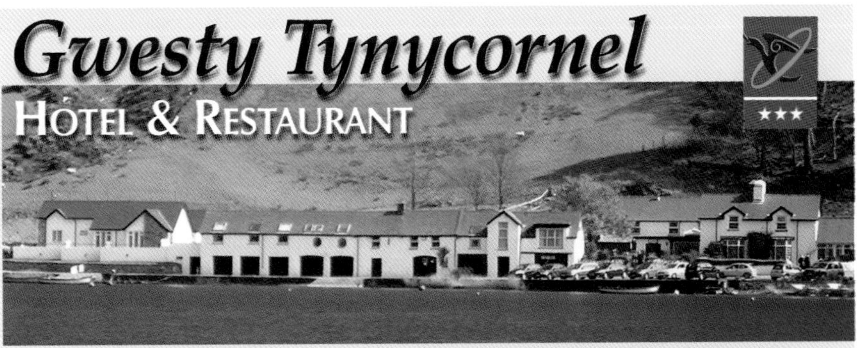

Tynycornel Hotel is set in a spectacular scenic location on the shores of its own lake at the foot of Cader Idris in Snowdonia National Park.

We offer a warm friendly welcome, high standards of accommodation, cuisine and service. We only use the freshest ingredients and source local produce wherever possible. Special diets catered for. 22 en suite bedrooms with lake or garden views. Totally a non-smoking hotel. Fly fishing for brown trout available on Talyllyn Lake.

Talyllyn, Tywyn, Gwynedd LL36 9AJ
Tel: 01654 782282 • Fax: 01654 782679
e-mail: reception@tynycornel.co.uk • www.tynycornel.co.uk

FULLY LICENSED. 22 BEDROOMS, ALL WITH PRIVATE BATHROOMS.
NON-SMOKING ACCOMMODATION AVAILABLE. CHILDREN WELCOME.
LEISURE FACILITIES CONFERENCE FACILITIES. CIVIL WEDDING CEREMONIES. TYWYN 8 MILES. S££, D££.

North Wales

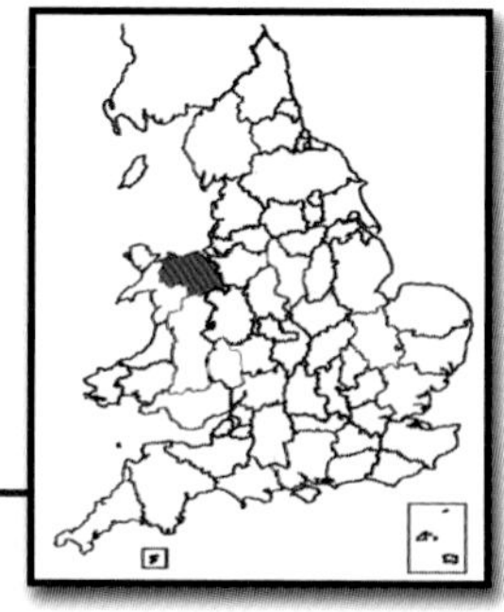

Truly individual ... truly magical ...
an extraordinary, romantic and historic hotel.

Only 23 miles from Chester, and situated by the River Clwyd, amongst acres of landscaped gardens, parkland and woods. All bedrooms have en suite bathroom and/or shower, many with four-poster bed and antique furniture. Gym and small health suite. Award-winning, creatively designed food served in a setting that suits romance, small business groups and celebration dinners. Ideally situated for exploring the North Wales coast, Snowdonia and Chester.

Choice of leisure and seasonal breaks available, including golf and beauty treatments. Well equipped conference centre.

Ruthin Castle, Ruthin, Denbighshire LL15 2NU • Tel: 01824 702664 • Fax: 01824 703435
www.ruthincastle.com • e-mail: reservations@ruthincastle.com

OPEN ALL YEAR. FULLY LICENSED. 62 BEDROOMS, ALL WITH PRIVATE BATHROOMS.
CHILDREN WELCOME. LEISURE FACILITIES. CONFERENCE FACILITIES. CIVIL WEDDING CEREMONIES.
WREXHAM 14 MILES. S££££, D£££/££££.

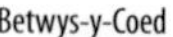
Betwys-y-Coed

Pembrokeshire

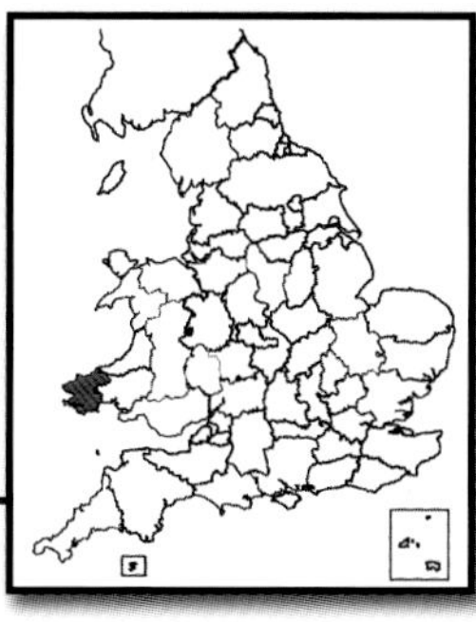

PEMBROKESHIRE'S entire coastline is a designated National Park, with its sheltered coves and wooded estuaries, fine sandy beaches and some of the most dramatic cliffs in Britain. The islands of Skomer, Stokholm and Grasholm are home to thousands of seabirds, and Ramsey Island, as well as being an RSPB Reserve boasts the second largest grey seal colony in Britain. Pembrokeshire's mild climate and the many delightful towns and villages, family attractions and outdoor facilities such as surfing, water skiing, diving, pony trekking and fishing make this a favourite holiday destination.

Powys

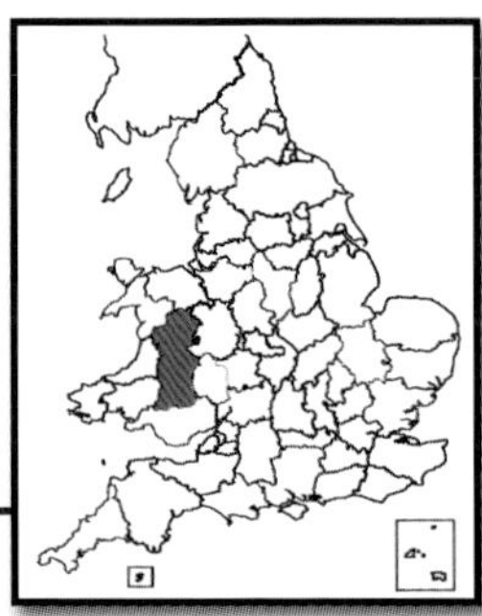

Lake Vyrnwy Hotel Llanwddyn, Powys SY10 0LY

Tel: 01691 870692 • Fax: 01691 870259
e-mail: info@lakevyrnwyhotel.co.uk • www.lakevyrnwy.com

Set within a 24000 acre estate, Lake Vyrnwy Hotel commands breathtaking views of the lake, mountains and moorland. All bedrooms are individually furnished and decorated, some with balconies, jacuzzis and antiques. All public rooms enjoy panoramic views over the lake. Enjoy award-winning cuisine in the restaurant, or, for more informal dining, the Tavern lounge serves traditional bar meals. Archery, clay shooting, fishing, paint balling, rafting, sailing, canoeing, walking, cycling are all available on site or near by. ***WTB ★★★, AA ★★★ and Rosette.***

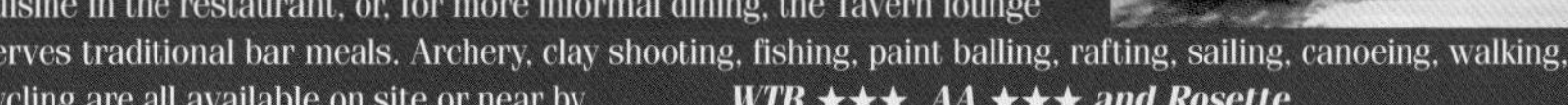

The new Spa & Thermal Suite offers a range of therapies and treatments, and facilities including an 8-person spa pool with views over the Lake, and a dry sauna. Also technogym fitness room

OPEN ALL YEAR. FULLY LICENSED. 52 BEDROOMS, ALL WITH PRIVATE BATHROOMS. CHILDREN AND PETS WELCOME. LEISURE FACILITIES. CONFERENCE FACILITIES. CIVIL WEDDING CEREMONIES. S££££, D££££.

Brynafon COUNTRY HOUSE HOTEL

South Street, Rhayader, Powys LD6 5BL
Tel: 01597 810735
e-mail: info@brynafon.co.uk • www.brynafon.co.uk

Once a workhouse and now a beautiful and very comfortable hotel, Brynafon has great character and charm. It is set against the dramatic backdrop of Gwastedyn Hill and the Druid's Circle, and is a stone's throw from the River Wye. Sitting in the very heart of the beautiful and still yet undiscovered Elan Valley, Brynafon is a must to visit any time of year. We cook fresh food each day, and change our set two and three-course menus five times per week, as well as offering a daily specials board. Our aim is to have a balanced menu which always has several vegetarian, meat and fish options. Brynafon has a total of 20 en suite bedrooms; three are family suites containing an extra bedroom, which brings the total number of bedrooms to 23. All are different, and most have beautiful views of the surrounding countryside.

B&B prices range from £61-£88 for two sharing, with family suites from £88. Brochure and tariff on request.

OPEN ALL YEAR. FULLY LICENSED. 20 BEDROOMS, ALL WITH PRIVATE BATHROOMS.
NON-SMOKING ACCOMMODATION AVAILABLE. CHILDREN WELCOME. CONFERENCE FACILITIES.
CIVIL WEDDING CEREMONIES. LLANDRINDOD WELLS 13 MILES. S£££.

FREE or REDUCED RATE entry to Holiday Visits and Attractions – see our **READERS' OFFER VOUCHERS** on pages 149-172

South Wales

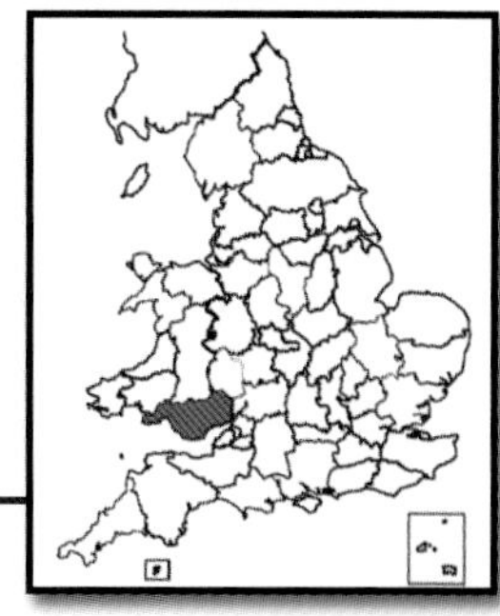

Bryngarw House

Brynmenyn, Near Bridgend CF32 8UU

Tel: 01656 729009 • Fax: 01656 729007

Conveniently located just two miles off the M4 (Junction 36) midway between Cardiff and Swansea, this charismatic old house is a fine base for the many attractions of South Wales. Built in 1744 in Tudorbethan style, the house lies resplendent in 113 acres of glorious parkland overlooked by the elegant award-winning Harlequin Restaurant, where the cuisine is something of a legend: light refreshments are served in the coffee lounge/terrace. In common with the high standard of furnishings throughout, guest rooms of de luxe style incorporate en suite facilities, satellite television, direct-dial telephone, hairdryer and hospitality tray.

e-mail: bryngarw.house@bridgend.gov.uk • www.bryngarwhouse.co.uk

OPEN ALL YEAR. LICENSED. 19 BEDROOMS, ALL WITH PRIVATE BATHROOMS.
NON-SMOKING ACCOMMODATION AVAILABLE. CHILDREN WELCOME. CONFERENCE FACILITIES.
CIVIL WEDDING CEREMONIES. BRIDGEND 3 MILES. S££/£££, D£££/££££.

Egerton Grey

Porthkerry, Vale of Glamorgan, Near Cardiff CF62 3BZ

Tel: 01446 711666 • Fax: 01446 711690

e-mail: info@egertongrey.co.uk • www.egertongrey.co.uk

★★★

A recommended centre from which to explore the lovely and uncrowded Gower Peninsula and the Brecon Beacons, this stylish and distinguished country house was opened as a small and luxurious hotel in 1988. Only 10 miles from Cardiff, it is set in a secluded, wooded valley in seven acres of gardens, with views down to Porthkerry Park and the sea. The excellent facilities accorded guests include exquisitely furnished bedrooms (all with private bathrooms), two dining rooms, library and magnificent Edwardian drawing room. Only a short stroll away is a well-maintained country park with an 18-hole pitch and putt course. The cuisine is outstanding and dining here by candlelight is a memorable experience. Recommended by many national and international hotel and restaurant guides.

VisitWales ★★★★ Gold Award

Taste of Wales Cuisine

RESIDENTIAL LICENCE. 10 BEDROOMS, ALL WITH PRIVATE BATHROOMS.
NON-SMOKING ACCOMMODATION AVAILABLE. CHILDREN AND PETS WELCOME.
CONFERENCE FACILITIES. CIVIL WEDDING CEREMONIES. CARDIFF 7 MILES. S£££, D££/£££.

Looking for Holiday Accommodation?

for details of hundreds of properties throughout the UK, visit our website

www.holidayguides.com

This is a selection of hotels which cater for meetings, conferences and seminars of varying sizes.

See individual entries in the main section of the book for a full listing.

Brief details only are included here – please see the main entry under the appropriate county heading for a fuller description

ARMATHWAITE HALL
COUNTRY HOUSE HOTEL
Bassenthwaite Lake, Keswick,
Cumbria CA12 4RE
Tel: 017687 76551
Fax: 017687 76220
reservations@armathwaite-hall.com
www.armathwaite-hall.com

4 meeting rooms available

LANGTRY MANOR
Derby Road, East Cliff,
Bournemouth, Dorset BH1 3QB
Tel: 01202 553887
lillie@langtrymanor.com
www.langtrymanor.com

4 meeting rooms; up to 150 delegates, 54 residential

HARDWICKE HALL
MANOR HOTEL
Hesleden, Hartlepool,
Durham TS27 4PA
Tel: 01429 836326 • Fax: 01429 837676
enquiries@hardwickehallmanor.co.uk
www.hardwickehallmanor.co.uk

3 meeting rooms, up to 50 delegates, 15 residential.

TORTWORTH COURT
FOUR PILLARS HOTEL
Tortworth, Wotton-under-Edge,
South Gloucs GL12 8HH
Tel: 01454 263000 • Fax: 01454 263001
tortworth@four-pillars.co.uk
www.four-pillars.co.uk

Choice of conference rooms for up to 400 delegates. Dedicated business support team.

WROXTON HOUSE
HOTEL
Wroxton St Mary, near Banbury
Oxfordshire OX15 6QB
Tel: 01295 730777
Fax: 01295 730800
events@wroxtonhousehotel.com
www.wroxtonhousehotel.com

Two meeting rooms, accommodating up to 45 theatre style.

ARDENCOTE
MANOR HOTEL
Lye Green Road, Claverdon,
Warwickshire CV35 8LT
Tel: 01926 843111
hote@ardencote.com
www.ardencote.com

Function rooms and suites catering from 8 to 300 delegates.

RAVEN HALL

COUNTRY HOUSE HOTEL

Ravenscar, Scarborough,
North Yorkshire YO13 0ET
Tel: 01723 870353 • Fax: 01723 870072
enquiries@ravenhall.co.uk
www.ravenhall.co.uk

6 meeting rooms available; up to 160 delegates, 100 residential.

THE CONISTON HOTEL

Coniston Cold, Skipton,
North Yorkshire BD23 4EB
Tel: 01756 748080 • Fax: 01756 749487
sales@theconistonhotel.com
www.theconistonhotel.com

8 meeting rooms with natural light and presentation equipment facilities for 2-200 delegates.

MOORPARK HOUSE HOTEL

Kilbirnie, Ayrshire KA25 7LD
Tel: 01505 683503
reception@moorparkhouse.co.uk
www.moorparkhouse.co.uk

3 meeting rooms available, up to 100 delegates, 20 residential

LOCKERBIE MANOR

COUNTRY HOTEL

Boreland Road, Lockerbie
Dumfries & Galloway DG11 2RG
Tel: 01576 202610/203939
Fax: 01576 203046
info@lockerbiemanorhotel.co.uk
www.lockerbiemanorhotel.co.uk

Choice of conference, meeting, exhibition and banquet facilities.

LAKE VYRNWY HOTEL

Llanwddyn, Powys SY10 0LY
Tel: 01691 870692
info@lakevyrnwyhotel.co.uk
www.lakevyrnwy.com

Choice of 5 meeting rooms catering for over 200 delegates, 104 residential.

Bryngarw House

Brynmenyn, Near Bridgend,
South Wales CF32 8UU
Tel: 01656 729009 • Fax: 01656 729007
bryngarw.house@bridgend.gov.uk
www.bryngarwhouse.co.uk

4 meeting rooms; up to 80 delegates in the lounge, Traherne Suite or Conference Room.

This is a selection of hotels which offer indoor/outdoor leisure facilities.

See individual entries in the main section of the book for a full listing.

Brief details only are included here – please see the main entry under the appropriate county heading for a fuller description

WHIPSIDERRY HOTEL

Trevelgue Road, Porth,
Newquay, Cornwall TR7 3LY
Tel: 01637 874777
info@whipsiderry.co.uk
www.whipsiderry.co.uk

Outdoor heated swimming pool.

ARMATHWAITE HALL COUNTRY HOUSE HOTEL

Bassenthwaite Lake, Keswick,
Cumbria CA12 4RE
Tel: 017687 76551
Fax: 017687 76220
reservations@armathwaite-hall.com
www.armathwaite-hall.com

Indoor swimming pool, sauna, gym and jacuzzi; tennis; clay pigeon shooting; quad bike safaris

BEST WESTERN VENTOR TOWERS HOTEL

54 Madeira Road, Ventnor,
Isle of Wight PO38 1QT
Tel: 01983 852277
Fax: 01983 855536
www.ventnortowers.com

Outdoor swimming pool; tennis.

HEDGEFIELD HOUSE HOTEL

Stella Road, Ryton on Tyne,
Tyne & Wear NE21 4LR
Tel/Fax: 0191 4137373
david@hedgefieldhouse.co.uk
www.hedgefieldhouse.co.uk

Sauna, gym and relaxtion area with aromatherapy/Swedish massage available.

RAVEN HALL COUNTRY HOUSE HOTEL

Ravenscar, Scarborough,
North Yorkshire YO13 0ET
Tel: 01723 870353 • Fax: 01723 870072
enquiries@ravenhall.co.uk
www.ravenhall.co.uk

Indoor swimming pool, sauna, gym; golf and tennis available; croquet, crown green bowls.

GREYWALLS

Muirfield, Gullane,
East Lothian EH31 2EG
Tel: 01620 842144
Fax: 01620 842241
hotel@greywalls.co.uk
www.greywalls.co.uk

Tennis, putting and croquet available on site.

This is a selection of hotels which are licensed to hold Civil Wedding Ceremonies.

See individual entries in the main section of the book for a full listing.

Brief details only are included here – please see the main entry under the appropriate county heading for a fuller description

GREEN LAWNS HOTEL

Falmouth, Cornwall TR11 4QJ

Tel: 01326 312374 • Fax: 01326 211427

www.greenlawnshotel.com

Civil wedding licence. Four function suites accommodating from 4 to 150 persons. Beautiful gardens.

POLURRIAN HOTEL

Mullion, Cornwall TR12 7EN

Tel: 01326 240421 • Fax: 01326 240083

relax@polurrianhotel.com

www.polurrianhotel.com

Weddings may be held in the Dining room with stunning sea views or in the smaller more intimate Marconi Room.

PENMORVAH MANOR HOTEL & COURTYARD COTTAGES

Falmouth, Cornwall TR11 5ED

Tel: 01326 250277

reception@penmorvah.co.uk

www.penmorvah.co.uk

Tailormade civil ceremonies and 1st class receptions. Free wedding information pack.

HOTEL TRESANTON

St Mawes, Cornwall TR2 5DR

Tel: 01326 270055

Fax: 01326 270053

info@tresanton.com

www.tresanton.com

Licensed for civil ceremonies, max 50 guests.

ARMATHWAITE HALL COUNTRY HOUSE HOTEL

Bassenthwaite Lake, Keswick, Cumbria CA12 4RE

Tel: 017687 76551

Fax: 017687 76220

reservations@armathwaite-hall.com

www.armathwaite-hall.com

4 rooms available for civil ceremonies. The Lake Room accommodates up to 100 guests. Evening function room. Dedicated co-ordinator

HARDWICKE HALL MANOR HOTEL

Hesleden, Hartlepool, Durham TS27 4PA

Tel: 01429 836326 • Fax: 01429 837676

enquiries@hardwickehallmanor.co.uk

www.hardwickehallmanor.co.uk

Licensed for civil ceremonies.

TORTWORTH COURT
FOUR PILLARS HOTEL

Tortworth, Wotton-under-Edge, South Gloucs GL12 8HH

Tel: 01454 263000 • Fax: 01454 263001

tortworth@four-pillars.co.uk

www.four-pillars.co.uk

Many rooms licensed for civil wedding ceremonies, and a range of banquetting rooms for receptions.

TYRRELLS FORD
MANOR HOUSE COUNTRY INN

Avon, Near Ringwood, New Forest, Hampshire BH23 7BH
Tel: 01425 672646
info@tyrrellsfordcountryinn.co.uk
www.tyrrellsford.co.uk

2 rooms licensed for civil ceremonies. The Minstrels Galleried Lounge accommodates 60, Avon Suite 80.

WOODLANDS LODGE

Ashurst, Hampshire SO40 7GN

Tel: 023 80292257 • Fax:023 80293090
reception@woodlands-lodge.co.uk
www.woodlands-lodge.co.uk

Civil wedding ceremonies in Woodlands or Wedgwood rooms for up to 60 persons. Receptions for up to 80.

THE PRIORY BAY HOTEL

Priory Drive, Seaview, Isle of Wight PO34 5BU
Tel: 01938 613146
e-mail: enquiries@priorybay.co.uk
www.priorybay.co.uk

Licensed for civil weddings. Tailor-made packages available.

WROXTON HOUSE
HOTEL

Wroxton St Mary, near Banbury Oxfordshire OX15 6QB
Tel: 01295 730777
Fax: 01295 730800
events@wroxtonhousehotel.com
www.wroxtonhousehotel.com

2 rooms licensed for civil ceremonies. The Wroxton Room accommodates 26 and the Broughton Room up to 46 guests.

BATCH COUNTRY HOTEL

Lympsham, Near Weston-super-Mare, Somerset BS24 0EX
Tel: 01934 750371 • Fax: 01934 750501
www.batchcountryhotel.co.uk

Outdoor civil ceremonies available. 2 banqueting rooms.

RAVEN HALL
COUNTRY HOUSE HOTEL

Ravenscar, Scarborough, North Yorkshire YO13 0ET
Tel: 01723 870353 • Fax: 01723 870072
enquiries@ravenhall.co.uk
www.ravenhall.co.uk

Several rooms licensed for civil weddings; arrangements to be made through local registrar and the hotel. Chapel, ideal for blessings.

THE CONISTON HOTEL

Coniston Cold, Skipton, North Yorkshire BD23 4EB
Tel: 01756 748080 • Fax: 01756 749487
sales@theconistonhotel.com
www.theconistonhotel.com

Several rooms licensed for wedding ceremonies including Winston's 17th Century Barn, The Coniston Hall sitting room and the high beamed restaurant.

ROSELY COUNTRY HOUSE HOTEL.

Forfar Road, Arbroath,
Angus & Dundee DD11 3RB
Tel/Fax: 01241 876828
enq@theroselyhotel.co.uk
www.theroselyhotel.co.uk

Licensed for civil ceremonies.

MOORPARK HOUSE HOTEL

Kilbirnie, Ayrshire KA25 7LD
Tel: 01505 683503
reception@moorparkhouse.co.uk
www.moorparkhouse.co.uk

3 rooms licensed for civil ceremonies. New conservatory and in the grounds.

THE HARVIESTOUN COUNTRY HOTEL & RESTAURANT

Dollar Road, Tillicoultry,
Clackmannanshire FK13 6PQ
Tel: 01259 752522
harviestounhotel@aol.com
www.harviestouncountryhotel.com

Registered for civil ceremonies. Tobermory function suite caters for 20-95 guests; a marquee can be erected for larger parties.

LOCKERBIE MANOR COUNTRY HOTEL

Boreland Road, Lockerbie
Dumfries & Galloway DG11 2RG
Tel: 01576 202610/203939
Fax: 01576 203046
info@lockerbiemanorhotel.co.uk
www.lockerbiemanorhotel.co.uk

Civil and religious ceremonies. 20-100 guests catered for; marquee available.

GREYWALLS

Muirfield, Gullane,
East Lothian EH31 2EG
Tel: 01620 842144
Fax: 01620 842241
hotel@greywalls.co.uk
www.greywalls.co.uk

Civil and religious ceremonies in sun room or garden, maximum 40 people, daytime only.

CULCREUCH CASTLE HOTEL

Fintry,
Stirlingshire G63 0LW
Tel: 01360 860228/860555
Fax: 01360 860556
info@culcreuch.com
www.culcreuch.com

3 rooms licensed for wedding ceremony, for 2-50 persons. Catering for up to 110. Outside areas available.

LAKE VYRNWY HOTEL

Llanwddyn, Powys SY10 0LY
Tel: 01691 870692
info@lakevyrnwyhotel.co.uk
www.lakevyrnwy.com

3 suites available catering from 2 - 200 persons. Dedicated marriage room.

Bryngarw House

Brynmenyn, Near Bridgend,
South Wales CF32 8UU
Tel: 01656 729009 • Fax: 01656 729007
bryngarw.house@bridgend.gov.uk
www.bryngarwhouse.co.uk

Traherne Suite licensed for civil weddings; accommodates 80 for ceremony, 50 for Wedding Breakfast; marquee available April to September.

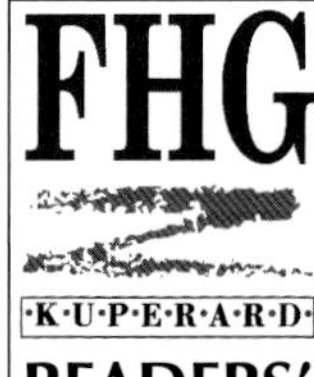

READERS' OFFER 2008

LEIGHTON BUZZARD RAILWAY

Page's Park Station, Billington Road,
Leighton Buzzard, Bedfordshire LU7 4TN
Tel: 01525 373888
e-mail: info@buzzrail.co.uk
www.buzzrail.co.uk

One FREE adult/child with full-fare adult ticket
Valid 11/3/2008 - 28/10/2008

NOT TO BE USED IN CONJUNCTION WITH ANY OTHER OFFER

READERS' OFFER 2008

THE LIVING RAINFOREST

Hampstead Norreys,
Berkshire RG18 0TN
Tel: 01635 202444 • Fax: 01635 202440
e-mail: enquiries@livingrainforest.org
www.livingrainforest.org

One FREE child with each full paying adult.
Valid during 2008.

NOT TO BE USED IN CONJUNCTION WITH ANY OTHER OFFER

BEKONSCOT MODEL VILLAGE & RAILWAY

Warwick Road, Beaconsfield,
Buckinghamshire HP9 2PL
Tel: 01494 672919
e-mail: info@bekonscot.co.uk
www.bekonscot.com

One child FREE when accompanied by full-paying adult
Valid February to October 2008

NOT TO BE USED IN CONJUNCTION WITH ANY OTHER OFFER

BUCKINGHAMSHIRE RAILWAY CENTRE

Quainton Road Station, Quainton,
Aylesbury HP22 4BY
Tel & Fax: 01296 655720
e-mail: bucksrailcentre@btopenworld.com
www.bucksrailcentre.org

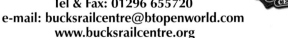

BUCKINGHAMSHIRE RAILWAY CENTRE

One child FREE with each full-paying adult
Not valid for Special Events

NOT TO BE USED IN CONJUNCTION WITH ANY OTHER OFFER

A 70-minute journey into the lost world of the English narrow gauge light railway. Features historic steam locomotives from many countries.

PETS MUST BE KEPT UNDER CONTROL AND NOT ALLOWED ON TRACKS

Open: Sundays and Bank Holiday weekends 11 March to 28 October. Additional days in summer.

Directions: on A4146 towards Hemel Hempstead, close to roundabout junction with A505.

FHG GUIDES, ABBEY MILL BUSINESS CENTRE, PAISLEY PA1 1TJ • www.holidayguides.com

Discover the exotic collection of tropical plants and animals inhabiting this living re-creation of the rainforest under glass. Explore your impact on the world's ecosystems using interactive displays. All-weather attraction. Children's play area.

Open: daily 10am to 5.15pm. Closed over Christmas period.

Directions: clearly signposted from J13 of M4. From Oxford take A34, exit at East Ilsley and follow signs. Nearest mainline station Newbury (8 miles). £1 'green discount' for visitors arriving by bus or bike.

FHG GUIDES, ABBEY MILL BUSINESS CENTRE, PAISLEY PA1 1TJ • www.holidayguides.com

Be a giant in a magical miniature world of make-believe depicting rural England in the 1930s. "A little piece of history that is forever England."

Open: 10am-5pm daily mid February to end October.

Directions: Junction 16 M25, Junction 2 M40.

FHG GUIDES, ABBEY MILL BUSINESS CENTRE, PAISLEY PA1 1TJ • www.holidayguides.com

A working steam railway centre. Steam train rides, miniature railway rides, large collection of historic preserved steam locomotives, carriages and wagons.

Open: Sundays and Bank Holidays April to October, plus Wednesdays in school holidays 10.30am to 4.30pm.

Directions: off A41 Aylesbury to Bicester Road, 6 miles north west of Aylesbury.

FHG GUIDES, ABBEY MILL BUSINESS CENTRE, PAISLEY PA1 1TJ • www.holidayguides.com

READERS' OFFER 2008

NATIONAL SEAL SANCTUARY

Gweek, Helston,
Cornwall TR12 6UG
Tel: 01326 221361
e-mail: seals@sealsanctuary.co.uk
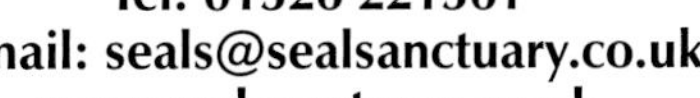
www.sealsanctuary.co.uk

TWO for ONE - on purchase of another ticket of equal or greater value. Valid until December 2008.

NOT TO BE USED IN CONJUNCTION WITH ANY OTHER OFFER

READERS' OFFER 2008

TAMAR VALLEY DONKEY PARK

St Ann's Chapel, Gunnislake,
Cornwall PL18 9HW
Tel: 01822 834072
e-mail: info@donkeypark.com
www.donkeypark.com

50p OFF per person, up to 6 persons
Valid from Easter until end October 2008

NOT TO BE USED IN CONJUNCTION WITH ANY OTHER OFFER

READERS' OFFER 2008

DUCKY'S PARK FARM

Moor Lane, Flookburgh, Grange-over-Sands
Cumbria LA11 7LS
Tel: 015395 59293 • Fax: 015395 58005
e-mail: donna@duckysparkfarm.co.uk
www.duckysparkfarm.co.uk

10% OFF admission price
Valid during 2008

NOT TO BE USED IN CONJUNCTION WITH ANY OTHER OFFER

READERS' OFFER 2008

CARS OF THE STARS MOTOR MUSEUM

Standish Street, Keswick,
Cumbria CA12 5HH
Tel: 017687 73757
e-mail: cotsmm@aol.com
www.carsofthestars.com

One child free with two paying adults
Valid during 2008

NOT TO BE USED IN CONJUNCTION WITH ANY OTHER OFFER

Britain's leading grey seal rescue centre	**Open:** daily (except Christmas Day) from 10am **Directions:** from A30 follow signs to Helston, then brown tourist signs to Seal Sanctuary.

FHG GUIDES, ABBEY MILL BUSINESS CENTRE, PAISLEY PA1 1TJ • www.holidayguides.com

Cornwall's only Donkey Sanctuary set in 14 acres overlooking the beautiful Tamar Valley. Donkey rides, rabbit warren, goat hill, children's playgrounds, cafe and picnic area. New all-weather play barn.	**Open:** Easter to end Oct: daily 10am to 5.30pm. Nov to March: weekends and all school holidays 10.30am to 4.30pm **Directions:** just off A390 between Callington and Gunnislake at St Ann's Chapel.

FHG GUIDES, ABBEY MILL BUSINESS CENTRE, PAISLEY PA1 1TJ • www.holidayguides.com

Children's open farm animal interaction centre. Large indoor soft play, bouncy castle, go-karts, driving school, playground, cafe. Full disabled facilities, wheelchair-friendly.	**Open:** March to October 10.30am to 4pm **Directions:** M6 J36. Follow A590 through Grange-over-Sands on the B5277. From Barrow-in-Furness turn right at Haverthwaite on to the B278 and follow signs to Flookburgh.

FHG GUIDES, ABBEY MILL BUSINESS CENTRE, PAISLEY PA1 1TJ • www.holidayguides.com

A collection of cars from film and TV, including Chitty Chitty Bang Bang, James Bond's Aston Martin, Del Boy's van, Fab1 and many more. **PETS MUST BE KEPT ON LEAD**	**Open:** daily 10am-5pm. Open February half term, Ist April to end November, also weekends in December. **Directions:** in centre of Keswick close to car park.

FHG GUIDES, ABBEY MILL BUSINESS CENTRE, PAISLEY PA1 1TJ • www.holidayguides.com

READERS' OFFER 2008

ESKDALE HISTORIC WATER MILL

Mill Cottage, Boot, Eskdale,
Cumbria CA19 1TG
Tel: 019467 23335
e-mail: david.king403@tesco.net
www.eskdale.info

Two children FREE with two adults
Valid during 2008

NOT TO BE USED IN CONJUNCTION WITH ANY OTHER OFFER

READERS' OFFER 2008

CRICH TRAMWAY VILLAGE

Crich, Matlock
Derbyshire DE4 5DP
Tel: 01773 854321 • Fax: 01773 854320
e-mail: enquiry@tramway.co.uk
www.tramway.co.uk

One child FREE with every full-paying adult
Valid during 2008

NOT TO BE USED IN CONJUNCTION WITH ANY OTHER OFFER

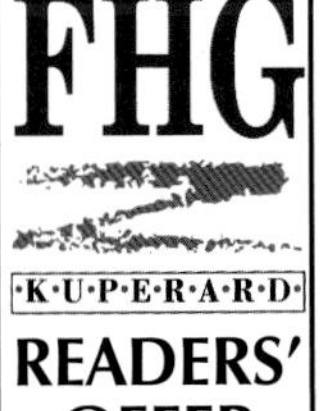

READERS' OFFER 2008

WOODLANDS

Blackawton, Dartmouth,
Devon TQ9 7DQ
Tel: 01803 712598 • Fax: 01803 712680
e-mail: fun@woodlandspark.com
www.woodlandspark.com

12% discount off individual entry price for up to 4 persons. No photocopies. Valid 15/3/08 – 1/11/08

NOT TO BE USED IN CONJUNCTION WITH ANY OTHER OFFER

READERS' OFFER 2008

KILLHOPE LEAD MINING MUSEUM

Cowshill, Upper Weardale,
Co. Durham DL13 1AR
Tel: 01388 537505
e-mail: killhope@durham.gov.uk
www.durham.gov.uk/killhope

One child FREE with full-paying adult
Valid April to October 2008

NOT TO BE USED IN CONJUNCTION WITH ANY OTHER OFFER

The oldest working mill in England with 18th century oatmeal machinery running daily.

DOGS ON LEADS

Open: 11am to 5pm April to Sept. (may be closed Saturdays & Mondays)

Directions: near inland terminus of Ravenglass & Eskdale Railway or over Hardknott Pass.

FHG GUIDES, ABBEY MILL BUSINESS CENTRE, PAISLEY PA1 1TJ • www.holidayguides.com

A superb family day out in the atmosphere of a bygone era. Explore the recreated period street and fascinating exhibitions. Unlimited tram rides are free with entry. Play areas, woodland walk and sculpture trail, shops, tea rooms, pub, restaurant and lots more.

Open: daily April to October 10 am to 5.30pm, weekends in winter.

Directions: eight miles from M1 Junction 28, follow brown and white signs for "Tramway Museum".

FHG GUIDES, ABBEY MILL BUSINESS CENTRE, PAISLEY PA1 1TJ • www.holidayguides.com

All weather fun - guaranteed! Unique combination of indoor/outdoor attractions. 3 Watercoasters, Toboggan Run, Arctic Gliders, boats, 15 Playzones for all ages. Biggest indoor venture zone in UK with 5 floors of play and rides. New Big Fun Farm with U-drive Tractor ride, Pedal Town and Yard Racers. Falconry Centre.

Open: mid-March to November open daily at 9.30am. Winter: open weekends and local school holidays.

Directions: 5 miles from Dartmouth on A3122. Follow brown tourist signs from A38.

FHG GUIDES, ABBEY MILL BUSINESS CENTRE, PAISLEY PA1 1TJ • www.holidayguides.com

This award-winning Victorian mining museum makes a great day out for all the family. Hands-on activities plus unforgettable mine tour. Green Tourism Gold Award 2007.

Open: Easter weekend +April 1st to October 31st 10.30am to 5pm daily.

Directions: alongside A689, midway between Stanhope and Alston in the heart of the North Pennines.

FHG GUIDES, ABBEY MILL BUSINESS CENTRE, PAISLEY PA1 1TJ • www.holidayguides.com

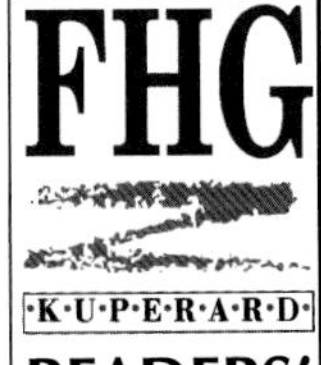

READERS' OFFER 2008

TWEDDLE CHILDREN'S ANIMAL FARM

Fillpoke Lane, Blackhall Colliery,
Co. Durham TS27 4BT
Tel: 0191 586 3311
e-mail: info@tweddle-farm.co.uk
www.tweddle-farm.co.uk

FREE bag of animal food to every paying customer.
Valid until end 2008

NOT TO BE USED IN CONJUNCTION WITH ANY OTHER OFFER

READERS' OFFER 2008

ST AUGUSTINE'S FARM

Arlingham
Gloucestershire GL2 7JN
Tel & Fax: 01452 740277
staugustines@btconnect.com
www.staugustinesfarm.co.uk

ST AUGUSTINES FARM

One child FREE with paying adult.
Valid March to October 2008.

NOT TO BE USED IN CONJUNCTION WITH ANY OTHER OFFER

READERS' OFFER 2008

THE HOP FARM AT THE KENTISH OAST VILLAGE

Beltring, Paddock Wood,
Kent TN12 6PY
Tel: 01622 872068 • Fax: 01622 870800
e-mail: info@thehopfarm.co.uk
www.thehopfarm.co.uk

Admit one child HALF PRICE with a full paying adult.
Valid until March 2008.

NOT TO BE USED IN CONJUNCTION WITH ANY OTHER OFFER

READERS' OFFER 2008

MUSEUM OF KENT LIFE

Lock Lane, Sandling, Maidstone,
Kent ME14 3AU
Tel: 01622 763936 • Fax: 01622 662024
e-mail: enquiries@museum-kentlife.co.uk
www.museum-kentlife.co.uk

MUSEUM OF KENT LIFE

One child FREE with one full-paying adult
Valid during 2008

NOT TO BE USED IN CONJUNCTION WITH ANY OTHER OFFER

Children's farm and petting centre with lots of farm animals and exotic animals too, including camels, otters, monkeys, meerkats and lots more. Lots of hands-on, with bottle feeding, reptile handling and bunny cuddling happening daily.	**Open:** March to Oct: 10am-5pm daily; Nov to Feb 10am to 4pm daily. Closed Christmas, Boxing Day and New Year's Day. **Directions:** A181 from A19, head towards coast; signposted from there.

FHG GUIDES, ABBEY MILL BUSINESS CENTRE, PAISLEY PA1 1TJ • www.holidayguides.com

A real working organic dairy farm in the Severn Vale. St Augustine's is a typical dairy farm of over 100 acres where the everyday farm life will go on around you.	**Open:** March to October open daily 11am to 5pm (except term-time Mondays). **Directions:** leave M5 by J13 to A38. Half a mile south turn right on B4071 and follow brown tourist signs.

FHG GUIDES, ABBEY MILL BUSINESS CENTRE, PAISLEY PA1 1TJ • www.holidayguides.com

Set in 400 acres of unspoilt Kent countryside, this once working hop farm is one of Kent's most popular attractions. The spectacular oast village is home to an indoor and outdoor play area, interactive museum, shire horses and an animal farm, as well as hosting special events throughout the year.	**Open:** 10am-5pm daily (last admission 4pm). **Directions:** A228 Paddock Wood

FHG GUIDES, ABBEY MILL BUSINESS CENTRE, PAISLEY PA1 1TJ • www.holidayguides.com

Kent's award-winning open air museum is home to a collection of historic buildings which house interactive exhibitions on life over the last 150 years.	**Open:** seven days a week from February to start November, 10am to 5pm. **Directions:** Junction 6 off M20, follow signs to Aylesford.

FHG GUIDES, ABBEY MILL BUSINESS CENTRE, PAISLEY PA1 1TJ • www.holidayguides.com

READERS' OFFER 2008

DOCKER PARK FARM

Arkholme, Carnforth,
Lancashire LA6 1AR
Tel & Fax: 015242 21331
e-mail: info@dockerparkfarm.co.uk
www.dockerparkfarm.co.uk

One FREE child per one paying adult (one voucher per child)
Valid from January to December 2008

NOT TO BE USED IN CONJUNCTION WITH ANY OTHER OFFER

READERS' OFFER 2008

SKEGNESS NATURELAND SEAL SANCTUARY

North Parade, Skegness,
Lincolnshire PE25 1DB
Tel: 01754 764345
e-mail: natureland@fsbdial.co.uk
www.skegnessnatureland.co.uk

Natureland Seal Sanctuary

Free entry for one child when accompanied by full-paying adult. Valid during 2008.

NOT TO BE USED IN CONJUNCTION WITH ANY OTHER OFFER

THE BEATLES STORY

Britannia Vaults, Albert Dock
Liverpool L3 4AD
Tel: 0151-709 1963 • Fax: 0151-708 0039
e-mail: info@beatlesstory.com
www.beatlesstory.com

One FREE child with one full paying adult
Valid during 2008

NOT TO BE USED IN CONJUNCTION WITH ANY OTHER OFFER

READERS' OFFER 2008

BRESSINGHAM STEAM & GARDENS

Low Road, Bressingham, Diss,
Norfolk IP22 2AB
Tel: 01379 686900 • Fax: 01379 686907
e-mail: info@bressingham.co.uk
www.bressingham.co.uk

One child FREE with two paying adults
Valid Easter to October 2008

NOT TO BE USED IN CONJUNCTION WITH ANY OTHER OFFER

We are a working farm, with lots of animals to see and touch. Enjoy a walk round the Nature Trail or refreshments in the tearoom. Lots of activities during school holidays.

Open: Summer: daily 10.30am- 5pm. Winter: weekends only 10.30am- 4pm.

Directions: Junction 35 off M6, take B6254 towards Kirkby Lonsdale, then follow the brown signs.

FHG GUIDES, ABBEY MILL BUSINESS CENTRE, PAISLEY PA1 1TJ • www.holidayguides.com

Well known for rescuing and rehabilitating orphaned and injured seal pups found washed ashore on Lincolnshire beaches. Also: penguins, aquarium, pets' corner, reptiles, Floral Palace (tropical birds and butterflies etc).

Open: daily from 10am. Closed Christmas/Boxing/New Year's Days.

Directions: at the north end of Skegness seafront.

FHG GUIDES, ABBEY MILL BUSINESS CENTRE, PAISLEY PA1 1TJ • www.holidayguides.com

A unique visitor attraction that transports you on an enlightening and atmospheric journey into the life, times, culture and music of the Beatles. See how four young lads from Liverpool were propelled into the dizzy heights of worldwide fame and fortune to become the greatest band of all time. Hear the story unfold through the 'Living History' audio guide narrated by John Lennon's sister, Julia.

Open: daily 10am to 6pm (last admisssion 5pm) all year round (excl. 25/26 December)

Directions: located within Liverpool's historic Albert Dock.

FHG GUIDES, ABBEY MILL BUSINESS CENTRE, PAISLEY PA1 1TJ • www.holidayguides.com

Explore one of Europe's leading steam collections, take a ride over 5 miles of narrow gauge steam railway, wander through beautiful gardens, or visit the only official 'Dads' Army' exhibition. Two restaurants and garden centre.

Open: Easter to October 10.30am - 5pm

Directions: 2½ miles west of Diss and 14 miles east of Thetford on the A1066; follow brown tourist signs.

FHG GUIDES, ABBEY MILL BUSINESS CENTRE, PAISLEY PA1 1TJ • www.holidayguides.com

FHG

·K·U·P·E·R·A·R·D·

READERS' OFFER 2008

FERRY FARM PARK

Ferry Farm, Boat Lane, Hoveringham
Nottinghamshire NG14 7JP
Tel & Fax: 0115 966 4512
e-mail: enquiries@ferryfarm.co.uk
www.ferryfarm.co.uk

20% OFF admission price.
Valid during 2008.

NOT TO BE USED IN CONJUNCTION WITH ANY OTHER OFFER

·K·U·P·E·R·A·R·D·

READERS' OFFER 2008

EXMOOR FALCONRY & ANIMAL FARM

Allerford, Near Porlock, Minehead,
Somerset TA24 8HJ
Tel: 01643 862816
e-mail: exmoor.falcon@virgin.net
www.exmoorfalconry.co.uk

10% off entry to Falconry Centre
Valid during 2008

NOT TO BE USED IN CONJUNCTION WITH ANY OTHER OFFER

·K·U·P·E·R·A·R·D·

READERS' OFFER 2008

THE HELICOPTER MUSEUM

The Heliport, Locking Moor Road,
Weston-Super-Mare BS24 8PP
Tel: 01934 635227• Fax: 01934 645230

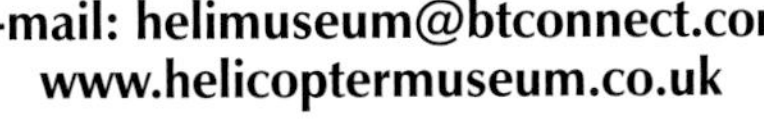

e-mail: helimuseum@btconnect.com
www.helicoptermuseum.co.uk

One child FREE with two full-paying adults
Valid from April to October 2008

NOT TO BE USED IN CONJUNCTION WITH ANY OTHER OFFER

·K·U·P·E·R·A·R·D·

READERS' OFFER 2008

YESTERDAY'S WORLD

High Street, Battle, E. Sussex TN33 0AQ
Tel: 01424 775378 (24hr info)
Enquiries/bookings: 01424 893938
e-mail: info@yesterdaysworld.co.uk
www.yesterdaysworld.co.uk

One child FREE when accompanied by one full-paying adult. Valid until end 2008

NOT TO BE USED IN CONJUNCTION WITH ANY OTHER OFFER

Family-run farm park set in beautiful countryside next to river. 20-acre site with animal handling, large indoor soft play area, go-karts, trampolines, pedal tractors, swings, slides, zipline and assault course.	**Open:** daily 10am to 5.30pm April to end September. Closed Mondays except Bank Holidays and during school holidays. Please check for winter opening hours. **Directions:** off A612 Nottingham to Southwell road.

FHG GUIDES, ABBEY MILL BUSINESS CENTRE, PAISLEY PA1 1TJ • www.holidayguides.com

Falconry centre with animals - flying displays, animal handling, feeding and bottle feeding - in 15th century NT farmyard setting on Exmoor. Also falconry and outdoor activities, hawk walks and riding.	**Open:** 10.30am to 5pm daily **Directions:** A39 west of Minehead, turn right at Allerford, half a mile along lane on left.

FHG GUIDES, ABBEY MILL BUSINESS CENTRE, PAISLEY PA1 1TJ • www.holidayguides.com

The world's largest helicopter collection - over 70 exhibits, includes two royal helicopters, Russian Gunship and Vietnam veterans plus many award-winning exhibits. Cafe, shop. Flights. **PETS MUST BE KEPT UNDER CONTROL**	**Open:** Wednesday to Sunday 10am to 5.30pm. Daily during school Easter and Summer holidays and Bank Holiday Mondays. November to March: 10am to 4.30pm **Directions:** Junction 21 off M5 then follow the propellor signs.

FHG GUIDES, ABBEY MILL BUSINESS CENTRE, PAISLEY PA1 1TJ • www.holidayguides.com

The past is brought to life at one of the South East's best loved family attractions. 100,000+ nostalgic artefacts, set in a charming 15th century house and country garden. New attractions and tearooms.	**Open:** 9.30am to 6pm (last admission 4.45pm, one hour earlier in winter). Closing times may vary – phone or check website. **Directions:** just off A21 in Battle High Street opposite the Abbey.

FHG GUIDES, ABBEY MILL BUSINESS CENTRE, PAISLEY PA1 1TJ • www.holidayguides.com

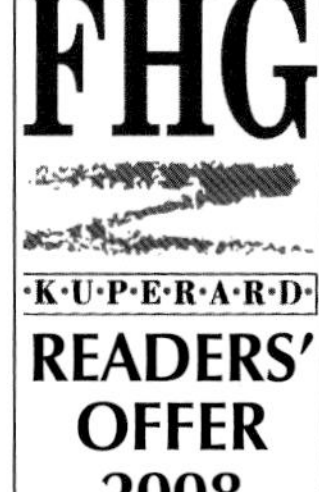

READERS' OFFER 2008

PARADISE PARK & GARDENS

Avis Road, Newhaven,
East Sussex BN9 0DH

PARADISE PARK

Tel: 01273 512123 • Fax: 01273 616000
e-mail: enquiries@paradisepark.co.uk
www.paradisepark.co.uk

Admit one FREE child with one adult paying full entrance price. Valid during 2008

NOT TO BE USED IN CONJUNCTION WITH ANY OTHER OFFER

READERS' OFFER 2008

WILDERNESS WOOD

Hadlow Down, Near Uckfield,
East Sussex TN22 4HJ
Tel: 01825 830509• Fax: 01825 830977
e-mail: enquiries@wildernesswood.co.uk
www.wildernesswood.co.uk

one FREE admission with a full-paying adult Valid during 2008 (not for Special Events/Bank Holidays)

NOT TO BE USED IN CONJUNCTION WITH ANY OTHER OFFER

READERS' OFFER 2008

EARNLEY BUTTERFLIES & GARDENS

133 Almodington Lane, Earnley, Chichester,
West Sussex PO20 7JR
Tel: 01243 512637
e-mail: earnleygardens@msn.com
www.earnleybutterfliesandgardens.co.uk

Earnley Butterflies & Gardens

£2 per person offer normal entry prices. Valid late March to end October 2008.

NOT TO BE USED IN CONJUNCTION WITH ANY OTHER OFFER

READERS' OFFER 2008

STRATFORD BUTTERFLY FARM

Swan's Nest Lane, Stratford-upon-Avon
Warwickshire CV37 7LS
Tel: 01789 299288 • Fax: 01789 415878
e-mail: sales@butterflyfarm.co.uk
www.butterflyfarm.co.uk

STRATFORD-UPON-AVON Butterfly Farm

Admit TWO for the price of ONE Valid until 31/12/2008

NOT TO BE USED IN CONJUNCTION WITH ANY OTHER OFFER

Discover 'Planet Earth' for an unforgettable experience. A unique Museum of Life, Dinosaur Safari, beautiful Water Gardens with fish and wildfowl, plant houses, themed gardens, Heritage Trail, miniature railway. Playzone includes crazy golf and adventure play areas. Garden Centre and Terrace Cafe.	**Open:** open daily, except Christmas Day and Boxing Day. **Directions:** signposted off A26 and A259.

FHG GUIDES, ABBEY MILL BUSINESS CENTRE, PAISLEY PA1 1TJ • www.holidayguides.com

Wilderness Wood is a unique family-run working woodland park in the Sussex High Weald. Explore trails and footpaths, enjoy local cakes and ices, try the adventure playground. Many special events and activities. Parties catered for. Green Tourism Gold Award.	**Open:** daily 10am to 5.30pm or dusk if earlier. **Directions:** on the south side of the A272 in the village of Hadlow Down. Signposted with a brown tourist sign.

FHG GUIDES, ABBEY MILL BUSINESS CENTRE, PAISLEY PA1 1TJ • www.holidayguides.com

3 attractions in 1. Tropical butterflies, exotic animals of many types in our Noah's Ark Rescue Centre. Theme gardens with a free competition for kids. Rejectamenta - the nostalgia museum.	**Open:** 10am - 6pm daily late March to end October. **Directions:** signposted from A27/A286 junction at Chichester.

FHG GUIDES, ABBEY MILL BUSINESS CENTRE, PAISLEY PA1 1TJ • www.holidayguides.com

Wander through a tropical rainforest with a myriad of multicoloured butterflies, sunbirds and koi carp. See fascinating animals in Insect City and view deadly spiders in perfect safety in Arachnoland.	**Open:** daily except Christmas Day. 10am-6pm summer, 10am-dusk winter. **Directions:** on south bank of River Avon opposite Royal Shakespeare Theatre. Easily accessible from town centre, 5 minutes' walk.

FHG GUIDES, ABBEY MILL BUSINESS CENTRE, PAISLEY PA1 1TJ • www.holidayguides.com

READERS' OFFER 2008

AVONCROFT MUSEUM

AVONCROFT
MUSEUM OF HISTORIC BUILDINGS

Stoke Heath,
Bromsgrove,
Worcestershire B60 4JR
Tel: 01527 831363 • Fax: 01527 876934
www.avoncroft.org.uk

One FREE child with one full-paying adult
Valid from March to November 2008

NOT TO BE USED IN CONJUNCTION WITH ANY OTHER OFFER

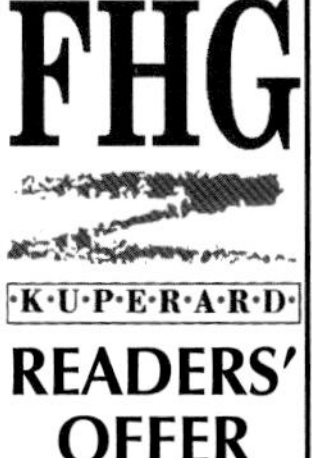

READERS' OFFER 2008

EMBSAY & BOLTON ABBEY STEAM RAILWAY

EMBSAY &
BOLTON ABBEY
STEAM RAILWAY

Bolton Abbey Station, Skipton,
North Yorkshire BD23 6AF
Tel: 01756 710614
e-mail: embsay.steam@btinternet.com
www.embsayboltonabbeyrailway.org.uk

One adult travels FREE when accompanied by a full fare paying adult (does not include Special Event days). Valid during 2008.

NOT TO BE USED IN CONJUNCTION WITH ANY OTHER OFFER

READERS' OFFER 2008

WORLD OF JAMES HERRIOT

HERRIOT

23 Kirkgate, Thirsk,
North Yorkshire YO7 1PL
Tel: 01845 524234
Fax: 01845 525333
www.worldofjamesherriot.org

Admit TWO for the price of ONE (one voucher per transaction only). Valid until October 2008

NOT TO BE USED IN CONJUNCTION WITH ANY OTHER OFFER

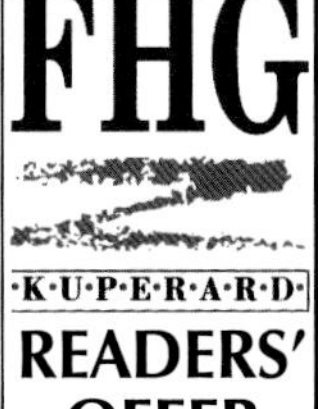

READERS' OFFER 2008

YORKSHIRE DALES FALCONRY & WILDLIFE CONSERVATION CENTRE

YORKSHIRE DALES
FALCONRY & WILDLIFE CONSERVATION CENTRE

Crow's Nest, Giggleswick, Near Settle LA2 8AS
Tel: 01729 822832• Fax: 01729 825160
e-mail: info@falconryandwildlife.com
www.falconryandwildlife.com

One child FREE with two full-paying adults
Valid until end 2008

NOT TO BE USED IN CONJUNCTION WITH ANY OTHER OFFER

A fascinating world of historic buildings covering 7 centuries, rescued and rebuilt on an open-air site in the heart of the Worcestershire countryside. **PETS ON LEADS ONLY**	**Open:** July and August all week. March to November varying times, please telephone for details. **Directions:** A38 south of Bromsgrove, near Junction 1 of M42, Junction 5 of M5.

FHG GUIDES, ABBEY MILL BUSINESS CENTRE, PAISLEY PA1 1TJ • www.holidayguides.com

Steam trains operate over a 4½ mile line from Bolton Abbey Station to Embsay Station. Many family events including Thomas the Tank Engine take place during major Bank Holidays.	**Open:** steam trains run every Sunday throughout the year and up to 7 days a week in summer. 10.30am to 4.30pm **Directions:** Embsay Station signposted from the A59 Skipton by-pass; Bolton Abbey Station signposted from the A59 at Bolton Abbey.

FHG GUIDES, ABBEY MILL BUSINESS CENTRE, PAISLEY PA1 1TJ • www.holidayguides.com

Visit James Herriot's original house recreated as it was in the 1940s. Television sets used in the series 'All Creatures Great and Small'. There is a children's interactive gallery with life-size model farm animals and three rooms dedicated to the history of veterinary medicine.	**Open:** daily. Easter-Oct 10am-5pm; Nov-Easter 11am to 4pm **Directions:** follow signs off A1 or A19 to Thirsk, then A168, off Thirsk market place

FHG GUIDES, ABBEY MILL BUSINESS CENTRE, PAISLEY PA1 1TJ • www.holidayguides.com

All types of birds of prey exhibited here, from owls and kestrels to eagles and vultures. Special flying displays 12 noon, 1.30pm and 3pm. Bird handling courses arranged for either half or full days. **GUIDE DOGS ONLY**	**Open:** 10am to 4.30pm summer 10am to 4pm winter **Directions:** on main A65 trunk road outside Settle. Follow brown direction signs.

FHG GUIDES, ABBEY MILL BUSINESS CENTRE, PAISLEY PA1 1TJ • www.holidayguides.com

READERS' OFFER 2008

DINOSTAR - THE DINOSAUR EXPERIENCE

28-29 Humber Street
Hull HU1 1TH
Tel: 01482 320424
e-mail: info@dinostar.co.uk
www.dinostar.co.uk

Children FREE with a full paying adult.
Valid between April and September (incl)

NOT TO BE USED IN CONJUNCTION WITH ANY OTHER OFFER

READERS' OFFER 2008

STORYBOOK GLEN

Maryculter,
Aberdeen
Aberdeenshire AB12 5FT
Tel: 01224 732941
www.storybookglenaberdeen.co.uk

10% discount on all admissions
Valid until end 2008

NOT TO BE USED IN CONJUNCTION WITH ANY OTHER OFFER

READERS' OFFER 2008

THE GRASSIC GIBBON CENTRE

Arbuthnott, Laurencekirk,
Aberdeenshire AB30 1PB
Tel: 01561 361668
e-mail: lgginfo@grassicgibbon.com
www.grassicgibbon.com

TWO for the price of ONE entry to exhibition (based on full adult rate only). Valid during 2008 (not groups)

NOT TO BE USED IN CONJUNCTION WITH ANY OTHER OFFER

READERS' OFFER 2008

INVERARAY JAIL

Church Square, Inveraray,
Argyll PA32 8TX
Tel: 01499 302381 • Fax: 01499 302195
e-mail: info@inveraryjail.co.uk
www.inverarayjail.co.uk

One child FREE with one full-paying adult
Valid until end 2008

NOT TO BE USED IN CONJUNCTION WITH ANY OTHER OFFER

Dinostar features an exhibition of dinosaurs and fossils. Highlights include a T-Rex skull, Triceratops bones you can touch, and our unique dinosaur sound box.

Open: 11am to 5pm Wednesday to Sunday.

Directions: in the Fruit Market area of Hull's Old Town, close to The Deep and Hull Marina.

FHG GUIDES, ABBEY MILL BUSINESS CENTRE, PAISLEY PA1 1TJ • www.holidayguides.com

28-acre theme park with over 100 nursery rhyme characters, set in beautifully landscaped gardens. Shop and restaurant on site.

Open: 1st March to 31st October: daily 10am to 6pm; 1st Nov to end Feb: Sat/Sun only 11am to 4pm

Directions: 6 miles west of Aberdeen off B9077

FHG GUIDES, ABBEY MILL BUSINESS CENTRE, PAISLEY PA1 1TJ • www.holidayguides.com

Visitor Centre dedicated to the much-loved Scottish writer Lewis Grassic Gibbon. Exhibition, cafe, gift shop. Outdoor children's play area. Disabled access throughout.

Open: daily April to October 10am to 4.30pm. Groups by appointment including evenings.

Directions: on the B967, accessible and signposted from both A90 and A92.

FHG GUIDES, ABBEY MILL BUSINESS CENTRE, PAISLEY PA1 1TJ • www.holidayguides.com

19th century prison with fully restored 1820 courtroom and two prisons. Guides in uniform as warders, prisoners and matron. Remember your camera!

Open: April to October 9.30am-6pm (last admission 5pm); November to March 10am-5pm (last admission 4pm)

Directions: A83 to Campbeltown

FHG GUIDES, ABBEY MILL BUSINESS CENTRE, PAISLEY PA1 1TJ • www.holidayguides.com

READERS' OFFER 2008

SCOTTISH MARITIME MUSEUM

Harbourside, Irvine,
Ayrshire KA12 8QE
Tel: 01294 278283
Fax: 01294 313211
www.scottishmaritimemuseum.org

Scottish Maritime Museum

TWO for the price of ONE
Valid from April to October 2008

NOT TO BE USED IN CONJUNCTION WITH ANY OTHER OFFER

READERS' OFFER 2008

GALLOWAY WILDLIFE CONSERVATION PARK

Lochfergus Plantation, Kirkcudbright,
Dumfries & Galloway DG6 4XX
Tel & Fax: 01557 331645
e-mail: info@gallowaywildlife.co.uk
www.gallowaywildlife.co.uk

One FREE child or Senior Citizen with two full paying adults.
Valid Feb - Nov 2008 (not Easter weekend and Bank Holidays)

NOT TO BE USED IN CONJUNCTION WITH ANY OTHER OFFER

READERS' OFFER 2008

CREETOWN GEM ROCK MUSEUM

Chain Road, Creetown, Newton Stewart
Dumfries & Galloway DG8 7HJ
Tel: 01671 820357 • Fax: 01671 820554
e-mail: enquiries@gemrock.net
www.gemrock.net

10% discount on admission.
Valid during 2008.

NOT TO BE USED IN CONJUNCTION WITH ANY OTHER OFFER

READERS' OFFER 2008

CLYDEBUILT SCOTTISH MARITIME MUSEUM

Braehead Shopping Centre, King's Inch Road,
Glasgow G51 4BN
Tel: 0141-886 1013 • Fax: 0141-886 1015
e-mail: clydebuilt@scotmaritime.org.uk
www.scottishmaritimemuseum.org

HALF PRICE admission for up to 4 persons.
Valid during 2008.

NOT TO BE USED IN CONJUNCTION WITH ANY OTHER OFFER

Scotland's seafaring heritage is among the world's richest and you can relive the heyday of Scottish shipping at the Maritime Museum.	**Open:** 1st April to 31st October - 10am-5pm **Directions:** situated on Irvine harbourside and only a 10 minute walk from Irvine train station.

FHG GUIDES, ABBEY MILL BUSINESS CENTRE, PAISLEY PA1 1TJ • www.holidayguides.com

The wild animal conservation centre of Southern Scotland. A varied collection of over 150 animals from all over the world can be seen within natural woodland settings. Picnic areas, cafe/gift shop, outdoor play area, woodland walks, close animal encounters.	**Open:** 10am to dusk 1st February to 30 November. **Directions:** follow brown tourist signs from A75; one mile from Kirkcudbright on the B727.

FHG GUIDES, ABBEY MILL BUSINESS CENTRE, PAISLEY PA1 1TJ • www.holidayguides.com

A fantastic display of gems, crystals, minerals and fossils. An experience you'll treasure forever. Gift shop, tearoom and AV display.	**Open:** Summer - 9.30am to 5.30pm daily; Winter - 10am to 4pm daily. Closed Christmas to end January. **Directions:** follow signs from A75 Dumfries/Stranraer.

FHG GUIDES, ABBEY MILL BUSINESS CENTRE, PAISLEY PA1 1TJ • www.holidayguides.com

The story of Glasgow and the River Clyde brought vividly to life using AV, hands-on and interactive techniques. You can navigate your own ship, safely load your cargo, operate an engine, and go aboard the 130-year-old coaster 'Kyles'. Ideal for kids young and old wanting an exciting day out. New - The Clyde's Navy.	**Open:** 10am to 5.30pm daily **Directions:** Green Car Park near M&S at Braehead Shopping Centre.

FHG GUIDES, ABBEY MILL BUSINESS CENTRE, PAISLEY PA1 1TJ • www.holidayguides.com

FHG

·K·U·P·E·R·A·R·D·

READERS' OFFER 2008

SPEYSIDE HEATHER GARDEN & VISITOR CENTRE

Speyside Heather Centre, Dulnain Bridge,
Inverness-shire PH26 3PA
Tel: 01479 851359 • Fax: 01479 851396
e-mail: enquiries@heathercentre.com
www.heathercentre.com

Speyside HEATHER GARDEN

FREE entry to 'Heather Story' exhibition
Valid during 2008

NOT TO BE USED IN CONJUNCTION WITH ANY OTHER OFFER

READERS' OFFER 2008

LLANBERIS LAKE RAILWAY

Gilfach Ddu, Llanberis,
Gwynedd LL55 4TY
Tel: 01286 870549
e-mail: info@lake-railway.co.uk
www.lake-railway.co.uk

One pet travels FREE with each full fare paying adult
Valid Easter to October 2008

NOT TO BE USED IN CONJUNCTION WITH ANY OTHER OFFER

READERS' OFFER 2008

ANIMALARIUM

Borth,
Ceredigion
SY24 5NA
Tel: 01970 871224
www.animalarium.co.uk

FREE child with full paying adult.
Valid during 2008.

NOT TO BE USED IN CONJUNCTION WITH ANY OTHER OFFER

READERS' OFFER 2008

FELINWYNT RAINFOREST CENTRE

Felinwynt, Cardigan,
Ceredigion SA43 1RT
Tel: 01239 810882/810250
e-mail: dandjdevereux@btinternet.com
www.butterflycentre.co.uk

TWO for the price of ONE (one voucher per party only)
Valid until end October 2008

NOT TO BE USED IN CONJUNCTION WITH ANY OTHER OFFER

Award-winning attraction with unique 'Heather Story' exhibition, gallery, giftshop, large garden centre selling 300 different heathers, antique shop, children's play area and famous Clootie Dumpling restaurant.	**Open:** all year except Christmas Day. **Directions:** just off A95 between Aviemore and Grantown-on-Spey.

FHG GUIDES, ABBEY MILL BUSINESS CENTRE, PAISLEY PA1 1TJ • www.holidayguides.com

A 60-minute ride along the shores of beautiful Padarn Lake behind a quaint historic steam engine. Magnificent views of the mountains from lakeside picnic spots. **DOGS MUST BE KEPT ON LEAD AT ALL TIMES ON TRAIN**	**Open:** most days Easter to October. Free timetable leaflet on request. **Directions:** just off A4086 Caernarfon to Capel Curig road at Llanberis; follow 'Country Park' signs.

FHG GUIDES, ABBEY MILL BUSINESS CENTRE, PAISLEY PA1 1TJ • www.holidayguides.com

A collection of unusual and interesting animals, including breeding pairs and colonies of exotic and endangered species whose natural environment is under threat. Many were unwanted exotic pets or came from other zoos.	**Open:** 10am - 6pm April to October **Directions:** only a short walk from the railway station and beach in Borth, which lies between Aberystwyth and Machynlleth.

FHG GUIDES, ABBEY MILL BUSINESS CENTRE, PAISLEY PA1 1TJ • www.holidayguides.com

Mini-rainforest full of tropical plants and exotic butterflies. Personal attention of the owner, Mr John Devereux. Gift shop, cafe, video room, exhibition. Suitable for disabled visitors. VisitWales Quality Assured Visitor Attraction. **PETS NOT ALLOWED IN TROPICAL HOUSE ONLY**	**Open:** daily Easter to end October 10.30am to 5pm **Directions:** West Wales, 7 miles north of Cardigan off Aberystwyth road. Follow brown tourist signs on A487.

FHG GUIDES, ABBEY MILL BUSINESS CENTRE, PAISLEY PA1 1TJ • www.holidayguides.com

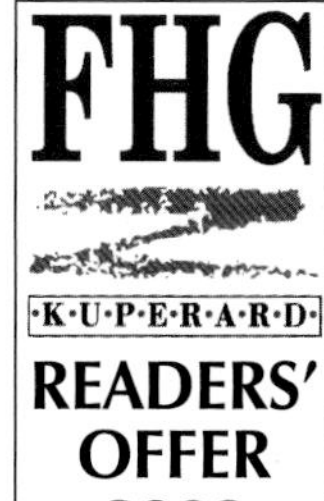

READERS' OFFER 2008

NATIONAL CYCLE COLLECTION

Automobile Palace, Temple Street,
Llandrindod Wells, Powys LD1 5DL
Tel: 01597 825531
e-mail: cycle.museum@powys.org.uk
www.cyclemuseum.org.uk

TWO for the price of ONE
Valid during 2008 except Special Event days

NOT TO BE USED IN CONJUNCTION WITH ANY OTHER OFFER

READERS' OFFER 2008

RHONDDA HERITAGE PARK

Lewis Merthyr Colliery, Coed Cae Road,
Trehafod, Near Pontypridd CF37 2NP
Tel: 01443 682036

e-mail: info@rhonddaheritagepark.com
www.rhonddaheritagepark.com

Two adults or children for the price of one when accompanied by a full paying adult. Valid until end 2008 for full tours only. Not valid on special event days/themed tours.

NOT TO BE USED IN CONJUNCTION WITH ANY OTHER OFFER

Other specialised holiday guides from FHG

Recommended **INNS & PUBS** OF BRITAIN

Recommended **COUNTRY HOTELS** OF BRITAIN

Recommended **SHORT BREAK HOLIDAYS** IN BRITAIN

The bestselling and original **PETS WELCOME!**

The GOLF GUIDE, *Where to Play, Where to Stay* IN BRITAIN & IRELAND

COAST & COUNTRY HOLIDAYS

SELF-CATERING HOLIDAYS IN BRITAIN

BED & BREAKFAST STOPS

CARAVAN & CAMPING HOLIDAYS

CHILDREN WELCOME! Family Holiday & Days Out Guide

BRITAIN'S BEST LEISURE & RELAXATION GUIDE

Published annually: available in all good bookshops or direct from the publisher:
FHG Guides, Abbey Mill Business Centre, Seedhill, Paisley PA1 1TJ
Tel: 0141 887 0428 • Fax: 0141 889 7204
E-mail: admin@fhguides.co.uk • Web: www.holidayguides.com

Journey through the lanes of cycle history and see bicycles from Boneshakers and Penny Farthings up to modern Raleigh cycles. *Over 250 machines on display* **PETS MUST BE KEPT ON LEADS**	**Open:** 1st March to 1st November daily 10am onwards. **Directions:** brown signs to car park. Town centre attraction.

FHG GUIDES, ABBEY MILL BUSINESS CENTRE, PAISLEY PA1 1TJ • www.holidayguides.com

Make a pit stop whatever the weather! Join an ex-miner on a tour of discovery, ride the cage to pit bottom and take a thrilling ride back to the surface. Multi-media presentations, period village street, children's adventure play area, restaurant and gift shop. Disabled access with assistance.	**Open:** Open daily 10am to 6pm (last tour 4pm). Closed Mondays Oct - Easter, also Dec 25th to early Jan. **Directions:** Exit Junction 32 M4, signposted from A470 Pontypridd. Trehafod is located between Pontypridd and Porth.

FHG GUIDES, ABBEY MILL BUSINESS CENTRE, PAISLEY PA1 1TJ • www.holidayguides.com

Index of Towns and Counties

Inverurie, Aberdeen, Banff & Moray	SCOTLAND
Ireby, Cumbria	NORTH WEST
Keswick, Cumbria	NORTH WEST
Kidderminster, Worcestershire	MIDLANDS
Kilbirnie, Ayrshire & Arran	SCOTLAND
Kinclaven, Perth & Kinross	SCOTLAND
King's Lynn, Norfolk	EAST
Kingsbridge, Devon	SOUTH WEST
Kirriemuir, Angus & Dundee	SCOTLAND
Langar, Nottinghamshire	MIDLANDS
Langdon, Devon	SOUTH WEST
Lifton, Devon	SOUTH WEST
Llanbedr, Anglesey & Gwynedd	WALES
Llanwddyn, Powys	WALES
Loch Harray, Scottish Islands/Orkney	SCOTLAND
Lochinver, Highlands	SCOTLAND
Lockerbie, Dumfries & Galloway	SCOTLAND
Lostwithiel, Cornwall	SOUTH WEST
Lulworth Cove, Dorset	SOUTH WEST
Lyme Regis, Dorset	SOUTH WEST
Lynmouth, Devon	SOUTH WEST
Lynton, Devon	SOUTH WEST
Lynton/Lynmouth, Devon	SOUTH WEST
Mevagissey, Cornwall	SOUTH WEST
Mullion, Cornwall	SOUTH WEST
New Forest, Hampshire	SOUTH EAST
Newquay, Cornwall	SOUTH WEST
Newton Stewart, Dumfries & Galloway	SCOTLAND
Oakham, Leicester & Rutland	MIDLANDS
Oban, Argyll & Bute	SCOTLAND
Paignton, Devon	SOUTH WEST
Porlock, Somerset	SOUTH WEST
Redruth, Cornwall	SOUTH WEST
Rhayader, Powys	WALES
Ruthin, North Wales	WALES
Rye, East Sussex	SOUTH EAST
Ryton on Tyne, Tyne & Wear	NORTH EAST
Sandbach, Cheshire	NORTH WEST
Scarborough, North Yorkshire	YORKSHIRE

Scone, Perth & Kinross	SCOTLAND
Seaview, Isle of Wight	SOUTH EAST
Skipton, North Yorkshire	YORKSHIRE
Somerton, Somerset	SOUTH WEST
St Agnes, Cornwall	SOUTH WEST
St Fillans, Perth & Kinross	SCOTLAND
St Ives, Cornwall	SOUTH WEST
St Mawes, Cornwall	SOUTH WEST
Staffin, Scottish Islands/Skye.	SCOTLAND
Stow-on-the-Wold, Gloucestershire	SOUTH WEST
Studland, Dorset	SOUTH WEST
Talyllyn, Anglesey & Gwynedd	WALES
Taunton, Somerset	SOUTH WEST
Taynuilt, Argyll & Bute	SCOTLAND
Tenbury Wells, Worcestershire	MIDLANDS
Tenby, Pembrokeshire	WALES
Tenterden, Kent	SOUTH EAST
The Lizard, Cornwall	SOUTH WEST
Thirsk, North Yorkshire	YORKSHIRE
Tillicoultry, Stirling & Trossachs	SCOTLAND
Tongue, Highlands	SCOTLAND
Totland Bay, Isle of Wight	SOUTH EAST
Tring, Hertfordshire	EAST
Tywyn, Anglesey & Gwynedd	WALES
Uplawmoor, Renfrewshire	SCOTLAND
Ventnor, Isle of Wight	SOUTH EAST
Wadebridge, Cornwall	SOUTH WEST
Wadhurst, East Sussex	SOUTH EAST
Wareham, Dorset	SOUTH WEST
Wem, Shropshire	MIDLANDS
Weston-super-Mare, Somerset	SOUTH WEST
Winchester, Hampshire	SOUTH EAST
Windermere, Cumbria	NORTH WEST
Woodbridge, Suffolk	EAST
Woodhall Spa, Lincolnshire	MIDLANDS
Woolacombe, Devon	SOUTH WEST
Wooler, Northumberland	NORTH EAST
Worleston, Cheshire	NORTH WEST
Wotton-under-Edge, Gloucestershire	SOUTH WEST

Other FHG titles for 2008

FHG Guides Ltd have a large range of attractive holiday accommodation guides for all kinds of holiday opportunities throughout Britain. They also make useful gifts at any time of year. Our guides are available in most bookshops and larger newsagents but we will be happy to post you a copy direct if you have any difficulty. POST FREE for addresses in the UK. We will also post abroad but have to charge separately for post or freight.

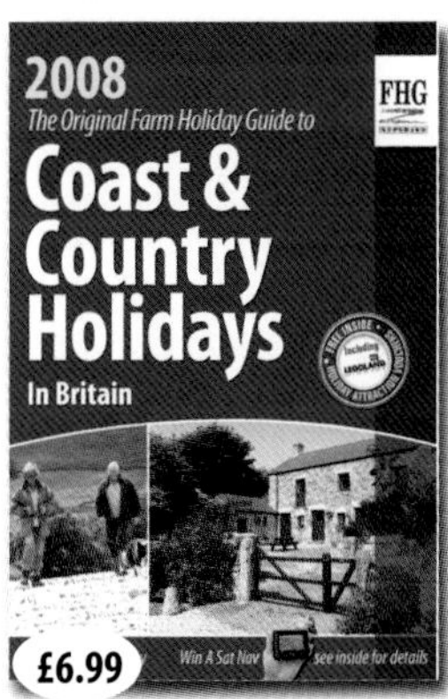

The original Farm Holiday Guide to COAST & COUNTRY HOLIDAYS
in England, Scotland, Wales and Channel Islands. Board, Self-catering, Caravans/Camping, Activity Holidays.

BED AND BREAKFAST STOPS
Over 1000 friendly and comfortable overnight stops. Non-smoking, Disabled and Special Diets Supplements.

BRITAIN'S BEST LEISURE & RELAXATION GUIDE
A quick-reference general guide for all kinds of holidays.

The Original PETS WELCOME!
The bestselling guide to holidays for pet owners and their pets.

Recommended INNS & PUBS of Britain
Including Pubs, Inns and Small Hotels,

SELF-CATERING HOLIDAYS in Britain
Over 1000 addresses throughout for self-catering and caravans in Britain.

CHILDREN WELCOME! Family Holidays and Days Out guide.
Family holidays with details of amenities for children and babies.

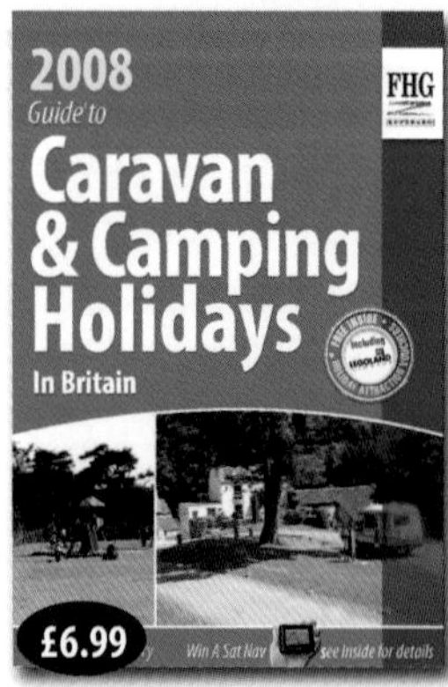

The FHG Guide to CARAVAN & CAMPING HOLIDAYS
Caravans for hire, sites and holiday parks and centres.

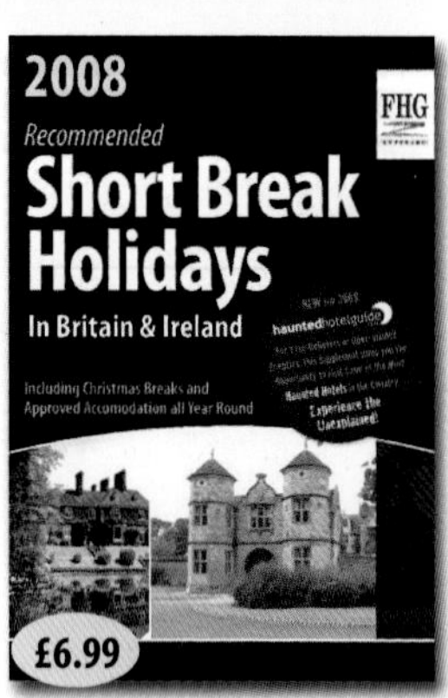

Recommended SHORT BREAK HOLIDAYS IN BRITAIN & IRELAND
"Approved" accommodation for quality bargain breaks.

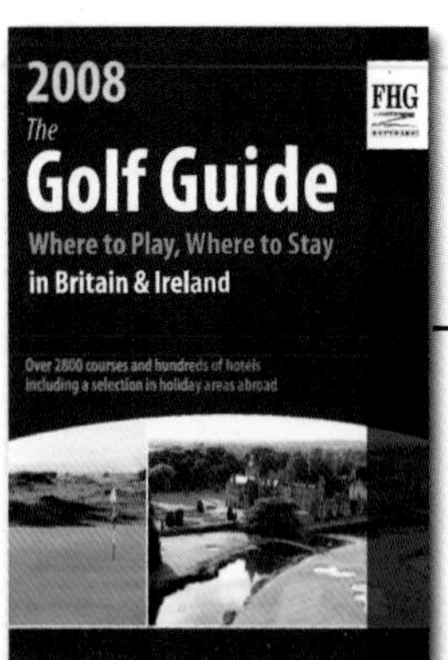

The GOLF GUIDE – *Where to play Where to stay*
In association with GOLF MONTHLY. Over 2800 golf courses in Britain with convenient accommodation. Holiday Golf in France, Portugal, Spain, USA and Thailand.

£9.99

Tick your choice above and send your order and payment to

FHG Guides Ltd. Abbey Mill Business Centre
Seedhill, Paisley, Scotland PA1 1TJ
TEL: 0141- 887 0428 • FAX: 0141- 889 7204
e-mail: admin@fhguides.co.uk

Deduct 10% for 2/3 titles or copies; 20% for 4 or more.

Send to: NAME ....

ADDRESS ....

....

....

POST CODE ....

I enclose Cheque/Postal Order for £ ....

SIGNATURE ....DATE ....

Please complete the following to help us improve the service we provide.

How did you find out about our guides?:

☐ Press ☐ Magazines ☐ TV/Radio ☐ Family/Friend ☐ Other